The Novel & Society

The Novel & Society
DEFOE to GEORGE ELIOT

GRAHAME SMITH

Barnes & Noble Books, Totowa, New Jersey

For Ieuan Williams and
in memory of Brian Way

© Grahame Smith 1984
First published in the USA 1984 by
Barnes & Noble Books
81 Adams Drive
Totowa, New Jersey, 07512

ISBN 0-389-20440-4

Library of Congress Cataloging in Publication Data

Smith, Grahame.
  The novel and society.

  1. English fiction—18th century—History and
criticism. 2. English fiction—19th century—History
and criticism. 3. Literature and society—England.
4. Social history in literature. I. Title.
PR851.S55 1984   823'.009'355   83-22286
ISBN 0-389-20440-4

Printed in Great Britain

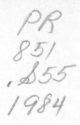

Contents

Preface

Although my 'story of the novel' is very different from George Watson's book of that name, some words of his apply directly to my own enterprise:

> I have concerned myself with novels that are famous, or at least known;
> and some of my assertions about the primacy of events may seem
> over-bold and omissive unless seen in the light of that guiding principle
> ...it is compelled upon the historian...by a body of evidence so vast that
> his own knowledge is necessarily partial and imperfect.[1]

It is surely more interesting to discuss great works and great writers than to scrutinise the less good in however much detail. If this view seems frivolous, however, a more theoretical point is to hand. The relation of lesser works to society is often a matter of unconscious assimilation, a reflection of reality of a fairly unmediated kind. Much can be learned in this way of a directly sociological nature, but the great writer complicates the issue by his critical stance towards social reality. Even great works are mimetic to some degree, or allow elements of their social context to slip unquestioned through the writer's imagination into the text. But great novels characteristically raise difficult questions about their relation to a social context because they subject it to a demanding scrutiny. In doing so they fulfil, rather than deny, an important part of their aesthetic purpose; and so the problem becomes one of the connection between the aesthetic and the social, a more challenging level of intellectual enquiry than a sociological examination of fictional content.

A general argument is set out in the first chapter which is pursued throughout the book as a whole. Thus while later chapters seek to illuminate specific novels and novelists, a connecting line of thought is also intended. I have not attempted a strict balance of space and attention within my field. The chapters on *Persuasion* and *Vanity Fair* are long because these novels raise acutely interesting problems for this study which can only be dealt with at some length. Where a novel lends itself to brevity of treatment, no attempt is made to pad this out. I hold stubbornly to the view that writers such as Fanny Burney, and the novelists of the Gothic and Jacobin schools, are minor. But their presence is acknowledged in terms of the argument, if not in discussion of their work. I thus hope to suggest comprehensiveness without a tediously lengthy completeness.

What follows will try to keep several aims in view. Another chapter will be added to the perennially interesting story of the rise of the novel in England. And an attempt will be made to suggest a socially oriented history of the form. Both efforts will be placed within a theoretical framework in the first chapter. But the heart of the enterprise is aesthetic; this is a work of literary criticism. Theoretical and practical criticism will be brought to bear on specific works and writers in the conviction that a social reading does no violence to artistry. A true social reading of a work of literature is not a hunt for scraps of historical fact or information, but an engagement with issues that belong entirely within the fictional world. Such readings are not second order, in contrast to first order readings which concentrate exclusively on language or literary techniques. The very richness of literature invites a wealth of readings of which the only final test is the illumination they provide. The following pages hope to demonstrate that a social reading of works of fiction can be as artistically enlightening as any other.

This book has benefited greatly from the interest of friends and colleagues. I am particularly grateful to Robert Rehder, Susan Reid, Bill and Sue Barnes-Gutteridge and, above all, Ieuan Williams. Without the minute scrutiny of my wife and colleague, Angela Smith, the book would have been longer and poorer. Its remaining faults are entirely my own responsibility.

Grahame Smith
Zomba, Malawi
November 1982

1

Problems in the Relationship of
Literature and Society

Introduction

The house of fiction has many rooms and the energies of the formalist critic are devoted to the discovery of its internal intricacies as well as its external architecture. The task exerts a continual fascination and is often seen as the critic's area of professional expertise: the carpet can be examined both for fit and pattern. And so the formalist craftsman hammers away, happy in the pleasures of close scrutiny. But such delights have their dangers. The plumbing in the older establishments may be found to be faulty, the roof a trifle leaky. No doubt the best houses can withstand such surveys, but even the inventory of their beauties becomes tiresome if the detail is too minute. On the other hand, the recognition that they exist within a landscape has its dangers, too; the interest of the surroundings may be allowed to dominate, the object of attention viewed only distantly. However, a balance can be struck between these positions which may be of benefit to the study of literature. There is surely some middle ground between critics who see nothing but the work itself and those for whom it recedes in a vista dominated by its historical context.

The mediaeval manor and the Georgian mansion had complex relationships to the worlds of which they were a part, relationships which embraced art and economics, social function and craftsmanship. And the connections between literature and society are no less complex. New Criticism has taught us that the study of literature should begin and end with close attention to the text, but we can speculate about what might occur between these initial and terminal events. An extreme advocate of the New Critical position might reply: 'Nothing! Read the text, read and read again.' We are hardly likely to accuse ourselves of reading a masterpiece too many times;

on the other hand, once discussion of literature begins it is hard to know where, or perhaps why, it should stop. The uses of literature are too manifold to be restricted solely to consideration of the words on the page. Common-sense suggests that the humane discussion of literature involves questions of psychology, politics and social forces, as well as the analysis of imagery and the tracing of literary influences. And this common-sense widening of the area of discussion is not something foisted on a virginally unwilling literature. Great books and great writers invite such a robust communion because they spring from, and continue to exist, in a world of public interests as well as private imagination. In fact, imagination as I wish to use the term embraces the public no less than the private. This relation of literature to the wider world is enforced with classical lucidity by F. R. Leavis:

> For to insist that literary criticism is, or should be, a specific discipline of intelligence is not to suggest that a serious interest in literature can confine itself to the kind of intensive local analysis associated with 'practical criticism' – to the scrutiny of the 'words on the page' in their minute relations, their effects of imagery, and so on: a real literary interest is an interest in man, society and civilization, and its boundaries cannot be drawn.[1]

This book attempts explanations of the form of certain eighteenth and nineteenth century English novels, and literary criticism usually makes such explanations in one of two ways: by trying to reveal how content demands a specific shape for the fullest expression of all its subtleties; or by tracing the development of large-scale changes in technique by reference to the fluctuations of literary tradition. My claim is that it is also possible to trace, in different periods of history, a connection between even the details of artistic technique and elements wider than those of literature considered in isolation. Two classic passages of English writing may help to make the point: one of Shakespeare's greatest soliloquies and a brilliant few lines from Pope. The first is Macbeth's impassioned consideration of the issues involved in the murder of Duncan:

> If it were done when 'tis done, then 'twere
> well
> It were done quickly. If th' assassination
> Could trammel up the consequence, and catch,
> With his surcease, success: that but this blow
> Might be the be-all and end-all – here

> But here, upon this bank and shoal of time,
>   We'd jump the life to come..........
>   ....I have no spur
> To prick the sides of my intent, but only
> Vaulting ambition, which o'erleaps itself
> And falls on the other. (I, vii, 1-28)

The second is the series of death-bed vignettes from *Moral Essays*, 'Epistle 1. To Richard Temple, Viscount Cobham':

> 'Odious! in woollen! 'twould a saint provoke,
> (Were the last words that poor Narcissa spoke)
> No. let a charming Chintz, and Brussels lace
> Wrap my cold limbs, and shade my lifeless face:
> One would not, sure, be frightful when one's dead –
> And – Betty – give this Cheek a little Red.'
>   ....
> 'I give and I devise, (old Euclio said,
> And sigh'd) my land and tenements to Ned.'
> 'Your money, Sir?' 'My money, Sir, what all?
> Why, – if I must – (then wept) I give it Paul.'
> 'The manor, Sir?' – 'The manor! hold,' he cry'd,
> 'Not that, – I cannot part with that' – and dy'd. (242-7, 256-61)

These passages are separated by only some 130 years, but the differences between them are clearly vast and may illuminate the commonplace that renaissance and neo-classic writers have widely divergent views of the nature of man. But – our New Critic might exclaim – this is to leap immediately to the wider issues: what about the texts themselves? Their differences as poetry are, of course, fascinating. Both poets are gripped by the problem of human evil, but their means of expression are worlds apart. Shakespeare's primary concern is with the moral implications of the psychology and emotions of his individual character, although these cannot be divorced from the light they throw on humanity in general. Pope's moral interest, on the other hand, is focused on a typical human vice, representative of the evils of society. And this difference is embodied in the characteristic features of their chosen form.

Macbeth's soliloquy is a presentation of the surface of human evil which is, simultaneously, an exploration of its depths. The literal burden of the speech is that Macbeth would chance his immortal soul in killing Duncan if only he could be sure of escaping judgement in this life. But this explicit risking of the after-life ('We'd jump the life to come') is denied by our privileged insight into his

11

inner world. The imagery which Shakespeare makes rise to his lips with such apparent naturalness is fraught with references to the Day of Judgement (19-23) and is a concrete instance of that split between the mundane Macbeth who is so influenced by his wife and the Macbeth whose moral imagination takes the form of the 'air-drawn dagger'. Shakespeare achieves this complexity through his manipulation of the total resources of poetic language and the capacity of blank verse to be extended over a long passage without any loss of poetic discipline. Pope, in contrast, uses the precision and epigrammatic force of each unit of the heroic couplet to move from one glancing blow to another at the surface of man's ruling passions and social hypocrisies. In both cases we feel that form is fully adequate to the expressive need. More, it is responding to the pressure of meaning in ways that almost exhaust its capacity for further development. The changes of direction within a single line ('"Your money, Sir?"...and dy'd'), the delicately stopped pause of 'old Euclio said, And sigh'd', reveal an artistic control dazzling in its virtuosity. Freedom in chains could hardly go further. And, similarly, the sheer richness of a Shakespearian soliloquy from line to line is extraordinary. The opening puns of the *Macbeth* passage, the submerged metaphor of the sea of eternity implied by 'this bank and shoal of time', the religiously loaded reference to a cup as a poisoned 'chalice', the almost incredible convolution of the metaphor of Macbeth's 'horrid deed' as a piece of grit that will make the collective eye of Scotland pour rain, so producing the common natural phenomenon of the wind dropping – all this is of a richness to beggar description, let alone a full analysis.

Verbal analysis is, then, the basic method by which we seek to explore the meaning and artistry of these passages. They are, of course, part of the wider context of the play and poem, and we hope that analysis will further our understanding of the larger structures. But works of literature stand in a *series* of contexts: in their place in the writer's life and within his complete output, as examples of a genre, as facts of literary history. The reversal of a statement by Roy Harvey Pearce suggests another context, the social life of which they are a part and which may, to some extent, have helped them into existence: 'Studying history, we study culture. Studying a culture, we study its poetry. Studying its poetry, we study its language. The system is one and whole.'[2] This reinforces one's sense that the writer and his work have a social as well as a private dimension. After all, the basic raw material of the passages from Shakespeare and Pope, blank verse and the heroic couplet, did not spring fully formed from the void. In both cases we have the inheritance of other writers, Marlowe and Dryden, who developed the already existing and somewhat crude form to a level that permitted the daring experiments of the greater poets. A social context of literary influences is undeniably at work here. But if, as I would claim, these passages embody, as well as their more personal aspects, the aspiration of the renaissance hero and the social functioning of eighteenth-century man in the very texture of their language and style, we are forced to consider a wide context indeed.

We may then be struck by the intersection of a series of lines of force. On the one hand, there is the dominance of a popular dramatic form capable of tragic intensity, a highly developed interest in individual psychology, a poetic language with the extension in time characteristic of the natural speaking voice; on the other, the dominance of the mock-epic, the absence of a tragic view of personal life, a poetic language that catches, rather than penetrates, the surfaces of things. These observations might, in their turn, prompt such questions as why dramatic blank verse should be the characteristically great poetic technique of the early seventeenth century and the heroic couplet that of the eighteenth. The endlessly invoked swing of the pendulum *could* be brought into play, the mechanically determined view that the dominance of a form, idea, world view is bound to lead to its opposite, but this, of course, answers nothing. A more serious response, in terms of the development of poetic styles, might be attempted, but that is not my subject. It might seem, then, that there is no more to be said unless, that is, we are prepared to accept the idea that human culture is, at least in the short term, more than a matter of random events, that reasons and explanations are assignable to things. In this, I agree with Ian Watt that, so far as understanding is concerned, the 'terms "genius" and "accident"' are the 'twin faces of the Janus of the dead ends of literary history.'[3] This is not to deny that such explanations are ultimately limited in their scope, if only because we can never hope to exhaust the possible factors involved, but this is no reason for shrinking from the attempt.

As my subject is the form of some English novels in relation to society, a full-scale examination of Shakespeare and Pope would be inappropriate, but it is encouraging that specialists are willing to risk generalizations of a social nature. A. R. Humphreys, for example: 'Augustan literary characters can be great figures, but their power comes from the fact that they are not subtly understood individuals but representatives of a type, with a kind of collective force.'[4] Theodore Spencer is even prepared to suggest an explanation of the very emergence of Elizabethan drama:

> The contrast between the theoretical good and evil goes very deep into the thought and feeling of Shakespeare's age...To a large extent it was expressed in drama...and one of the assumptions I shall make...is that the existence at the end of the sixteenth century of the basic conflict about the nature of man is perhaps the deepest underlying cause for the emergence of the great drama of that time.[5]

Theoretically conditioned hackles rise at the mention of 'cause' – the quicksand of necessity threatens the unwary – but such statements, and my own earlier analysis of the passages, at least hint at the possibility of seeing these writers in a context wider than that of literature itself. There is no suggestion that width implies pre-eminence, of course, that this context should annihilate or even displace other contexts of a more purely literary kind. But if we read literature with the aspiration of reaching as near to a total understanding of it as is possible, then this context should take its place side by side with the others. At the lowest level, there must be some connection between the technical features of the passages quoted and the view of man held by Shakespeare and Pope because the social medium of language, however refined by genius, is the essential vehicle for the expression of such a view.

Beginning with poetic examples rests on the strategy of using the form which is furthest in some minds from the vulgar incursions of the social. Such an emphasis should also make clear that this is a work of literary criticism: I have no interest in rummaging through the content of novels looking for bits and pieces of social 'relevance'. My intention is to remove the wedge driven between the social and the aesthetic; to show, in fact, that they are inseparably related. What precisely is involved, then, in seeking to demonstrate the importance of a social dimension to literature? A well edited collection of essays, *The Sociology of Literature*, is helpful in clarifying this point. Its editors suggest five main ways in which the relationship between literature and society may be conceived: the question of 'how literature arises in society;' how literature affects 'society and [is] continually involved in the process of social development;' how literature has been used '*as a kind of sociology*;' and how literature may 'affect society, and affect social change.' There is

14

much to be gained from these lines of enquiry, but they are not my major concern. This book aims to be what the editors of *The Sociology of Literature* call a '*sociologically aware* study of literature. Social problems or the development of theory are not at issue in such work: the focus of the study is literature.' [6] This is well put and illuminates a crucial problem of all inter-disciplinary study, the question of what constitutes the centre of an intellectual enquiry. To attempt a serious contribution to knowledge necessitates working from a centre, no matter how widely one may range from it. To be simultaneously a literary critic and a social historian is not just difficult; it may ultimately hinder understanding by failing to strike an emphasis, thus obscuring the area to be understood. The problem is familiar in certain kinds of literary history: works are listed, plots summarized, characters anatomized, but little is illuminated. And this highlights the necessity of another kind of centre for intellectual enquiry. At a certain point, the merely random accumulation of knowledge for its own sake begins to seem barren in the face of the human desire for order and pattern, for explanation. That something to be explained constitutes the disciplining centre of study against which forays into other fields can be measured and controlled, a point made by the French historian, Marc Bloch: 'In other words, every historical research supposes that the inquiry has a direction at the very first step. In the beginning, there must be the guiding spirit.'[7] Presumably all knowledge would co-exist as a total form in the mind of God, but human attempts at understanding must have a starting point that delineates the area of investigation. Two recent books may, in their different ways, help to clarify the point.

Real and Imagined Worlds: The Novel and Social Science is by a sociologist of very wide reading whose respect for literature is clear on every page and who is obviously fitted to use sociology in the way envisaged by C. Wright Mills: 'The sociological imagination enables its possessor to understand the larger historical scene in terms of its meaning for the inner life and the external career of a variety of individuals.'[8] Monroe Berger is, in short, at the furthest possible remove from the tough wielder of statistics who refuses to accord any special status to the creative imagination, for whom even the greatest literary work is merely one piece of evidence that must take its place amongst possibly hundreds of others. Without impertinence, one might suggest that a major purpose of his book is to make the excessively specialized social scientist aware that the insights in which he is interested exist everywhere in the novel.

Berger's basic method is to cite passages, very frequently of authorial commentary, which bear on the concerns of sociology. This is of general interest, but the literary critic is bound to feel a pang of disappointment when he reads the following, fairly well on in the book:'"Direct" authorial commentary has contributed much to a knowledge of human behavior, although some writers and critics believe that the "indirect" meaning conveyed by the novel as a unity is more satisfying aesthetically.'[9] There is surely a false dichotomy at work here in the opposition between knowledge and the aesthetic. A suggestion of limitation is explicit in Berger's view of the literary critic's preference, but for the critic this pinpoints the fact that Berger has been using his novels as examples, rather in the manner of some moral philosophers, for nuggets of insight totally divorced from their context, a procedure that violates the unity central to any real work of art. What this leads to in the end is a version, albeit enormously more sophisticated, of the collections of wisdom culled by the Victorians from their literary sages. Although humane, then, and no doubt useful to its specialist audience, Berger's work must seem limited to the critic because of a use of literature which is for him inadmissible. Berger's study has its own centre of enquiry which permits his sociologically disciplined exploration of literature, but his method is unsatisfactory to the critic because of its unproblematic attitude to narrative commentary. Even in the case of George Eliot, a novelist for whom this technique is central, commentary is complicated by being the expression of an idealized narrative voice rather than that of the 'real' author; and it is refined, amplified, sometimes qualified even, by the dramatic embodiment of plot, action and dialogue in the novel as a whole.

Similarly, the work of literary criticism and scholarship may disappoint in a different, but related, way. One approached John Speirs's *Poetry Towards Novel* with high expectations for the fascinating promise of its title. The displacement of poetry from a central position in European literature by the novel is a problem of perennial interest, but Speirs's treatment of it is, paradoxically, too narrowly literary. The book's central point is that the great nineteenth-century English novelists are the descendants of Shakespeare by way of Romantic poetry, a richly suggestive argument. It is certainly clear that Dickens and George Eliot, say, are saturated in both Shakespeare and Wordsworth, but Mr Speirs does little to show how this process of inheritance took place in detail. Also, the movement from poetry to the novel seems altogether too complex a process to be accounted for in purely literary terms and the context which forms the book's argument is only one of several that would need to be considered if the problems were to be done justice to. *Poetry Towards Novel* exemplifies the formalist position expressed by Eichenbaum:

> Literature, like any other specific order of things, is not generated from facts belonging to other orders and therefore *cannot be reduced* to such facts...the facts of the literary order and facts extrinsic to it cannot simply be causal relations but can only be the relations of correspondence, interaction, dependency, or conditionality.[10]

This is trenchantly put and Speirs's work can be admired, not only for its local insights, but for its determination to stay within its own area of competence, and for the interest of its conclusion:

> The three poets of the beginning of the nineteenth century who have seemed to me to have most affinities with the novelists are Wordsworth, Crabbe (...of his *Verse Tales*) and Byron (...of *Don Juan*)...the pervasive and profound creative effect of Shakespeare on both the poets and the novelists of the nineteenth century...could not be ignored.[11]

But this is in the end limited, and in too many ways. The degree of specificity suggested here demands a demonstration that all these works have been read by his novelists, but Mr Speirs is unable to show this in detail. Of course, he is right to suggest that it is highly likely: 'The novelists did not only read novelists.'[12] But one questions if this is a high enough degree of demonstrable relationship. Again, and more important, too much is left out to serve as an adequate explanation of the development of the novel in the nineteenth century. Early on, the point is made that the novel 'as part of the nineteenth century developments in consciousness, took on a new dimension of greatness' and it is here that one senses a major gap to be filled. What, specifically, are these 'developments in consciousness' and how do they relate to the growth of the novel? These are legitimate questions, but the book ignores them. A way into the area is suggested by the statement that 'the pains of growing up and arriving at mature manhood or womanhood...[is] one of the main recurrent themes in the novels of the nineteenth century.'[13] But this remains undeveloped and no link is made, crucial though one would have thought it to be, with the wider Continental perspective. The arrival at 'mature manhood or womanhood' is surely 'one of the main recurrent themes' in nineteenth-century European fiction, as the mention of Balzac and Stendhal is enough to show. Despite its interest, then, *Poetry Towards Novel* fails in several ways. When we read, 'there is a sense, of course, in which as works of imaginative literature, all novels are poems'[14] we know immediately that the book belongs to a specific moment in English literary criticism. Mr Speirs is a disciple of Leavis and for those disciples the reduction of all literary forms to poetry is an article of faith. The sense in which a Shakespeare play is a 'dramatic poem', to use the accepted phrase, is complex, but it is not impossible to see the point. In what way, though, *Emma* or *Middlemarch* are poems is an entirely different matter. At the very least, the claim would need to be argued in detail; even so, the value of this generic reductiveness remains doubtful. Another limitation of this discipleship is that its followers are more Leavisite than the master himself, above all in how they see the relationship of literature to forces outside itself. We have seen that Leavis insists that literary study cannot be limited to 'the words on the page', but it is precisely this disabling weakness, given its subject, that *Poetry Towards Novel* displays.

A way of expressing one's disappointment with Speirs's and Berger's work is to say that their models of intellectual enquiry are insufficient for the task in hand. Speirs's is the more seriously limited in that his book lacks any sociological dimension at all, an omission exacerbated by the thinness of evidence within his chosen field of literary study. Berger is more wide-ranging, but his view of literature as something to be cut up for slices of sociological insight is too simplistic to be of value to the literary critic. The confusion generated by false or weak models is just as great when we turn to the relationship between individual works and society. In one model, the literary work is seen as causally created by a variety of pressures – social, economic or generic—which are separated from the work in a different universe of being. Similarly, on a simple mimetic view the work reflects an already existing and separable social reality. Diagrammatically, both might be understood in terms of a circle representing human life in its widest sense, within which the smaller circles of the literary work and social forces interact. Again, a criticism which stresses the total primacy of works of art suggests that they create reality, by the construction of new forms of social relationship, for example. To illustrate these models, *The Great Gatsby*, say, is read as causally created by the moral and social chaos following the First World War; as a reflection of these conditions in the mirror of Fitzgerald's prose; or as creating our image of the period through a process of naming and definition.

The basic weakness of these models is their externality, the distancing of elements which are, in fact, inextricably inter-related. In recognizing this totality of experience we face an unavoidable dilemma. Totality is irrecoverable and so a study which attempts to remove even a small segment of the past for investigation is doomed to incompleteness. But we must begin by accepting that there is only one history, that the past is a seamless garment which we are, paradoxically, forced to unpick if we wish to examine a small piece of the material. This abstraction from the whole is bound to lead to an incompleteness which can only be filled by speculation, especially if the segment of history for examination is a selection of eighteenth and nineteenth-century novels whose artistry is to be viewed from a social standpoint. In this case, especially, the stress must be on internality, both in the relations between the works and their total context and, decisively, in their specifically artistic embodiment of a social dimension.

Any attempt to deal with a group of novels over a chronological spread involves the writing of a history within the larger history to which I have just referred and, intellectual enquiry being the complex matter it is, this could take several forms. (In practice, of course, such forms of enquiry overlap, even where only one is central.) A purely aesthetic investigation might pursue changes in some of the techniques of fiction; point-of-view, characterization, and so on. Literary history, in its traditional sense, might trace the patterns of influence and reaction between novels themselves. But if, as George Watson claims, form is 'a complex of devices for representing reality'[15] the way is open for a study which tries to show how individual novels, and a history of the genre, may be understood by placing them where they surely belong, within their social world. If this social world is part of history in the widest sense, the novel also claims a place there not simply as a historical fact, in the least interesting kind of way, but in its very nature. In the introduction to his *Popular Literature*, Victor Neuburg points out that:

> It is more than thirty years since a French historian, Lucien Febvre, urged a change in the direction of historical studies, so that what he described as 'l'histoire des mentalités collectives' should be given greater prominence. By this phrase he meant the assumptions, beliefs, feelings and modes of thought of men and women in the past.[16]

In other words, human consciousness is part of the raw material of history and this surely gives a crucial role to the novel, a form in which the complexities of human consciousness can be rendered with subtle exactness and the widest social generality.

The third section of this chapter will attempt to pursue these issues at a theoretical level, but for the moment a specific example might be in order. In his study of ennui in western literature, *The Demon of Noontide*, Reinhard Kuhn presents a methodological justification for his book:

> Ennui is not just an idea about which authors have written. Inextricably linked with the notion of time and space, ennui is not only the subject of certain works of art but also a part of their temporal fabric and spatial structure.[17]

He suggests, in other words, that ennui is a form of consciousness widespread in European culture and, above all, that it is not simply a part of the subject matter of literary works, but that it is crucial to their artistry. This is the internality to which I referred earlier: the work of art and a mode of consciousness are fused, and this fusion arises from the relationship between the artist's creative imagination and an objective aspect of his culture. This phenomenon is social in several ways. Ennui is expressed in individual lives, whether in artistic creations such as Byron's gloomy heroes, or in the episode where it apparently afflicted Wordsworth, in his disappointment at the violent outcome of the French Revolution. However different these manifestations may be, in sharing a diffused mode of consciousness they are inescapably social in their origins. But there is a social relationship of another kind here, that of the engagement of a creative mind with an aspect of its society. And these points are worth stressing if only because, despite Febvre, one still encounters resistance to the idea of consciousness as a suitable subject for intellectual enquiry. In the following section, I shall try to demonstrate the widespread incidence of a mode of consciousness – melodrama – in the nineteenth century as a way of beginning to justify the validity, and interest, of seeing novels (and by implication literature in general) within a social context.

Melodrama and the nineteenth century

Writing to his mother in 1869, Matthew Arnold made a personal assertion which has a general bearing on the problems before us:

> My poems represent, on the whole, the main movement of mind of the last quarter of a century, and thus they will probably have their day as

people become conscious to themselves of what that movement of mind is, and interested in the literary productions which reflect it. It might fairly be argued that I have less poetical sentiment than Tennyson, and less intellectual vigour and abundance than Browning; yet, because I have perhaps more of a fusion of the two than either of them, and have more regularly applied that fusion to the main line of modern development, I am likely enough to have my turn, as they have had theirs.[18]

Arnold's use of the word 'reflect' might be seized on as theoretically naive, but although expressed with unfashionable lucidity the passage relates directly to many of the issues that motivate this book. Arnold is in no doubt that consciousness, at the level of feeling as well as ideas, is a detectable element in the historical process, even if not immediately apparent, and that literature is one way in which significant patterns of thought and feeling are expressed. But it is clearly a large leap from this personal response to a rigorously convincing demonstration of what these patterns are and how they relate to works of literature. What I think must be dismissed at the outset is any hope of scientific verifiability in this area. Even if novels are excluded as a feasible kind of evidence, ideas about consciousness will not be provable from, for example, statistical tables. This is not to say that they are without value in such an investigation, but the information they provide will of necessity have to be generalized in language, a process that can only be accomplished through interpretation and judgement. In short, evidence of consciousness has to be sought in letters, memoirs, autobiography, journalism, and so on, forms of writing which are themselves the product of the very mental processes which are the object of investigation. It is a commonplace that such material yields latent as well as surface significances, and their discovery can only be accomplished by a process of interpretation governed by a sense of the meaning of the evidence before one. In short, the discovery of patterns in this area is similar to that of discovering patterns in works of art themselves. Works of literature are analysable in terms of patterns of extraordinary variety, capable of demonstration with an evidential reference to the text that should convince anyone not a fool or madman. It seems hard to deny, for example, that the dramatic structure of Shakespeare's *Henry IV Part 1* is related to a patterning of character, scene and setting which is based on the court, the tavern and the rebels. And it is well known that at a verbal level Dickens's novels reveal a pattern in which the inanimate is realized in terms of the animate, and vice versa.[19] It goes without saying that

21

such examples do not exhaust the possibilities of pattern within these works; the reader will concentrate on the pattern, or patterns, which seem most important to him, rather than possessing some absolute, totally verifiable rightness. There are difficulties here, but they are minimal compared to the problems involved when we interpret these patterns into meaning. *Macbeth* contains an important image pattern centred on the notion that in killing Duncan, Macbeth takes on 'borrowed robes' which are too big for him. What is the precise meaning and effect of lines such as these?

> Now does he feel his title
> Hang loose about him, like a giant's robe
> Upon a dwarfish thief. (V, ii, 20-2)

Do we find Macbeth sinister in this metaphorical get-up, or is there something absurdly comic in his Chaplin-like trailing of outsize garments? Or, a favourite move in New Criticism, are we meant to hold both possibilities together in a paradoxical, and yet somehow harmonious, duality? I have suggested a similarity between the detecting of such patterns in works of literature and in social life; formidable difficulties certainly seem common to both. From a literary standpoint we may appear to be trapped within Spitzer's 'philological circle'.[20] In other words, our interpretation of works of literature begins from an often intuitive grasping of a fragment (sometimes what David Lodge calls a 'key word,'[21] although an aspect of the work's larger structure may be just as useful) which we add to by a process of accretion, from within the work itself, until an interpretative pattern forms in our minds. But just as E. D. Hirsch has suggested ways of breaking this circle by the use of what he considers relevant factors from outside the work,[22] so a similar possibility may exist for social history. Keeping these qualifications in view, let us return to Arnold. We shall have to cut a very thin slice of the social world of even a specific historical period if we hope to trace some connections between literature and society, but if the slice is thin enough patterns may emerge which entitle us to believe that we are dealing with something more than an arbitrary 'reading into' the past.

What, then, are some of the main movements of mind in the Victorian period? It is possible to isolate, amongst many, two major lines of development that coincide with two widely held popular views. The Victorians have been criticized on two large counts: for a solemn and sober-minded earnestness; and for an absurd indulgence in emotion of a suspect kind. The recent comprehensive revaluation of the nineteenth century makes it unnecessary to combat such vulgar misconceptions. But they can be adapted to suggest a main current in Victorian consciousness; putting it crudely, an opposition between intellect and emotion. Since the argument will bear most heavily on the second, it is salutary to remember the genuine distinction of mind in the period: the mental rigour of John Stuart Mill, the moral subtlety of George Eliot, the urbane critical insight of Matthew Arnold. We need also to remember that these qualities of mind are to an extent representative in the sense that an educated public supported such immensely serious periodicals as the *Westminster Review.* On the other hand, it seems tenable to suggest, George Eliot being the great exception, that this intellectuality did not find its way into creative literature, which is not to say that Victorian literature is not intelligent, as opposed to intellectual. At its best, it is supremely so – Dickens comes readily to mind. But the general point may hold if we see Matthew Arnold as representative in a sense different from what he himself intended. He claimed for his poetry a 'fusion' of 'poetical sentiment...and...intellectual vigour', but at this stage we may be struck by a lack of wholeness if we consider the full range of his writing career. There is an evident, and quite widely admitted, split between the poetry and the literary and social criticism, even allowing for the wide difference in the nature of the forms, a split highlighted by Arnold's well-known dissatisfaction with the contemporary state of English poetry: 'More and more I feel bent against the modern English habit (too much encouraged by Wordsworth) of using poetry as a channel for thinking aloud, instead of making anything.' If there is an absence of mental rigour in Arnold's poetry compared with his prose, this has nothing to do with the poetry's avoidance of explicit ideas. Explicitness is the substance of Arnold's charge against modern poetry, an explicitness which for him blurs, instead of sharpening, the poetic focus. Indeed, the very concept of the poet as a maker of something presupposes mental activity the reverse of subjective meandering. Arnold did create well-made poems which embody thought and emotion with beautiful objectivity – *Thyrsis* and *Dover Beach*, for example – but his poetic impulse as a whole lacks the sustained power of much of his prose writing.

This split between intellect and emotion leads into such areas of Victorian life as obsessive activity, and a sometimes hysterical-seeming exaggeration of action and feeling.[23] This is a rich soil, I would argue, for the growth of such phenomena as melodrama and sentimentality; such widespread manifestations of Victorian feeling must have come from somewhere. If their presence in the period requires any justification, the most obvious way to do so would be through a series of literary examples, the juicier the better. The death of Little Nell would demand inclusion and also, perhaps, this passage from *In Memoriam* which offers some objective correlatives for the poet's sense of loss:

> That loss is common would not make
> My own less bitter, rather more:
> Too common! Never morning wore
> To evening, but some heart did break.
> . . . .
>
> O somewhere, meek, unconscious dove,
> That sittest ranging golden hair;
> And glad to find thyself so fair,
> Poor child, that waitest for thy love!
>
> For now her father's chimney glows
> In expectation of a guest;
> And thinking 'this will please him best,'
> She takes a riband or a rose;
>
> For he will see them on tonight;
> And with the thought her colour burns;
> And, having left the glass, she turns
> Once more to set a ringlet right;
>
> And, even when she turned, the curse
> Had fallen, and her future Lord
> Was drowned in passing through the ford
> Or killed in falling from his horse.(VI)

The ghost of Lytton Strachey does not need to be invoked to find an almost absurd vagueness in that fatal closing alternative. *In Memoriam* is an impressive poem, but our relatively new-found respect for the Victorians should not blind us to the inadequacy of this conventionalised tear-jerking as an embodiment of Tennyson's agonizing grief. It is tempting to stay within the world of literary examples, in the narrow sense, at this point, but if we do we are condemned to remain within a circle that is, if not vicious, certainly of little ultimate value, theoretically or even practically. It would be easy to compile an almost inexhaustible list of examples of melodrama from Victorian literature. But the end result would be mere description. An infinite list of appropriate examples would do no more than show that Victorian literature is full of melodrama. It would do nothing to explain this preponderance, and meaning is the elusive quarry here. If we can move even one step outside the charmed circle of creative works we can perhaps begin to set up a connection between literature and something other than itself which may give us a firmer foothold than the endless rotation of Spitzer's circle.

A good place to begin is Carlyle's wonderful description of Tennyson at the age of 34, in a letter to Emerson:

> Alfred is one of the few British or Foreign Figures... who are and remain beautiful to me; – a true human soul, or some authentic approximation thereto... a man solitary and sad, as certain men are, dwelling in an element of gloom, – carrying a bit of Chaos about him, in short, which he is manufacturing into Cosmos!... In this way he lives still, now here, now there... One of the finest-looking men in the world. A great shock of rough dusty-dark hair; bright-laughing hazel eyes; massive aquiline face, most massive yet most delicate; of sallow-brown complexion, almost Indian-looking; clothes cynically loose, free-and-easy; – smokes infinite tobacco. His voice is musical metallic, – fit for loud laughter and piercing wail, and all that may lie between... We shall see what he will grow to. He is often unwell; very chaotic, – his way is through Chaos and the Bottomless and Pathless.[24]

The problems of evidence here are very complex. There is, for example, an undoubted element of literary convention in Carlyle's invocation of a Byronic strain in Tennyson, although there is no question but that Byronic attitudes did actually pass into what might for once validly be called 'life-styles' in the first half of the nineteenth century, a fact observable on a European scale. If we can assume, as seems legitimate, that Carlyle's impression has a basis in objective reality, then there is nothing inappropriate in seeing strong elements of melodrama in Tennyson, physically, psychologically and spiritually. This sense of melodrama is similar to that sketched by Christopher Prendergast in *Balzac: Fiction and Melodrama:*

> One of the initial advantages of this approach to 'melodrama' as a loose, general category is that it enables one to bypass the rather arid territory of fine taxonomic distinctions and generic definitions... Seen as a general mode, 'melodrama' may manifest itself in a whole variety of different ways.[25]

As Prendergast points out, melodrama as a general mode is marked by 'the systematic use of two elementary rhetorical figures, antithesis and hyperbole. Antithesis serves to organize the universe in terms of…preconceived polarities…while hyperbole reinforces this naive antithetical ordering of experience by ensuring that each side…is represented in an extreme, intensely magnified form.'[26] It is not difficult to trace these qualities working through Carlyle's description: Tennyson is 'solitary and sad' with 'bright-laughing hazel eyes', 'most massive yet most delicate', expresses both 'loud laughter and piercing wail'. It might be claimed that Carlyle himself is melodramatic in his hyperbolic organization of Tennyson's personality in terms of Chaos and Cosmos, yet biographical evidence suggests that his Tennyson is not entirely a personal construct.[27] But, in the last analysis, the point does not hang on whether Tennyson's personal life and character were melodramatic in some objective sense. The very fact that Carlyle makes use of antithesis and hyperbole, whether unconsciously or because he thinks it peculiarly appropriate to his subject, is enough to show that this mode of consciousness has some general currency.

This discussion is clearly highly speculative and so imposes the necessity of finding a wide range of reinforcing examples. The following is, perhaps, sufficiently different:

> The bourgeoisie, wherever it has got the upper hand, has put an end to all feudal, patriarchal, idyllic relations. It has pitilessly torn asunder the motley feudal ties that bound man to his 'natural superiors', and has left no other nexus between man and man than naked self-interest, than callous 'cash payment'. It has drowned the most heavenly ecstacies of religious fervour, of chivalrous enthusiasm, of philistine sentimentalism, in the icy water of egotistical calculation. It has resolved personal worth into exchange value, and in place of the numberless indefeasible chartered freedoms, has set up that single, unconscionable freedom – Free Trade. In one word, for exploitation, veiled by religious and political illusions, it has substituted naked, shameless, direct, brutal exploitation.[28]

And so on. This amazing outburst is from *The Communist Manifesto* and with its language we seem almost in the world of melodrama in the strictly technical sense. Images of villainy, of foreclosure, of threatened innocence, hover insistently around the passage as the personified bourgeoisie gets the upper hand, pitilessly tears asunder and drowns virtue, while its indecent revelation of past exploitation is a raping of the veiled in favour of the naked, shameless, direct and brutal. The last act of the as yet uncompleted drama will presumably see the triumph of the proletarian hero over the bourgeois villain in a manner that echoes the dénouement of countless popular plays throughout the nineteenth century.[29]

From the glare of the footlights we move to the more intimately personal realm of John Stuart Mill's emotional crisis, as recorded in his *Autobiography:*

> In all probability my case was by no means so peculiar as I fancied it, and I doubt not that many others have passed through a similar state; but the idiosyncrasies of my education had given to the general phenomenon a special character, which made it seem the natural effect of causes that it was hardly possible for time to remove. I frequently asked myself if I could, or if I was bound to go on living, when life must be passed in this manner. I generally answered to myself, that I did not think I could possibly bear it beyond a year. When, however, not more than half that duration of time had elapsed, a small ray of light broke in upon my gloom. I was reading, accidentally, Marmontel's *Mémoires*, and came to the passage which relates his father's death, the distressed position of the family, and the sudden inspiration by which he, then a mere boy, felt and made them feel that he would be everything to them – would supply the place of all that they had lost. A vivid conception of that scene and its feelings came over me, and I was moved to tears. From this moment my burden grew lighter.[30]

One is again struck by the resemblance between the outline of this situation and the stage ('A vivid conception of that scene'): the death of the father, the distressed family, the boy's heroism and, of course, the effect of all this on the audience, Mill himself. These ingredients are also universal in their appeal, reminding us that melodrama has its roots in the same human soil as tragedy, however debased it may have become in the nineteenth century. But the actual existence of melodrama as a fact of the period makes it impossible to ignore this configuration and its related sentimentalism, for sentimentality 'so integral a part of the melodramatic formula, was an international phenomenon in Western Europe.'[31]

Can any conclusions legitimately be drawn from all this? I have offered three examples from different kinds of non-creative writing – an informal character sketch in a letter, politics, and auto-biography – which on analysis contain inescapably melodramatic elements in their style and structure. They exhibit sufficient variety, but are pitifully few in number, a thinness which focuses the problem of evidence in literary writing. An immense number of figures can be accommodated in tables, but verbal quotation is expensive of space. What are the alternatives? The reader can be referred to the appropriate sections of a work such as W. E.

Houghton's *The Victorian Frame of Mind,* a lifetime's compilation of passages from many sources which illustrate aspects of Victorian consciousness. Alternatively, or in addition, we can utilize Leavis's formulaic, 'This is so, isn't it?' That is, an appeal to the reader's general sense of the whole period, alerted and guided by my examples, that melodrama is a mode of behaviour, gesture, language – style in the widest sense—which is pervasive in its social life as well as its literature.

Even if the reader feels involved in a morass of speculation at this point, one fact is at least indisputable, that stage melodrama was a dominantly popular form throughout the nineteenth century. Here, at any rate, we are on the secure ground of a thoroughly documented social relationship between an audience and a theatrical experience which it found endlessly renewing. All I can offer here is a highly compressed version of processes whose details can be followed in the work of specialists in the field.[32] One way of making brief sense of the story is by abstracting its purely literary history. Elements of melodrama are to be found in the eighteenth-century English novel, above all in *Clarissa,* as I shall show later; these are absorbed into French writing through Richardson's immense popularity and influence on the Continent; they surface in popular Parisian drama in the years around the French Revolution and, by a process of translation, reappear in the English theatre shortly afterwards, where they maintain an unshakable hold on the popular imagination for the rest of the century.

Here, surely, is something to be explained, and the explanation cannot remain within the philistine limits of some such non-account as that melodrama was popular because it gave its audience what it wanted, and there is no more to be said. One possibility is that melodrama and sentimentality are found in European literature because they exist at a social, and even a psychic, level in the period itself; that they are, in fact, one of the significant strands of the epoch. Their depth and pervasiveness can be plausibly related, for example, to the most important historical event of the time:

> The origins of melodrama can be accurately located within the context of the French Revolution and its aftermath...the moment that symbolically, and really, marks the final liquidation of the traditional Sacred and its representative institutions (Church and Monarch), the shattering of the myth of Christendom, the dissolution of an organic and hierarchically cohesive society, and the invalidation of the literary forms – tragedy, comedy of manners – that depended on such a society.[33]

The emergence of stage melodrama in Paris may correctly be linked with the turmoil associated with the French Revolution, but I have already pointed out that the origins of melodrama lie farther back in the eighteenth century. And if the passage seems a trifle far-fetched or apocalyptic in tone it can be glossed by some comments of the soberly brilliant de Tocqueville:

> When the Revolution that changed the social and political state of an aristocratic people begins to penetrate into literature, it generally first manifests itself in the drama... The spectator of a dramatic piece is, to a certain extent, taken by surprise by the impression it conveys. He has no time to refer to his memory or to consult those more able to judge than himself. It does not occur to him to resist the new literary tendencies that begin to be felt by him; he yields to them before he knows what they are... If you would judge beforehand of a literature that is lapsing into democracy, study its dramatic productions.[34]

In its turn, this relates to an authoritative description of the audience for melodrama as an 'army of factory slaves, navvies, guttersnipes, emaciated counter-clerks and care-worn women suckling babes in arms.'[35] In short, we are witnessing the first mass popular entertainment in modern history, a partial explanation for which can be found in one of Wordsworth's underlying motives in writing the *Lyrical Ballads:*

> For a multitude of causes, unknown to former times, are now acting with a combined force to blunt the discriminating powers of the mind, and, unfitting it for all voluntary exertion, to reduce it to a state of almost savage torpor. The most effective of these causes are the great national events which are daily taking place, and the increasing accumulation of men in cities, where the uniformity of their occupations produces a craving for extraordinary incident, which the rapid communication of intelligence hourly gratifies. To this tendency of life and manners the literature and theatrical exhibitions of the country have conformed themselves.

Wordsworth is clearly disturbed by what he calls the 'degrading thirst after outrageous stimulation,'[36] the human impoverishment of the popular forms of entertainment of his own day, and in the long term we might be inclined to agree with him. But a complex series of responses is involved in contemporary hostility to melodrama, one of which is a fairly simple political dislike, as in Coleridge's comment: 'But the whole system of your drama is a moral and intellectual *Jacobinism* of the most dangerous kind and consists with you in the confusion and subversion of the natural order of things, their causes and their effects.'[37] One suspects that Coleridge's animus is engendered at least partly by the fact that the hero of melodrama was frequently a 'commoner...The phenomenon of the plebeian hero is a phase of that democratization of the drama which, having begun toward the end of the eighteenth century...was proceeding through the nineteenth, chiefly in the people's theatre – the theatre of melodrama.'[38] It is more instructive to turn to a profound passage from Melville's letters which bears even more forcibly on our situation perhaps than it did on his: 'They [the public] look not only for more entertainment, but, at bottom, even for more reality than real life itself can show. Thus, though they want novelty, they want nature, too; but nature unfettered, exhilarated, in effect transformed.'[39] The desire for a surrogate reality carries with it its own comment on the more than purely personal failure to find nourishment in ordinary living, but however much we confidently deplore fantasy it may in certain lives, and in historical periods even, be a saving link with an inner world, however debased or shadowy. If melodrama is a form designed to 'immortalize the innocent, persecuted by a stronger power'[40] it may have been a necessity for those who had the human desire to escape from the drabness of their surroundings into a world of peace and justice. What other recourse was open to that 'army of factory slaves'? The key literary figure in this more positive view of melodrama is, of course, Dickens, whose whole private and professional life was bound up in the form that provided one of the central links between him and his enormous public. Dickens's involvement with the theatre throughout his entire life is well known and his increasingly subtle use of melodrama in his novels is the mark of a great popular genius who strives to refine, rather than reject, the conventions dear to his audience. Dickens's attitude to popular entertainment is made clear in his Preliminary Word to the opening number of *Household Words* in which he states that the periodical will indulge no 'mere utilitarian spirit, no iron binding of the mind to grim realities' but 'cherish that light of Fancy which is inherent in the human breast' and defend any class against exclusion from 'the sympathies and graces of imagination.'[41] And the same number contains one of Dickens's most powerful, and amusing, defences of the popular theatre – his article, 'The Amusements of the People.'

Here, then, is a complex case of the rise of a literary mode which comes to intense popularity because it fulfils a need in new groups of humanity. But this is not a complete answer to the question of why melodrama and sentimentality should be so pervasive at all levels of Victorian consciousness, not just the popular. A possible line of approach is suggested by a passage in James Smith's *Melodrama:* 'Generations, bred in the narrow but familiar patterns of village life found themselves alone in a city of strangers, at the mercy of random and outrageous fortune.'[42] Again, if one accepts that a major influence on melodrama was the 'daily life of the times, particularly the kaleidoscopic spectacle of modern city life'[43] then we may also accept the implication that there is something melodramatic in the very nature of modern urban and industrialized existence itself. This is certainly the view of Eric Bentley in *The Life of the Drama:* 'I am arguing, then, up to a point, that melodrama is actually more natural that Naturalism, corresponds to reality, not least to modern reality, more closely than Naturalism.'[44] Of course, fate, chance, accident are timeless features of human life, although in some periods they might have seemed bearable or meaningful in relation to the gods, or Christianity, or Nature. But the economic accidents of modern urban living seemed to the nineteenth century mechanical in their impersonality, the working out of immutable laws. And the setting for this random play of forces, the great modern city, is a place of sentimental and melodramatic contrasts, of chance encounters and surprising revelations. This is how the urban vision is conveyed by a fine, if minor, novelist, Mrs Gaskell, in *Mary Barton:*

> It is a pretty sight to walk through a street with lighted shops; the gas is so brilliant, the display of goods so much more vividly shown than by day, and of all the shops a druggist's looks the most like the tales of our childhood, from Aladdin's garden of enchanted fruits to the charming Rosamund with her purple jar. No such associations had Barton: yet he felt the contrast between the well-filled, well-lighted shops and the dim gloomy cellar, and it made him moody that such contrasts should exist. They are a mysterious problem of life to more than him. He wondered if any in all the hurrying crowd had come from such a house of mourning. He thought they all looked joyous, and he was angry with them. But he could not, you cannot, read the lot of those who daily pass you by in the street. How do you know the wild romances of their lives: the trials, the temptations they are even now enduring, resisting, sinking under? You may be elbowed one instant by the girl desperate in her abandonment, laughing in her mad merriment with her outward gesture, while her soul is longing for the rest of the dead, and bringing itself to think of the cold-flowing river as the only mercy of God remaining to her here. You may pass the criminal, meditating crimes at which you will tomorrow shudder with horror as you read them. You may push against one,

humble and unnoticed, the last upon earth, who in Heaven will for ever be in the immediate light of God's countenance. Errands of mercy – errands of sin – did you ever think where all the thousands of people you meet are daily bound?[45]

This may lack the power of Balzac, Dickens or Dostoevsky – even, in a different way, Mayhew – but it encapsulates at its own level what can be regarded as one of the key insights into the consciousness of nineteenth-century Europe, in a way that precludes further comment. The sense of the city, and of the life within it, presented here could be duplicated in the period's great novelists, in its poets, historians, social commentators, journalists, and in the letters and memoirs of ordinary people. It conveys a vision of life radically unlike that of say, the Renaissance, one dependent on objectively verifiable changes in social life, above all the vast increase in the size of cities and the economic uncertainties engendered by the emergence of large-scale industrial capitalism. These are only two of the most important of Wordsworth's 'multitude of causes' which combined to make melodrama not merely the outstandingly popular art form of the day but, in a wider sense, an essential mode of being of human life itself.

Conclusions

At the very least the previous section shows the extreme complexity of demonstrating a relationship between literature and society at the practical level. But these problems are simple compared with the difficulty of theorizing the relationship. In fact, two recent authorities have cast doubt on the possibility of doing so at all, from the sociological and from the literary point of view. Thus Monroe Berger, whose book was discussed on p. 15 above: 'The search for general principles in the sociology of art has been unsuccessful in the century and a half since Hegel first pointed out the difficulties of this approach.'[46] And in his recent, and very thorough, *Literary Sociology and Practical Criticism* Jeffrey Sammons examines the whole problem from the standpoint of a mastery of the European, above all German, work in the field: 'There is at present no generally acceptable systematic theory of the nature of the correlation of literary events and complexities to core patterns of society...I am by no means convinced that such a general theory is even possible.'[47] If these qualifications seem faint-hearted or ideologically biased, the reader is referred to the long discussion of economic determinism in the book-length interviews with Raymond Williams, *Politics and Letters*, conducted by the editors of *New Left Review*.[48] The book traces in fascinating detail Professor Williams's move towards ultimate acceptance of Marxism, or historical materialism, in a full sense. At least part of the work's value is that the interviewers are not lay figures. They are intellectually committed and highly educated Marxists of a younger generation who, within a general context of respect, pursue Williams with questioning at a deep level. In doing so they may surprise readers more familiar with vulgar Marxism by the flexibility of their acceptance of the value of certain features of bourgeois life, above all culture. At one point they even give a spirited account of what they call the 'vitality and efficacy' of developments in Christianity. It is all the more surprising, then, to encounter the following.

> It is true that historical materialism does not possess any worked out theory, even for one epoch, let alone trans-epochally, of the exact connections between the economic and political and cultural or ideological orders. But to dwell at exclusive length on this point can be a way of burking and evading the central fact that we can in a perfectly reasonable and empirically verifiable way assert that the processes of physical production have till now exerted an ultimate power of constraint over all others.[49]

Even to those not committed to the position, Marxism has seemed the area of thought most likely to produce a fully comprehensive theory of the relations between literature and society. If this is yet to come then perhaps we can be forgiven for discussing the theoretical issues involved within a less than totalizing perspective; and also for grasping at the interviewers' stress on the empirical, although with possibly different emphases. Empirically, there is no reason to feel anything but gratitude, of course, for much of the Marxist thinking in this field. Goldmann's concept of an 'homology of structure'[50] – the close parallel between the inner structure of a literary work and related social structures – is of great interest; and Gramsci's use of hegemony, as it is being developed at the moment, is of particular value in avoiding the naive separatism involved in many social theories of art.[51] Raymond Williams puts the point clearly in *Marxism and Literature:* 'It is in just this recognition of the *wholeness* of the process that the concept of "hegemony" goes beyond "ideology." What is decisive is not only the conscious system of ideas and beliefs, but the whole lived social process as practically organized by specific and dominant meanings and values.'[52] The relation of the form of the novel to the 'whole lived social process' is central to my own enquiry. But Williams goes on to say that a 'Marxism without some conception of determination is in effect worthless.'[53] *Politics and Letters* reveals that this opposition between social wholeness – Williams has long rejected the model of economic base and cultural superstructure – and determinism causes intense difficulty for even convinced and sophisticated Marxists. In the last analysis, indeed, his interviewers seem unable to be fully persuaded by Williams's qualifications of what they call 'a central tenet of historical materialism: the primacy, or determination in the last instance, of the economic within any social totality.[54] For the uncommitted, determinism is probably the greatest stumbling block to an intellectual acceptance of Marxism. In its most limiting form it posits a one-to-one relationship which is denied by the sheer variety of literature within a single historical period. At the simplest, how can the work of Dickens and George Eliot be causally determined, at even a deep and remote level? It seems impossible, for example, to distinguish between them in terms of artistic greatness. Dickens might be seen as the greater writer of the two, but many would quarrel with the view that *Middlemarch* is in any sense inferior to the best of Dickens's novels. No two writers could be as eminent and different in artistry or general outlook, unless perhaps the Tolstoy *or* Dostoevski differentiated by George Steiner. But if the stress is laid on 'determination *in the last instance*' (my emphasis) then we are left with a concept not radically unlike that posited by Werner Stark's *The Sociology of Knowledge* in his discussion of Freud:

> Yet these wish-determined thought-processes start out from a picture of reality which is not, in and by itself, wish-determined – which is not para-theoretical, but genuine. In the late-Victorian Vienna where Freud grew up, life had realized, out of the indefinite number of potential family forms, one pattern in particular – the small family unit dominated by the male element, the breadwinner – imbued with the characteristic high-powered internal pressure-system which we find reflected, not only in Freud's world-picture, but generally in contemporary literature, scientific and artistic. In...this set-up, his thought is indeed socially determined... but it is not ideologically deflected from the truth; indeed, it *is* the truth precisely *because* of its social determination.[55]

There is no incompatibility between this general grounding in social life, which is true of all human existence, and concerns which are insistently personal and spiritual.

Wuthering Heights has recently become a test case for various forms of sociological criticism and it would be absurd to deny that it contains many important social features. The whole novel can be understood as a response to kinds of emotional deprivation highly characteristic of the period, and the detail of Catherine's rejection of Heathcliff for money and status is a typical gesture of Victorian social criticism. Again, the novel inhabits a social domain in its rapid, but richly detailed, sketching of a specific regional culture with its own language, habits of mind and religious beliefs. But can it seriously be maintained that these are the novel's central concerns? Although he calls them 'classic' Raymond Williams dismisses 'attempts to read Heathcliff as a figuration of the proletariat. It can't be done in that way.[56] The 'it', of course, is the attempt to give the novel a radically social emphasis. On this issue, and that of Dickens's production of 'virtue, almost magically, as in *Little Dorrit*,' the seriousness of *Politics and Letters* degenerates into solemnity and some high comedy ensues:

> All these questions revolve around a single problem which still
> preoccupies me to an extraordinary extent. How are we to explain the
> possibility of liberating responses to a system that do not seem to have in
> any obvious way been prepared by social conditions? Certain
> relationships occur which are very difficult to understand by normal
> canons, and which give force to metaphysical or subjectivist explanations
> because these remain virtually the only terms to hand for them. I am very
> keen to find alternative terms.[57]

There is something almost touching in that keenness. The fact is that goodness in, say, *Little Dorrit* and *Great Expectations* is part of a religious view of experience which is not external to the books' deepest concerns. It operates in terms of both structure and detail of language so that to unpick this aspect of the novels from the whole causes them to collapse. Some comments of Werner Stark on Haydn and Mozart are relevant:

> Nevertheless, one feels in this discussion that the limits of sociological
> interpretation are here in sight. When all social circumstances are taken
> fully into account and the sociology of knowledge is driven as far as it can
> reasonably be, there remains the irreducible fact that different
> personalities react differently to the same conditions – there remains the
> ineffable spontaneity of the individual.[58]

The final hallucinatory movement of Heathcliff towards Catherine in those passages where he is apparently staring at nothing is not reducible to anything other than itself, either psychologically or socially. The artistic statement here is complete within its own terms, and those terms have to do with a love which derives neither from personal frustration nor social need. Put simply, it is just not fruitful to discuss *Wuthering Heights* in social terms. Of course, this can and has been done, as it can with all works of literature. A social dimension is always present, in a lyric poem or in *Paradise Lost*, but whether it is always useful to pursue this dimension is quite another matter. There is a scale of profitability here, from the lyric poem to the novel, and common sense suggests that more will be gained from discussing the social aspects of the second rather than the first.

This section has demanded some confrontation of the theoretical issues involved in the relationship of literature and society, a demand equally necessary for history itself since, as I remarked earlier, to deal with a series of individual novels over a chronological spread is, in effect, to attempt a history of the form. Leavis, again, has a useful passage describing the ideal social historian: 'It is with such questions in mind [concerning the human implications of his work] – which is not to say he will come out with answers to them – that a social historian, in so far as his history is anything more than an assemblage of mechanically arranged external information, must define the changes and developments that he discerns.'[59] What are some of the implications of this view of knowledge? First, that knowledge is only meaningful if it is ordered by a theory of some kind. If history is more than 'an assemblage of mechanically arranged external information,' this can only be because the enquirer has a method for perceiving order in the apparently chaotic multiplicity of existence. For the historian Bloch, to take the past in unordered variety would be to 'sacrifice clarity, not to the true order of reality – which is composed of natural affinities and underlying connections – but to the purely superficial order of contemporaneousness.'[60] This unmodernist assumption, that order is present as an objective part of external reality, is at the opposite pole from Beckett's *Murphy* in a passage describing the 'hero's' ideal vision of existence: 'It was pleasant to kick the Ticklepennies and Miss Carridges simultaneously together into ghastly acts of love. It was pleasant to lie dreaming on the shelf beside Belacqua, watching the dawn break crooked. But how much more pleasant was the sensation of being a missile without provenance or target, caught up in a tumult of non-Newtonian motion.'[61] A non-Newtonian universe presumably lacks causation and predictability, substituting a realm of uncertainty for that of order and harmony. But there is no need to take sides between these positions, for even without the foundation of a metaphysic the recognition of at least a provisional order is inseparable from any intellectual endeavour. Literary history, for example, can only be written from a combination of selection and arrangement of the available material. Even within this comparatively narrow area there is no possibility of comprehensiveness. And if there were, its desirability would still be an open question. What would it mean to write a fully comprehensive history of English literature, or even of the English novel? The result would surely be an ultimately meaningless listing of facts. Any history worth the name involves selectivity, and selection means the imposition of order on one's material, a point made clearly by the Russian formalist, Boris Eichenbaum: 'Without theory no historical system would be possible, because there would be no principle for selecting and conceptualizing facts.'[62] This is not to suggest that reality is merely a construct of mind. Like the notes of the musical score, reality is 'out there' in some objective sense, but it comes fully into focus only when it is mediated and interpreted, as through the hands of the musician, by consciousness. The scope of any intellectual endeavour is imposed by the mind, but solutions to problems are discoverable in the real world, not just in subjective manipulation. Sammons has this in view, surely, in complaining of the subjectivist element in contemporary thinking: 'The study of the relations of literature and society, as part of the intellectual climate of our times, is deeply infected with the trend toward the absorption of reality by synthesizing intellect.'[63] Extreme positions in this area have suggested that reality is simply a projection of thought and/or language, an impertinent denial of the materiality of nature. Wordsworth memorably captured our relationship to reality as a duality composed of

> all the mighty world
> Of eye, and ear – both what they half create,
> And what perceive.[64]

And in a burst of Anglo-Saxon moderation, rather than Gallic fervour, Raymond Aron expresses a related idea in more strictly sociological terms:

> If Max Weber were right and all social facts were incoherent, then every interpretation would be superimposed on the facts and therefore bound up with the personality of the sociologist himself. On the other hand, if social reality were completely structured, if it had a complete unity...there would be only one true sociological theory.[65]

The second major implication of Leavis's statement is that knowledge is a series of inter-relationships; in Stark's words, knowledge is 'above all structured.' That is, discrete pieces of information are of interest as facts, but to constitute knowledge they need to be seen as ordered patterns of events. The danger here is clearly the imposition of subjective interpretation on material to which it is irrelevant. A way of avoiding this failure, and of thinking at the level necessary to perceive significant relationships, is provided by a wonderful passage from Auerbach, his concept of the epoch:

> When people realize that epochs and societies are...to be judged...in every case in terms of their own premises; when people reckon among such premises not only natural factors like climate and soil but also the intellectual and historical factors; when, in other words, they come to develop a sense of historical dynamics, of the incomparability of historical phenomena and of their constant inner mobility; when they come to appreciate the vital unity of individual epochs, so that each epoch appears as a whole whose character is reflected in each of its manifestations; when, finally, they accept the conviction that the meaning of events cannot be grasped in abstract and general forms of cognition and that the material needed to understand it must not be sought exclusively in the upper strata of society and in major political events but also in art, economy, material and intellectual culture, in the depths of the workaday world and its men and women, because it is only there that one can grasp what is unique, what is animated by inner forces, and what, in both a more concrete and a more profound sense, is universally valid: then...the present too will be seen...as a piece of history whose everyday depths and total inner structure lay claim to our interest.[66]

However tentatively, one criticism can be proffered here, that the concept has a certain rigidity in its suggestion of one epoch existing separately in a watertight compartment from another. But if we could combine this sense of the many-layered-ness of society with its continuous movement forward in time we would clearly have a marvellously subtle instrument for registering social complexity. Of course, to come within hailing distance of this depth and variety of understanding is obviously impossible for the ordinary scholar. It is an achievement only for the few such as G. M. Young in *Victorian England: Portrait of an Age*, which bears eloquent testimony to his claim of hearing the tones of the speaking voice of the period through his omnivorous reading. However, it may be possible to make use of Auerbach's method, if without his depth of knowledge, to solve an important difficulty in the relationship between literature and society: the opposition between a superstructure and its base. This opposition between a less important or secondary phenomenon, the superstructure, influenced or caused by the more essential, the base, is, as Raymond Williams remarks in *The Long Revolution*, 'a false meaning'; this is clarified by a passage remarkably close to Auerbach's:

> And at this point we find ourselves moving into a process which cannot be the simple comparison of art and society, but which must start from the recognition that all the acts of men compose a general reality within which both art and what we ordinarily call society are comprised.[67]

If we see the novel as existing within the complex wholes suggested by Auerbach and Williams, it becomes possible to suggest links between it and society which are not either reductionist or deterministic, in the sense that one is given priority over the other. And this opens the way to a history of the form which has an equally interesting social dimension.

It is striking that relatively few attempts have been made in recent years to write histories of the novel, especially in the light of Diana Spearman's statement that 'the impact of writers on each other was as important as the influence of sociological forces.'[68] But this claim must be placed in the context of her book, which is a highly polemical attack on the relationship of the novel to society. A contrary passage from Ian Watt will show that it is very much an open question: 'Defoe, Richardson, and Fielding do not in the usual sense constitute a literary school. Indeed their works show...little sign of mutual influence and are...different in nature.'[69] This is reinforced, for the nineteenth century, by Kathleen Tillotson in *Novels of the Eighteen-Forties:* 'I see the novelists of the forties as initiating rather than continuing, and am more aware of their legacy to succeeding novels than of their own inheritance from the novel's past.'[70] All kinds of influences, of a conventional nature, can of course be seen in the English novel, between Fanny Burney and Jane Austen, Smollett and early Dickens, and so on. On a more serious level, recent studies of such phenomena as the Jacobin novel at the end of the eighteenth and beginning of the nineteenth century have done something to fill gaps that appeared to exist between the great creative periods of English fiction.[71] Interesting as it is, though, such work does not really redraw the map of the English novel: the peaks and the plains remain as they were. Indeed, I would query even the second part of Mrs Tillotson's judgement, that concerning the novel's legacy to the future. My stress would fall on the essentially innovatory nature of the classic English novel. Novelists learn what they can from each other, and from literature in general, but I see English fiction as largely experimental, as making a series of fresh starts, each of which – this is true of the greatest works, at least – embodies in its own unique form its grasp on experience.

If the works making up the field of eighteenth and nineteenth-century fiction are in some real sense discrete, rather than homogeneously inter-related, this would suggest the inapplicability of the usual kind of literary history, with its tracing of influences. In this form of history the focus is on the relationship of books and writers to one another, but the focus might be altered so as to give a rather different historical reading. Another way of tracing the development of the English novel might be in terms of its relationship to society, and changes in novelistic form might be validly related to objective social change and to changes in the conceptions men and women have of their social world. This, at any rate, is the order my book will attempt to impose on its chosen field, an order that may not seem merely arbitrary, given the obviously social dimension that is present in many novels. Conventional literary history does, after all, sometimes have to manipulate unprovable assumptions about the reading habits of particular authors. My assumption is simply that great writers are aware of the nature of the world in which they live. A problem of method immediately presents itself as far as the demonstration of a relationship between fictional form and society is concerned, as Ian Watt is well aware:

> It is one of the general difficulties in applying social history to the interpretation of literature that, uncertain as our knowledge of any particular social change may be, our knowledge of its subjective aspects, the way it affected the thoughts and feelings of the individual concerned, is even more insecure and hypothetical. Yet the problem cannot altogether be avoided; however important the external facts about the complexities of the social situation of women may have been, they presented themselves to Richardson in the form of the largely unconscious presuppositions of the people around him; and it was presumably these social and psychological orientations which dictated the way his readers understood the thoughts and actions of the characters in *Pamela*.[72]

There is no way in which the total texture of a past historical period can be re-created, but this does not mean that we are completely at the mercy of subjective interpretation. It should be possible to point to some objectively agreed social factors that are in accord with specific aspects of novelistic form, and this book will do so wherever possible. But, as Ian Watt suggests, subjectivity is itself a crucial part of our understanding of the past, if we agree with Bloch that 'in the last analysis it is human consciousness which is the subject-matter of history.'[73] This is a point on which one can find agreement between the historian of the middle ages or of the eighteenth century, and the sociologist. Huizinga claims that 'for the history of civilization every delusion or opinion of an epoch has the value of an important fact.'[74] Dickinson states that 'for a full understanding of eighteenth-century politics we need to appreciate not just what historians now believe to be the objective reality, but how men at the time regarded the situation.'[75] And for Robert A. Nisbet 'the relations between events and ideas is never direct; it is always mediated by *conceptions* of the events.'[76]

There remains the final problem of the evidential basis of any attempt to trace the relations of literature and society. Total knowledge would, presumably, involve every last detail of interconnection, the world down to its finest detail. This impossibility for the mind of man is not even desirable, however, for there is a sense in which all knowledge is no knowledge. We realize what the artist is at when he tells the baffled man in the street that his work means itself. Picasso was right to say that we don't ask flowers for their meaning. On such a view, however, criticism would consist of a series of total responses to the complete work. So much the worse for criticism, some would say. But works of art do, after all, exist in a world of discourse. We want to speak of what we enjoy and, as soon as we do, we in some sense violate the wholeness of the created object. In any case, as I have suggested earlier, works of art are too robust to be damaged by the rough and tumble of public debate. Similarly, human attempts at historical understanding are forced to violate historical totality. We can begin the story of the novel a long way before Defoe, but a start must be made somewhere and to succumb to the demands of origins is to risk intellectual paralysis. Even working on a more limited scale, we cannot recreate a total picture of eighteenth and nineteenth-century social life in relation to any particular novel. This is, however, a literary study and novels can be grasped, through re-reading, with some approximation to completeness. My centre of interest is what

Auerbach calls the artist's 'active will to give the world a form'[77] and this suggests that novels themselves can legitimately be a centre of evidence. Support for this view can be found in both a Marxist and a non-Marxist literary critic. In discussing the question of novelistic authenticity, fictional truth to reality, David Craig remarks:

> But if a novel throws a clear and intense light on some walk of life... and if it succeeds artistically, it will contain within itself the knowledge needed to appreciate it and authenticate its truth to reality.[78]

The question-begging phrase here is, I think, 'if it succeeds artistically.' It is not always easy to command assent in literary discourse for what is artistically successful. And, assuming the assent to be given, is artistic success a sufficient guarantee of fidelity to objective reality? Would the knowledge contained within, say, an eighteenth-century novel be sufficient for a reader who knew nothing at all about the period to make a valid judgement about its success in portraying a social world? Perhaps not, but J. P. Stern carries the argument a stage further in a discussion of *Fortunata and Jacinta* by Galdos:

> And the ring of truth for which we have praised the novel? Now we understand that it is this coherence which fulfils our relatively uninformed yet never wholly ignorant expectation of what that human possibility called 'Madrid in the 1870's' might be like. It is the implicit affirmation *that* the thing works emerging from the explicit affirmation of *how* it works, which elicits our positive response and delight.[79]

Both writers agree that we must start from the coherence of the work of art itself. We cannot be persuaded that a formally incoherent novel will possess anything other than an incoherent vision of the world, that its relation to reality is not somehow fatally flawed. But Stern permits us to move out of the charmed circle of the autonomous by way of his empirically useful 'uninformed yet never wholly ignorant expectation' of external reality. We can thus move between a view of the novel as sealed-off within its 'literariness' and the demand that it be placed within such a detailed context that it is suffocated. What surely Craig and Stern have in mind is the competent reader, someone without the critical skills of a Leavis or the knowledge of an Auerbach but able, nonetheless, to bring to bear critical intelligence and a reasonably well-stocked mind in considering the question of how novels might relate to society. If the aura of British common-sense emanates from all this, it may be no bad thing as long as it avoids complacency.

There is also a more theoretical answer to the problems of any contextual study of literature. The first and last place to find an appropriate context is within the work itself. Any significant context will be internalized in the way that human beings internalize the social forces that impinge on them. The fact that we are social beings involves no fundamental loss of individuality, just as the fact that the novel may be a social form involves no loss of its artistic integrity. I said 'first and last' a moment ago because other activities can be pursued in between. If Spitzer's 'philological circle' is open to external verification, we can also look outside a novel to reinforce or elaborate our first, and essentially literary, response. The results, as in any critical activity, may be the enrichment of our 'last' reading by the enquiries prompted by a living response to the work in its social context. The studies that follow will attempt to justify a social reading of fiction that, far from violating artistry, arises out of the form of specific works. The validity of this approach is related to the technical problem of the contexts within which fictional characters can exist. In a work of any scale, characters relate to each other in ways wider than face-to-face confrontation. *The Canterbury Tales*, *Paradise Lost*, Shakespearian drama, all possess a landscape within which figures move and meet, but despite the social implications present in them in no case could these landscapes be given the status of representations of society. It is only with the advent of a 'rational' prose style that writers can amass the detail that is necessary to portray the ramifications of a social world. And the development of extended prose fiction in eighteenth-century England coincides with the beginnings of the process whereby society is recognised as something more than a given, unanalysed continuum, the moral battlefield whose victories and defeats are ultimately metaphysical in their scope. With the slow growth in the self-conscious recognition that society has a status of its own, a secular world at least partly created by man rather than simply God-given, comes the representation of this world in the long prose works we call novels. The relationship between the novel and society then becomes highly complex: in some cases an unconscious reflection of the social world, in others a critical vision of it. What does seem clear is that as society itself becomes more complex, and as man's awareness of society as an intellectual concept develops, so the form of the novel as an image of society becomes more elaborate. And by the very end of our period we may detect the first signs of a turning away from society as the seemingly unavoidable setting for the playing-out of personal dilemmas. My contention is, then, that the English novel comes into being with the idea of society and that the depiction of society is central to its artistic success, in its period of growth in the eighteenth century and its classic achievement in the nineteenth.

It may be argued that the concept of society itself is altogether too large, vague and all-embracing to satisfy the rigour necessary for a suggested relationship between it and the novel. Would it not be wiser, or intellectually more convincing, to attempt the demonstration through a segment of social life rather than society itself? A recent, and ambitious, attempt to do so is Tony Tanner's *Adultery and the Novel*.[80] Tanner believes that 'the novel tends to be drawn, all but irresistibly, to the problem of adultery' because the 'bourgeois novel is coeval and coterminous with the power concentrated in the central structure of marriage.'[81] When adultery ceases to be of significance, as in *Lady Chatterley's Lover*, 'sexuality, narration and society fall apart.'[82] Whatever interest these ideas may generate for novels such as *Anna Karenina* and *Madame Bovary*, Tanner's general thesis is hopelessly inadequate as an account of the novel as a whole. To take a single example: according to the book's index Dickens receives only one mention, in a footnote that has nothing to do with Tanner's controlling theme. Surely we are right to be suspicious of any general account of the novel that can find no place for Dickens? But this is the weakness of any attempt to account for the novel segmentally, even when the segment is as wide as Ian Watt's rise of the middle classes, as I shall argue in detail later. Any one thread of interest may illuminate even a group of novels, but it cannot do justice to a phenomenon with the range and variety of the novel as a whole. Anything less than the total context within which the novel comes into being is liable to partiality and its accompanying glaring exceptions. The nature of the relationship I am trying to clarify is hinted at in the words of an anonymous writer in the *Analytical Review* for 1798:

> The french (sic) revolution which has broken up the established forms of society, and destroyed the distinctions which generations had held in veneration, has very naturally called the attention of all men to the study of the social relations of life.[83]

Although I wish to push the story back earlier into the eighteenth century, it is precisely this self-conscious awareness of society which is, in my view, the overwhelmingly important accompaniment to the rise and development of the English novel.

Further Reading

The classic study of the development of the novel within a social context is *The Rise of the Novel* by Ian Watt (Penguin, 1972).

A start in the exploration of the social relations of literature is provided by:

Sociology of Literature and Drama edited by Elizabeth and Tom Burns (Penguin, 1973).

The Sociology of Literature by John Hall (London, 1979).

The Sociology of Literature by Diana Lawrenson and Allen Swingewood (London, 1972).
These works contain detailed bibliographies which will assist further study.

A rather more complex treatment is:

The Sociology of Literature: Theoretical Approaches edited by Jane Routh and Janet Wolff (University of Keele, 1977).

Advanced work in the field will be found in:

Sociology of Literature by Robert Escarpit (London, 1971), trans. Ernest Pick.

Towards a Sociology of the Novel by Lucien Goldmann (London, 1977), trans. Alan Sheridan.

Culture and Society by Raymond Williams (Penguin, 1971).

The Long Revolution by Raymond Williams (Penguin, 1971).

A humane discussion of the sociological dimension of culture in general is:

The Sociology of Knowledge by Werner Stark (London, 1958).

An introduction to Marxist thought in this area is provided by:

Marxists on Literature: An Anthology edited by David Craig (Penguin, 1975).

The full rigour of this position at a high intellectual level will be found in:

Marxism and Literature by Raymond Williams (Oxford University Press, 1977).

Those interested in melodrama should read:

The Melodramatic Imagination: Balzac, Henry James, Melodrama and the Mode of Excess by Peter Brooks (Yale University Press, 1977).

Balzac, Fiction and Melodrama by Christopher Prendergast (London, 1978).

Finally, a study of classic stature in this general field is:

Mimesis: The Representation of Reality in Western Literature by Erich Auerbach (Princeton Univeristy Press, 1953), trans. Willard Trask.

2

The Eighteenth Century:
Defoe, Smollett and the Rise
of the Novel

A pleasing irony at the expense of explanation is that the novel should be such a varied form from its eighteenth century beginnings. The major writers – Defoe, Smollett, Fielding, Richardson and Sterne – could hardly be more different from each other and this intractable individuality places a large obstacle in the way of any simple account of the form's development. Explanations frequently founder on the massive presence of Fielding, a failure analogous to advancing an account of nineteenth-century fiction which fails to accommodate either Dickens or George Eliot. That Fielding should be a radical or, at the very least, a bourgeois figure seems indispensable to many accounts of the novel's rise. It is, of course, possible to posit an element of social criticism in Fielding by concentrating on the plays and *Jonathan Wild*, although the limits of his radicalism are evident even here. But a writer is presumably to be judged by his greatest work and a later chapter will try to demonstrate the conservative nature of *Tom Jones*, a conservatism quite compatible with the most daring artistic originality. A comment from W. A. Speck's *Stability and Strife: England 1714-1760* is surely applicable to Fielding:

> One of the more significant signs that 'the middling sort' aspired to become gentlemen is that there was little if anything of a distinctly middle class culture or morality. The early novel, for instance, so often taken as a bourgeois art form, displays surprisingly genteel values...[It] reflects a society in which the dominant values are still overwhelmingly those of its landed proprietors.[1]

It is a tribute to the complexities involved in this area rather than simple inconsistency which leads the same writer at a later point to say something rather different about the success of Richardson and Fielding in the 1740s:

Such literature found a readership among merchants, tradesmen and craftsmen. Indeed it went further down the social scale, though how far is a question involving the spread of literacy and the economics of purchasing published matter in this period.[2]

It is surely hard to believe that a readership as wide as this could have existed for works which totally ignored the aspirations and world view of its audience. A similar shift of focus is evident in Pat Rogers's *The Augustan Vision*. In an extended passage Rogers takes issue with the idea that the novel is a middle class form and concludes:

The early novel is stuffed with violence, brutality, rape, crime and penury. There was a segment of eighteenth-century society to which such things were continually present, but it was assuredly not the 'economically, socially and politically influential middle class' of which Hauser writes.[3]

But only a few pages on Rogers gives a potted biography of Defoe which makes him seem a quintessentially bourgeois figure, and we read later of Crusoe's 'mercantile background' and that Moll Flanders is a 'perfect image of alienation.'[4]

The intention here is not to spot contradictions in distinguished writers, but to acknowledge the contradictions that exist within the problem of the rise of the novel itself. A single work may serve to bring out the difficulties of labelling the eighteenth century novel bourgeois, anti-bourgeois, or whatever. For reasons that are too obvious to elaborate, *Robinson Crusoe* is the masterpiece of the sociological-Marxist interpretation of the rise of the novel,[5] and yet close attention to the text reveals a pattern of references that seem to run counter to the 'Crusoe as economic man' aspect of the book. This is how Crusoe congratulates himself at a point when things are going well on the island:

I was lord of the whole manor; or if I pleased, I might call myself king or emperor over the whole country which I had possession of. There were no rivals; I had no competitor, none to dispute sovereignty or command with me. (139)[6]

Again, something touching and amusing is made of Crusoe's meals in the company of his cats, dog and parrot:

> It would have made a stoick smile to have seen me and my little family sit down to dinner; there was my majesty the prince and lord of the whole island; I had the lives of all my subjects at my entire command; I could hang, draw, give liberty, and take it away, and no rebels among all my subjects. (157)

Finally, Defoe rises to something like wit:

> My island was now peopled, and I thought myself very rich in subjects; and it was a merry reflection which I frequently made, how like a king I looked. First of all, the whole country was my own meer property; so that I had an undoubted right of dominion. 2ndly, my people were perfectly subjected: I was absolute lord and lawgiver; they all owed their lives to me, and were ready to lay down their lives, if there had been occasion of it, for me. It was remarkable too, we had but three subjects, and they were of three different religions. My man Friday was a Protestant, his father was a pagan and a cannibal, and the Spaniard was a Papist: however I allowed liberty of conscience throughout my dominions. (241)

It would be foolish to make too much of this, but it suggests an area of interest different from the assumptions of 'radical' readings of the novel. At the very least, Crusoe hardly appears in his 'progressive' guise at this point. Indeed, Defoe is working within an established tradition here, the most famous example of which is Gonzalo's celebration of an ideal commonwealth in *The Tempest* (II, i, 143-60). However superficially, Defoe is glancing at notions of the ideal state in these passages, the role of the ruler, the nature of tolerance, and so on. But unlike Gonzalo's island in which there is 'no sovereignty', Crusoe is clearly an absolute monarch. Generalizing about Defoe is notoriously difficult, partly because of his huge output and also because of his changes of view, but the salutariness of this reminder of his complexity is reinforced by a comment from his *Review* on that most fully accepted of 'bourgeois' elements in his work, the economic:

> And what if, being writing of commerce, I should tell you there is a kind of divinity in the original of trade, and if I spend one *Review* to put you in mind that God, in the order of nature... made trade necessary to the making of the life of man.[7]

This seems the clearest possible expression of the Augustan view of a universe divinely ordered in all its detail.

Returning to the 'problem' of Fielding, Ian Watt has provided his own brilliant account of the rise of the novel but here, too, the concentration on a single causal strand, the development of realism, leads to an imbalance in the critical evaluation of novelists and their work. I shall comment later on the inadequacies of Watt's discussion of Fielding,[8] a weakness that enforces the conclusion that theory must always be prepared to give way to fact. Is it not more satisfactory to recognize that English literature is as fortunate to possess the Fielding-Richardson opposition for the eighteenth century as it is to have Dickens and George Eliot for the nineteenth; in other words, that realist and non-realist elements are present in the English novel from the very start? Explanations like those of Watt and the Marxists fall into the trap of assuming that the general historical factors which lead to the rise of the novel must issue in one particular novelistic form. But there seems no necessary reason why this should be the case. The same conditions may facilitate the writing of novels in general, but the varieties of form they take in particular cases is a matter of individual genius. *Moll Flanders* can suggest reasons why the novel came into existence and also the necessity of certain qualities for it to exist successfully, but this does not mean that its form need be the same as that of *Tom Jones*.

In the Preface to his novel, Defoe makes a statement interesting in itself and also for the remarkably modern form of its expression:

> The second [part] is the life of her transported husband, a highwayman, who it seems, lived a twelve years' life of successful villainy upon the road, and even at last came off so well as to be a volunteer transport, not a convict, and in whose life there is an incredible variety. (4)[9]

A concern for the 'incredible variety' of human life reflects the pressure of a genuinely modern sensibility and there is reason to believe that it was a dominant concern of Defoe's, as we find the Preface to *Robinson Crusoe* claiming that 'the life of one man...[is] scarce capable of a greater variety' (25) than that of the book's hero. The point should not, of course, be exaggerated. The presence of 'God's plenty' in *The Canterbury Tales* is more than a critical cliché: at least part of Chaucer's purpose, clearly, is to create a rich sense of the possibilities of mediaeval life. Again, the world of *King Lear* is far from homogeneous; rich and poor, mad and sane, jostle one another with the energy of contrast. The fact that Chaucer and Shakespeare are exceptions to the attempt at generalization should cause no surprise; their intractability to pigeon-holing is inseparable from their fullness of genius. But an interest in the sheer oddity and strangeness of things for their own sake does seem to mark a step into the secular modern world. The quality I am reaching for is brilliantly expressed in one of Jane Austen's letters to Fanny Knight:

> You are inimitable, irresistable. You are the delight of my Life. Such
> Letters, such entertaining Letters as you have lately sent! Such a
> description of your queer little heart! Such a lovely display of what
> Imagination does. You are worth your weight in Gold, or even in the
> new Silver Coinage. I cannot express to you what I have felt in reading
> your history of yourself, how full of Pity & Concern & Admiration &
> Amusement I have been. You are the Paragon of all that is Silly &
> Sensible, commonplace & eccentric, Sad & Lively, Provoking &
> Interesting. Who can keep place with the fluctuations of your Fancy, the
> Capprizios of your Taste, the Contradictions of your Feelings? You are
> so odd! & all the time, so perfectly natural – so peculiar in yourself, & yet
> so like everybody else![10]

A delighted apprehension of idiosyncrasy is also central to the life
and work of Dickens.

But although there is plenty of human diversity in, say, *The Pilgrim's
Progress*, this is ultimately in the service of an ordering of existence in
which individuality has a role only in relation to the higher purposes
of God. Defoe was born only some thirty years later than Bunyan,
but the contrast between Bunyan's God-centred universe and the
sociological, quasi-scientific side of Defoe is a large one, despite the
more traditional elements in him to which I referred earlier. An
analogy exists in a contrast that suggests itself between the treatment
of love in Spenser and Donne. For Spenser, human love is a power to
be understood as part of those supernatural and hierarchical forces
that, for him, almost literally make the world go round. Freed of this
burden, or responsibility, Donne is able to anatomize the thing itself.
If it is true that, as Donne's 'First Anniversary' claims, ''tis all in
pieces, all coherence gone' (1. 213), then one refuge from this
confusion lies in cleaving to the hoped-for certainty of human love
and, consequently, the delight in celebrating its nature in intricately
intimate detail. In fact Donne, Shakespeare and the sonneteers
suggest the discovery of the self, in its own right, as an object of
scrutiny. Defoe records the later, and connected, discovery not of
society, that is to put the point too strongly, but of a consuming
interest in how people live in groups when these are governed
mainly by acquisitive forces rather than spiritual sanctions. One
writer has, indeed, made important claims for Defoe as an
economist: 'It was Defoe's highest merit as an economist that he was
the first prominent English writer to see national concerns with the
eye of a social historian.'[11] This, in its turn, is related to his interest in

statistics:

> Defoe's passion for statistics…anticipated the modern scientific study of facts which had displaced the older theorizing about 'natural laws' of commerce and the attributes of 'the economic man.'[12]

It is surely clear that when, late in life, Defoe turned to fiction he did not abruptly abandon these earlier concerns.

The interest of his phrase 'incredible variety' is not, however, limited to its literal meaning. Its idiomatic flexibility contains an unmistakably modern colouring, a point related to a statement of Ian Watt's about the prose of *Moll Flanders*:

> The most remarkable thing…is perhaps the fact that it is Defoe's usual style. No previous author's normal way of writing could so credibly have passed for the characteristic utterance of such an uneducated person as Moll Flanders.[13]

The same point is made about Crusoe by Sir Walter Scott: 'The supposed situation of his hero was peculiarly favourable to the circumstantial style of De Foe' and he generalizes with magisterial force:

> It is greatly to be doubted De Foe could have changed his colloquial, circuitous, and periphrastic style for any other, whether more coarse or more elegant. We have little doubt it was connected with his nature, and the particular turn of his thoughts and ordinary expressions, and that he did not succeed so much by writing in an assumed manner, as by giving full scope to his own.[14]

The important question this raises is that of the conflict between notions of literary language as *decorous* or *mimetic*. The concept of literary decorum is complicated by a persistent dichotomy in its theory and practice. Once again, we need to remember that great writers, in their greatest work, almost always break the rules. In other words, Chaucer, Shakespeare and Donne are capable of using language in a way that embodies the fluctuating curves of thought and feeling (the Wife of Bath's prologue and the soliloquies of Shakespeare's tragic heroes are obvious examples). But theoretically the dominant literary ideal up to the Romantics was of a language true to itself, to its own internal laws of fitness. An obvious example in prose would be Sir Thomas Browne, whose convoluted style is both a richly apt vehicle for his meditative explorations of the universal themes of death and providence, and also a celebration of the baroque possibilities of language itself. If Browne's style is in any sense a mirror, it is inward-looking. The novel, on the other hand, marks the true beginning of the consistent movement of language out into the world, a view strengthened by the very persistence of other styles into the eighteenth century:

> Nevertheless the prose norm of the Augustan period remained much too literary to be the natural voice of Moll Flanders or Pamela Andrews; and although the prose of Addison, for example, or Swift, is simple and direct enough, its ordered economy tends to suggest an acute summary rather than a full report of what is described.[15]

Lawrence's dictum of trusting the tale rather than the teller might help to verify whether Defoe's prefatory interest in the variety of human life is validated by the novel itself, and it may be possible to do so in two major ways. Firstly, it seems reasonable to claim that we can see this quality asserting itself in the richness of individual incident so characteristic of the book:

> The servants all called him my lord, and I was her honour the countess, and thus we travelled to Oxford, and a pleasant journey we had; for, give him his due, not a beggar alive knew better how to be a lord than my husband. We saw all the rarities at Oxford, talked with two or three fellows of colleges about putting a nephew that was left to his lordship's care to the university, and of their being his tutors. We diverted ourselves with bantering several other poor scholars with the hopes of being at least his lordship's chaplain and putting on a scarf; and thus having lived like quality indeed as to expense, we went away for Northampton and, in a word, in about twelve days' ramble came home again, to the tune of about £93 expense. (53)

This little adventure of Moll and her gentleman-tradesman husband is wonderfully representative of the novel as a whole, above all perhaps in the 'diverting' quality of its celebration of the oddities of modern experience. That it is modern seems justified by the thought that this kind of deception is made possible by a more fluid social structure (the pair can pass themselves off on appearances alone) and greater mobility of travel than existed even in the seventeenth century. The very sketchiness of the treatment of the poor scholars belongs to the disconnected absurdities of the confidence-man. And, as always, no descriptive detail would be complete without a more or less precise indication of its cost.

But Defoe's preoccupation with variety is observable also on the larger scale, in the structure of the novel as a whole with its stress on the wandering nature of Moll's life. It is this sense of movement, of a particular kind, which is so crucial to the development of the novel as a modern literary form, a view justified by considering a work, *The Pilgrim's Progress* again, which would appear to subvert the argument. Human life considered as a journey is probably the basic narrative form in Western literature. Its origins are almost certainly two-fold, in the story of the expulsion of Adam and Eve from the Garden of Eden and also in its universal implications as an analogue of the process from birth to death. An important difference is discernible, however, between a crucial example of the form such as *The Pilgrim's Progress* and a work like *Moll Flanders*, a difference that might be summarized as the contrast between a closed and open-ended journey. The progress of Christian is within a framework that dissolves uncertainty. The alternatives conceivable to Bunyan's imagination, and so to us as fictional possibilities, are strictly limited: Christian will either be saved or damned. There are no other directions in which the story can move. It is of the very nature of Defoe's novel, and of the novel in general, that Moll's fate is problematic. The novelist's possibilities are governed by nothing but the artistic limits of credibility, psychological motivation and the rest. Apart from this, his choices are as multifarious as the world by which he is surrounded. Another literary comparison is relevant here. If we remember that London low-life is an important element in the subject-matter of *Moll Flanders*, then a legitimate comparison is with such plays of Ben Jonson's as *The Alchemist* and *Bartholomew Fair*. The thieving, gulling and whoring, the behind-the-scenes exposure of trickery in the two writers are remarkably similar. But for all their frenetic movement on the stage, Jonson's plays are essentially static in their portrayal of social groupings, and they deal with what seems to be an essentially known and knowable community. Some large and interesting questions are involved in all of this. Why did the relatively static give way to the relatively full of movement; why did the sense of community alter; why, we might even ask, did drama give way to fiction? On this last point, at least one explanation of the rise of the novel might be found in its capacity to deal with the mobility within and between social classes which began in the seventeenth century in a way that drama, by its very nature, could not. But the social implications of these questions have been dealt with, suggestively and by and large successfully, by Ian Watt[16] and so I shall concentrate on the artistic implications of Defoe's interest in the variety of human experience.

This interest is not merely a way of providing a sociological explanation of the rise of the novel; it is also the discovery of a quality crucial to the nature of fiction as an art form. I shall suggest later that Fielding's grasp of the importance of novelistic detail is a significant break-through in its technical implications; Defoe's realization that a novel can only exist if it is bodied forth in incident is of similar scope. But these early glimpses of the nature of the novel highlight the problems involved in novelistic creation itself. A double-edged difficulty faces the writer in his depiction of life's variety. On the one hand is the necessity of creating a sufficiently rich world of incident so that the skeleton of plot and theme will be free of offensive angularity. On the other is the danger of this richness swamping the novel, of the thematic wood being obscured by the incidental trees. The only way out of this dilemma is through artistry. Richness of incident must be disciplined, although not weakened, by some concern for pattern, for relating the richness of incident to a context of significance. This seems the best possible illustration of the fact that technique is never a superficial matter. The technical ability to structure a novel can only come, in the end, from the ability to pick and choose, to arrange and pattern, the materials of art. In its turn, this ability can only come from a vision of human life or, as I wish to suggest in the case of the eighteenth and nineteenth century novel, an image of society. One might usefully at this point see how far Defoe possesses this organizing ability in *Moll Flanders* by looking in some detail at a particular incident, the fascinating moment towards the end when we see Moll in her son's company:

> This was the substance of our first day's conversation, the pleasantest day that ever passed over my head in my life and which gave me the truest satisfaction. He came every day after this and spent great part of his time with me, and carried me about to several of his friends' houses, where I was entertained with great respect. Also I dined several times at his own house, when he took care always to see his half-dead father so out of the way that I never saw him or he me. I made him one present, and it was all I had of value, and that was one of the gold watches of which I said I had two in my chest, and this I happened to have with me and gave it him at his third visit. I told him I had nothing of value to bestow but that, and I desired he would now and then kiss it for my sake. I did not, indeed, tell him that I stole it from a gentle-woman's side at a meeting-house in London. That's by the way. (290-1)

There is, of course, the possibility of a delightful irony here in Moll solemnly adjuring her adored, and newly discovered, son to bestow an occasional kiss on this apparently stolen property. With characteristic moral callousness, Moll simply dismisses this unsavoury fact: 'That's by the way.' But as Ian Watt points out, this can only be a reference to an episode when Moll, in fact, failed to steal the watch and so 'we must surely infer that Defoe had a faint recollection of what he had written a hundred pages earlier... but forgot that it had failed.'[17] This could be regarded as an unimportant act of carelessness on Defoe's part, which seems to be the view taken by Watt himself in his somewhat external explanation of the mistake: 'These discontinuities strongly suggest that Defoe did not plan his novel as a coherent whole, but worked piecemeal, very rapidly, and without any subsequent revision.'[18] Such mistakes are perhaps explicable in terms of Defoe's work as a journalist and his attitude to the form he was helping to initiate, but it may be legitimate to dig a little deeper and suggest that the weakness is symptomatic of something wider, the absence of a controlling vision for the novel as a whole. If *Moll Flanders* has a larger intentional purpose it is surely contained in the novel's penultimate sentence with its resolve to 'spend the remainder of our years in sincere penitence for the wicked lives we have lived.' (295) But this aim is utterly subverted by the actual working out of the plot and by the entire sense of the work, both material and spiritual. For example, in the last pages Moll's husband is 'amazed' by the size of her fortune:

> At last he began thus: 'Hold, let's see,' says he, telling upon his fingers still and first on his thumb; 'there's £246 in money at first, then two gold watches, diamond rings, and plate,' says he, upon the forefinger. Then upon the next finger, 'Here's a plantation on York River, £100 a year, then £150 in money, then a sloop-load of horses, cows, hogs, and stores'; and so on to the thumb again. 'And now,' says he, 'a cargo cost £250 in England, and worth here twice the money.' 'Well' says I, 'what do you make of all that?' 'Make of it?' says he. 'Why, who says I was deceived when I married a wife in Lancashire? I think I have married a fortune, and a very good fortune too,' says he. (293-4)

Penitence at this level of comfort would be an easy matter for most of us, a point substantiated by the equally facile disposal of moral difficulties. Her husband's only reproach for Moll's earlier incest was 'to live with him as a wife after I knew that he was my brother; that, he said, was a vile part. Thus all these little difficulties were made easy, and we lived together with the greatest kindness and comfort imaginable.' (294-5) The transition from vileness to easiness is so smooth as to be almost imperceptible. It is impossible, in fact, to argue that *Moll Flanders* is thematically coherent in the way that

Defoe evidently intended, or in any other way if it comes to that. The centre of the novel's artistic success is to be found, rather, in the implications of the book's full title:

> Who was born in Newgate, and during a life of continue'd variety for three-score years, besides her childhood, was twelve year a whore, five times a wife (whereof once to her own brother), twelve year a thief, eight year a transported felon in Virginia, at last grew rich, liv'd honest, and died a penitent.

We notice in passing the order of riches, honesty and penitence, but particularly striking is the 'continued variety' which returns us to the 'incredible variety' with which this discussion began. The book's sub-title is itself an example in miniature of Defoe's fascination with incident for its own sake. It is surely the grippingly depicted randomness of a life rather than the articulation of an ordered pattern that is the source of our enjoyment in *Moll Flanders*. In short, Defoe falls short of the originality ascribed to the eighteenth-century novel by Diana Spearman:

> ...the eighteenth century writers introduced something really new in European fiction when they transformed story into plot. Instead of a series of adventures, Richardson and Fielding constructed books in which all the incidents contribute to the central design.[19]

Whether consciously or not, Defoe's recognition of the 'incredible variety' of human life shows a grasp of a momentous change in European civilization. His sense of life as heterogeneous is related to our domination by time and spatial mobility, both of which are given maximum play for expression in the context of a social framework structured by economics rather than hierarchy. It is fascinating to observe Defoe raising in an acute form questions of how art relates to life at such an early stage in the history of the novel, partly because he illustrates two essential characteristics of the form identified by Michel Zeraffa. As in an extreme modernist text like *Molloy*, his novels link 'people and things together, even if it is only by contiguity' and they run 'parallel to human events, following the thread of history and, above all, taking on the characteristics of speech.'[20] Just as *Robinson Crusoe* has continued to be of interest to Marxist and sociological critics, we can see also why it has exerted a spell over *avant-garde* writers. Defoe's statement in his Preface that *Robinson Crusoe* has no 'appearance of fiction in it' might be the battle-cry of all those who have sought to dissolve the barriers between art and reality.

Smollett's *Roderick Random* provides, as its hero's surname suggests, a continuity of interest from Defoe in its documentary impulse, the writer's need to record the surfaces of things in the life around him. The dangers of discussing subject-matter to the exclusion of art, of straying vaguely into the realm of 'life', are peculiarly tempting in the case of the novel and it may be a sign of Smollett's weakness as an artist that his work offers this as an almost irresistible temptation. On the other hand, part of a novel's *artistic* purpose may be to tell us something of the nature of its society and, even if this is not the case, it seems perverse to ignore the possibilities of information when they are presented with Smollett's force and precision. Could any social historian convey with such immediacy the gentlemanly solution to the problem of eating on the cheap as Smollett does in the 'diving' episode of *Roderick Random?*

> About dinner-time, our landlord asked us how we proposed to live, to which we answered that we would be directed by him. 'Well, then,' says he, 'there are two ways of eating in this town, for people of your condition – the one more creditable and expensive than the other; the first is, to dine at an eating-house, frequented by well-dressed people only; and the other is called diving, practised by those who are either obliged or inclined to live frugally.' I gave him to understand that, provided the last was not infamous, it would suit much better with our circumstances than the other. 'Infamous,' cried he, 'God forbid! . . . I will go along with you today and introduce you.' He accordingly carried us to a certain lane, where stopping, he bade us observe him and do as he did, and, walking a few paces, dived into a cellar, and disappeared in an instant.
>
> I followed his example, and, descending very successfully, found myself in the middle of a cook's shop, almost suffocated with the steams of boiled beef, and surrounded by a company of hackney coachmen, chairmen, draymen, and a few footmen out of place or on board wages, who sat eating shin of beef, tripe, cowheel, or sausages, at separate boards covered with cloths that turned my stomach. (13)[21]

There follows Strap's nightmarish misadventure with the soldier whose scalded legs are well rubbed with salt in the places where the skin has been stripped off with his stockings. A dram of gin eventually 'composed all animosities' and 'we sat down at a board and dined upon shin of beef most deliciously, our reckoning amounting to twopence halfpenny each, bread and small beer included.' This could be paralleled by many other scenes, the episode where Roderick is fastened to the deck during a sea battle, for example:

> I concealed my agitation as well as I could, till the head of the officer of
> marines who stood near me being shot off, bounced from the deck
> athwart my face, leaving me well-nigh blinded with brains. I could
> contain myself no longer, but began to bellow with all the strength of my
> lungs: when a drummer coming towards me asked if I was wounded? and
> before I could answer received a great shot in his belly, which tore out his
> entrails and he fell flat on my breast. (29)

The interesting question to ask is whether such moments have more
than a documentary value, whether they are invested with
imaginative commitment on Smollett's part. What we notice, of
course, is an extraordinary richness of detail, an almost obsessive
concentration on the physical, especially compared with Defoe, a
point substantiated by the relationship between Defoe and Locke:

> Defoe's style reflects the Lockean philosophy in one very significant
> detail: he is usually content with denoting only the primary qualities of
> the objects he describes – their solidity, extension, figure, motion, and
> number – especially number: there is very little attention to the
> secondary quality of objects, to their colours, sounds, or tastes. [22]

In retrospect, Defoe's vividness of detail is somewhat prosaic in the
face of this torrent and it may be possible to pursue the question by
wondering if Smollett's richness of detail is of particular relevance to
other areas of the novel. Character forms a link because there is a
real sense in which characterization for Smollett is simply a
continuation of description, as the following examples make clear.
This is how we are introduced to Lieutenant Bowling and then Crab
the surgeon:

> He was a strong built man, somewhat bandy-legged, with a neck like
> that of a bull and a face which, you might easily perceive, had withstood
> the most obstinate assaults of the weather. His dress consisted of a soldier's
> jacket... a pair of red breeches japanned with pitch, clean grey worsted
> stockings, large silver buckles that covered three-fourths of his shoes, a
> silver-laced hat whose crown overlooked the brims about an inch and a
> half, a black bob wig in buckle, a check shirt, a silk handkerchief, an
> hanger with a brass handle, girded to his thigh by a tarnished laced belt,
> and a good oak plant under his arm. (3)

The detail here is relatively neutral in its effect, whereas the
description of Crab has all of Smollett's grotesquerie:

> This member of the faculty was aged fifty, about five feet high, and ten
> round the belly, his face was capacious as a full moon and much of the
> complexion of a mulberry; his nose, resembling a powder-horn, was

swelled to an enormous size, and studded all over with carbuncles; and his little grey eyes reflected the rays in such an oblique manner that, while he looked a person full in the face, one would have imagined he was admiring the buckle of his shoe. (7)

In a well-known comment, George Orwell praised Dickens for his use of the 'unnecessary detail'[23], but there is a clear difference between the novelists in this respect, despite Smollett's acknowledged influence on Dickens's earlier work. Dickens's use of detail is, characteristically, humanizing, the breath of life into what would otherwise remain caricature; Smollett's figures are obsessively powerful almost by virtue of their lack of recognizable humanity. This aspect of *Roderick Random* is crystallized in Chapter 11 with its extraordinary little gallery of ancient Jewish moneylender, brash young whore and the 'formidable' Captain Weazel, the whole scene a brilliant example of Smollett's savage, externalized comedy.

This remarkable preoccupation with surfaces is evident above all in the manner in which Smollett clearly perceives no radical discontinuity between people and objects, and so it becomes interesting to speculate how far he penetrates, or wishes to penetrate, below the surfaces of things, a problem that could be tackled through the character of Roderick himself. With full awareness of the intentional fallacy, it might still be helpful to begin from Smollett's own conception, as presented in his Preface: 'I have attempted to represent merit struggling with every difficulty to which a friendless orphan is exposed, from his own want of experience, as well as from the selfishness, envy, malice, and base indifference of mankind.' How far is this 'modest merit' validated by the text itself? A passage in which Roderick is attempting to decide his course in life reveals a complete harmony between character and author on the question of the kind of young man we are dealing with: 'Neither should I succeed in my endeavours to rise in the state, inasmuch as I could neither flatter nor pimp for courtiers, nor prostitute my pen in defence of a wicked and contemptible administration.' (44) Modern techniques of reading suggest we should be on the look-out for irony, but an examination of the novel as a whole suggests an absence of this quality verging on the intolerable. We may be told that this is, in fact, an idealized portrait of Smollett himself, but the suggestion founders, or should do, on the fact that we are dealing with a novel which is presumably aiming at some degree of consistency. A certain rigour in our analysis of Random is justified by his own bland assumption of superiority backed up by his creator's claim of 'modest merit'. Roderick may not be able to flatter the great, but on entering Crab's household he resolved to study his 'temper with all the application, and manage it with all the address, in my power' and these attentions are also applied to Mrs Crab:

> I was on very good terms with my master's wife, whose esteem I acquired and cultivated, by representing Mrs Potion in the most ridiculous lights my satirical talents could invent, as well as by rendering her some Christian offices when she had been too familiar with the dram bottle. (7)

Again, although the eighteenth century's attitude to venereal disease may have been a little more robust than our own, one can hardly fail to be struck by Roderick's consignment of its acquisition to one misfortune amongst others:

> Thus I found myself, by the iniquity of mankind, in a much more deplorable condition than ever: for though I had been formerly as poor, my reputation was without blemish and my health unimpaired till now, but at present my good name was lost, my money gone, my friends were alienated, my body infected by a distemper contracted in the course of an amour, and my faithful Strap, who alone could yield me pity and assistance, absent I knew not where. (21)

A fundamental good-heartedness is one of the implicit claims made by and for Roderick; this is his response to some cruel teasing of the innocent Wagtail:

> Although everybody in the company affected the utmost surprise, I could easily perceive it was a scheme concerted among them to produce diversion at the doctor's expense, and being under no concern about the consequence I entered into the confederacy and enjoyed the distress of Wagtail, who, with tears in his eyes, begged the protection of the company, declaring himself as innocent of the crime laid to his charge as the foetus in utero, and hinting, at the same time, that nature had not put it in his power to be guilty of such a trespass. (46)

Finally, Roderick's inability to prostitute himself weakens when the possession of money is threatened by religion: 'as to the difference of religion, I looked upon it as a thing of too small moment to come into competition with a man's fortune.' (42) In short, like almost all of Smollett's heroes Roderick belongs to a group of what one critic has called 'uningratiating personages.'[24] It would be comforting, of course, if we felt that Roderick was being treated ironically or that he was capable of behaving in a more serious way or that we are supposed to see for ourselves what a nasty young brute he is. The reverse of Roderick's moments of brutality and cynicism are his excursions into the realm of sentiment and these are particularly evident in scenes of meeting and reunion. It would be tiresome to give all the possible examples of this; perhaps two are sufficient to make the point. Here is Roderick's utterly implausible 'reunion' with Strap:

> But when I declared my name was Random, he exclaimed in a rapture, 'How! Rory Random?' The same, I replied, looking at him with astonishment. 'What,' cried he, 'don't you know your old schoolfellow, Hugh Strap?' At that instant, recollecting his face, I flew into his arms, and in the transport of my joy gave him back one half of the suds he had so lavishly bestowed on my countenance. (8)

A similar scene occurs when it is discovered that Thomson, who has been out of sight and (even more) out of mind for a long time, is not dead after all:

> Perceiving my confusion, which was extreme, he clasped me in his arms and bedewed my face with tears. It was some time ere I recovered the use of my reason, overpowered with this event, and longer still before I could speak, so that all I was capable of was to return his embraces and to mingle the overflowings of my joy with his, while honest Brayl, affected with the scene, wept as fast as either of us, and signified his participation of our happiness by hugging us both and capering about the room like a madman. (36)

Clearly, these descriptions are notable for their almost hysterical exaggeration and inappropriateness. There is simply no objective correlative to justify the frenzy of Roderick's responses and so although we can feel the pressure of imaginative commitment, it is commitment gone quite awry. Smollett's obsession with surfaces, his treatment of people as objects and the sometimes unbalanced exaggeration of his descriptive prose can now be seen in relation to his novel's almost total lack of psychological inwardness. Mad caperings round a room indicates joy, and wild outbursts of tears grief, because Smollett has no grasp of any other way in which emotional states can be presented. Indeed it might be claimed that such outlandish physical gesturing acquired almost the status of a literary convention for a period which, by and large, seemed to have lost the knack of inwardness.

A key problem facing eighteenth-century novelists was their period's somewhat undernourished conception of human character and personality, a point that can be made in various ways. A comment on Hogarth by Pat Rogers is of obviously general application: he 'was not particularly interested in psychology: his aims were instructive and illustrative, rather than explanatory and exploratory.'[25] Commenting on the inadequacy of Addison's 'philosophical' writing in the *Spectator*, Leslie Stephen remarks that Addison 'fully shares the characteristic belief of the day, that abstract problems are soluble by common sense, when polished by academic culture and aided by a fine taste.'[26] Again, Basil Willey claims that the approach of the eighteenth century sees a 'steady decline in what has been called the tragic sense of life.'[27] This is a point difficult to make without doing serious insult to one of the creative periods of English literature; it may seem particularly unfair because the standard of judgement is that of the age of Shakespeare. There is plenty of tragic feeling in the lives of eighteenth century men – Pope, Swift and Dr Johnson, for example – but this is not on the whole presented in their work as a profound examination of individual human suffering. Men had had enough, for the time, of tragedy, perhaps above all because of its manifestation in the English Civil War. They hoped and believed that human problems could be resolved by rationality and common-sense. And so it is entirely appropriate that the influence 'whose thought everywhere pervades the eighteenth-century climate of opinion' and which 'blends spontaneously with the ordinary language of all educated men' should be that of John Locke. Leslie Stephen goes on to add that Locke had 'laid down the fundamental outlines of the creed, philosophical, religious, and political, which was to dominate English thought for the next century.'[28] We must surely add, to Stephen's list, psychology, for Locke's was still the dominant influence in shaping the eighteenth century's view of human character. Something of what this meant is indicated by A. R. Humphreys:

> By greatly simplifying the constitution of the mind, by stripping off notions of inherited reverences, prejudices, and beliefs supposedly grounded in its very nature, by clarifying what had seemed a complex so involved as to defy analysis, Locke had enabled 'the science of man' to stand forth as an intelligible subject of knowledge.[29]

The achievement is real, but like all advances in human thought it had to be paid for. Personality may have seemed in the seventeenth century a 'complex so involved as to defy analysis' but not to defy artistic embodiment, as Shakespeare demonstrates with Othello, Lear and the rest. It was against this background that the eighteenth-century novelist had to struggle in order to discover his own sense of the nature of human character, a fact which increases one's sense of Richardson's genius. Smollett's interest lies in his complete inability to make this discovery before *Humphry Clinker*. Without it, his characters are fated to move with the inhuman energy of puppets.

It remains to take a more detailed look at the possibility of irony in *Roderick Random*, of whether Smollett wants, or expects, us to realize Roderick's limitations, a question that involves some consideration of the novel's structure. Structure inevitably raises questions about Smollett's inventiveness in the detail of his plot. A problem of illustration presents itself here: theoretical considerations aside, it is tiresome to quote at length, especially in order to make a negative point. Just as there is an element of repetition in the novel's scenes of meeting and reunion, so there is in its more extended moments of action. Smollett is especially fond of inn scenes of violent confusion (Chapters 10, 11 and 19 all provide examples) and this suggests a lack of controlled variety in his deployment of action. Chapter 19 reveals Roderick in a particularly unpleasant light as he enjoys the discomfiture of Miss Lavement into whose bed he has cheated himself through a characteristic series of bedroom mistakes. Indeed, if we go on to consider the arrangement of the plot towards the end of the novel, it becomes ruthlessly clear that Smollett is not taking an ironic stance towards his hero (the very paucity of invention would suggest a problem for him in creating a plot of the requisite complexity for this effect). What I have in mind above all is Roderick's disposal of Miss Williams, who had previously almost tricked him into marriage, but who is now in a condition identical to his own, Roderick having acquired his 'distemper contracted in the course of an amour':

> After having moralized upon these particulars, I proposed that she should lodge in the same room with me, an expedient that would save some money, and assured her I would undertake her cure as well as my own, during which she should partake of all the conveniencies that I could afford to myself. (21)

However, by the time that Roderick is involved with Narcissa his distemper has been conveniently forgotten:

> I was not sorry for this precaution, because I could unbosom myself

without reserve before Miss Williams, who was the confidant of us both. I therefore gave a loose to the inspiration of my passion, which operated so successfully upon the tender affections of Narcissa, that she laid aside the constraint she had hitherto wore, and blessed me with the most melting declaration of her mutual flame...We spent the afternoon in all the ecstasy of hope that the most fervent love exchanged by mutual vows could inspire, and Miss Williams was so much affected with our chaste caresses, which recalled the sad remembrance of what she was, that her eyes were filled with tears. (57)

We are clearly far removed from the world of Sir Charles Grandison, but some hint of Roderick's state when we last saw him with Miss Williams might be in order. As part of the novel's rounding off, Miss Williams, whom Roderick had earlier noted as a woman of 'beauty, good sense, and education' (21) is married to Strap. Nothing is too bad for a fallen woman, of course, but there is no indication as to Miss Williams's views of the matter. It seems farcical to invoke the name of E. M. Forster in relation to the novel's scenes of pox-ridden brutality, but the injunction 'only connect' seems as needful to Roderick as it ever was for Mr Wilcox. Roderick is unable to make even the most elementary moral discriminations and the absence of irony in Smollett's treatment of him suggests that his is the real failure to connect: in a wider sense, the ability to connect is the artistic cement out of which novelistic form is made. The conjunction of vision and technique is, once more, relevant. Vision is the ability to take a coherent view of the world – even a coherently ambiguous view – one in which the constituent elements fuse in a unified, but not mechanical, pattern. And technique is the ability to imbue this vision with a sense of inter-connectedness so that the totality and the detail cohere to a common purpose. It is possible to agree with John Barth that *Roderick Random* is a novel of 'nonsignificant surfaces...The particular nature and order of Roderick's encounters...are without consistent point, incremental meaning, "inevitability", relevance to character, or cumulative force'[30] without agreeing with his conclusion that all of this can somehow be seen in a positive light.

It seems clear, then, that in his earlier picaresque work Smollett is unable to penetrate successfully below the surface level, but that this surface is presented with such ferocious energy that we are bound to ask questions about a preoccupation with detail that will not occur again in the English novel until Dickens. Dickens himself acknowledged a debt to Smollett, but their differences are evidently very great. Dickens lacks almost completely Smollett's savagery – the beating of the schoolmaster in *Nicholas Nickleby* is merely a pallid imitation of the nightmarish horror of the original scene in *Roderick Random* – and this is something more than a matter of personality. The brutality of *Roderick Random* is sufficient testimony to a pathological element in Smollett, although it is hard not to feel that this is something he shares with an aspect of his whole period. If Swift and Smollett are linked, neither appears such a special case: Augustan restraint and civility exist side by side with an unflinching recourse to scatology and physical barbarism. In the visual arts, the examples of Hogarth and Rowlandson come immediately to mind. In an etching from as late as 1811, 'A Midwife Going to a Labour,' Rowlandson creates a grotesquerie that anticipates Mrs Gamp but outdoes her in ferociously detailed horror. There is more to this, surely, than the conventionally remarked contrast of eighteenth-century elegance rubbing shoulders with prize-fighting. The eruptions of violence in Swift and Smollett, even the excremental side of *The Dunciad*, are the revenge of darker forces against a self-constraint felt to be humanly limiting – Blake is probably the first writer to be truly self-conscious about this.

However, the main concern here is with social, rather than psycho-analysis. Turning from personal explanations, one might suggest that Smollett's obsession with surface detail is an unconscious assimilation of social change at a level that profoundly affects his way of seeing the world and of recording it artistically. This relates to aspects of realism in Defoe, that sense of life as heterogeneous which stems from modern man's domination by time and spatial mobility. At the most basic level, this led to a change in the sheer physical appearance of the world in terms of the varied detail of the surfaces of things, a change embodied in the growth of London, the increasingly complex stratification within social groups, the development of new trades and occupations – all of the physical, human and economic consequences of a vastly increased sense of scale. This connects with an emphasis on variety in the eighteenth-century novel which looks like something new in literature, at least in its range and extent. We have to wait for a novel like *Bleak House*, say, for the full embodiment of the complexity of post-renaissance life. But John Barth catches it well in its eighteenth-century manifestation:

> Smollett may lack breadth of vision, but width he had aplenty, in all
> directions, more than Richardson and Fielding combined. Sailors,

soldiers, fine gentlemen and ladies, whores, homosexuals, cardsharpers, fortune hunters, tradesmen of all description, clerics, fops, scholars, lunatics, highwaymen, peasants, and poets both male and female – they crowd a stage that extends from Glasgow to Guinea, from Paris to Paraguay, and among themselves perpetrate battles, debaucheries, swindles, shanghais, duels, seductions, rescues, pranks, poems, ship-wrecks, heroisms, murders, and marriages.[31]

Again, both Defoe and Smollett are forerunners in a key area of novelistic realism, the presentation of people's lives *to themselves* in something like a direct manner. Of course, Robinson Crusoe and Moll Flanders are to an extent atypical figures and Smollett's world seems to us wildly distorted, although it is not unrelated to the actual texture of daily living in his own time. But an undeniably major concern of both is to capture something of the feel of life in their period. Such an ambition was not entirely foreign to earlier writers, but the essential greatness of, say, Elizabethan literature lies in its creation of imagined worlds as vehicles for the presentation of universal human values, a purpose for which the accumulation of realistic detail is largely irrelevant. The general point is that Defoe and Smollett record certain aspects of their world willy-nilly through the sheer fact of being alive in it. It is unnecessary to the argument that they should be self-consciously aware of what they are recording, although the greater formal and thematic unity of *Humphry Clinker* over his earlier novels suggests that Smollett did eventually reach this stage. Artistry is central to the position being advanced here. My point is that Defoe the novelist – as distinct from Defoe the man, the essayist, the quasi-economist – has no considered view of human life because his novels are themselves disordered and internally inconsistent: form and vision are indissoluble. If *Moll Flanders* was, in the well-known judgement of Ian Watt, a 'work of irony' rather than an 'ironic object',[32] one would have to think again. But the formal imperfections of Defoe and earlier Smollett are clear signs that their assimilation of the world is largely unconscious. This can be seen most clearly perhaps in their rudimentary conception of fictional structure. Their novels simply go on, in an order that could be largely rearranged, to purely arbitrary conclusions: the appalling 'adventure story' tacked on to the end of *Robinson Crusoe*, the moral *volte face* of *Moll Flanders*, the deadeningly predictable 'happy' endings of Smollett. The central interest of *Tom Jones*, on the other hand, is what Fielding *makes*, in the literal as well as the popular sense, of his world. Defoe and Smollett are not makers of this kind:

they are controlled by, rather than controlling, the material which surrounds them.

What exactly is the nature of this material? Can such phenomena as variety of incident, range of detail and the surface appearance of things be generalized in any useful way? A clue exists in an interesting passage from Sir William Petty, written towards the end of the seventeenth century. Petty, who has been described as one of the earliest 'sociological' thinkers,[33] is discussing ways of dealing with criminals in his 'Crimes and Punishments': 'That every man have and cary about him an uncounterfitable Tickett, expressing his name, the numero of his House, his Age, Trade, Stature, Haire, eye, and other peculiar marks of his Body.'[34] The language casts a certain halo of archaic charm around this, but the reality of the identity card is unmistakably present. 'What a piece of work is a man' is for Petty reducible to a series of pieces: name, age, and so on. And we note that his house is to be identified by its 'numero,' not by such a colourfully inexact formula as 'at the sign of.' This particular happy thought is a logical extension of the general method Petty advances in his *Political Arithmetick*, in a passage that bears on the relationship between Defoe and Locke mentioned earlier:

> The Method I take ... is not yet very usual; for instead of using only comparative and superlative Words, and intellectual Arguments, I have taken the course (as a specimen of the Political Arithmetick I have long aimed at) to express myself in terms of Number, Weight, or Measure; to use only Arguments of Sense, and to consider only such Causes, as have visible Foundations in Nature.[35]

As an apprehension of man and the world this is at the opposite pole from that of Shakespeare and lends some weight to the suggestion that the modern world really did originate in the seventeenth century despite the remoter antecedents that can be traced in various directions. What is implied by Petty's method is a separation of man and external reality, imposed by the necessity of human control of the world through measuring and counting. In the semi-magical universe of a pre-scientific era, man and nature exist in a continuum: Lear's madness and the storm are inextricably related. A quite different relationship is set up if one's interest is in the duration of time between lightning and thunderclap. Developments in the physical sciences and economic expansion both point in the direction of man's mastery of nature and this finds general expression in the desire to explore and control all aspects of life external to man.

Francis Place, the 'Radical tailor of Charing Cross,' remarked of the late seventeenth century that there 'was not then the same disposition to pry into the state of society.'[36] Place refers quite easily to the 'state of society,' but eighteenth-century novelists actually lived through the period when it became possible to use such a phrase. Werner Stark makes clear how relatively late it was before such a concept could be formulated:

> Another instructive example is the distinction first drawn in the late eighteenth century by authors such as Adam Ferguson and John Millar between man as a social being and man as a citizen. The traditional doctrine knew only the state: it had not yet discovered what was to become known as civil society.[37]

The prying Place refers to was necessitated by, *and* brought into being, the sense of a web of human relationships beyond the personal which it seemed possible might have laws of its own and also a life somehow independent of individuals. A key aspect of this is that the expansion of activities in the eighteenth century discussed earlier demanded a degree of organization in human affairs that had previously been unnecessary. After suggesting that theft was the 'archetypal Augustan crime,' for example, Pat Rogers goes on to discuss the myth and reality of Jonathan Wild, his conclusion being that Wild 'made crime into a bourgeois occupation': 'Beside the operatic excitement of the Elizabethan underworld, the humdrum efficiency of Hanoverian crime takes on the air of a minor state industry farmed out to private enterprise.'[38] Ian Watt suggests something very similar, that the growth of eighteenth-century crime involved a 'well-defined criminal class, and a complex system for handling it, with law-courts, informers and even crime reporters like Defoe.'[39] The extent and organization of eighteenth-century crime, either in reality or in people's minds, suggested the existence of a sub-world parallel to, but almost separate from, normal existence. It also raised the possibility that the everyday existence which we take as the 'natural' and unstructured ground of our being, the way things must be, might have its own structures and laws, might even be made by man himself instead of just happening. But as well as being seen as possibly made by man, 'society' could also seem alien to him. Speck says of late eighteenth-century charitable institutions that they were 'the forerunners of that philanthropic movement which eventually was to transform attitudes towards the lower classes in England,' and that they were 'typical of a new approach to social problems which recognized society as well as the offender as a culprit,'[40] This humanitarianism is obviously to be welcomed, but it has the incidental effect of giving society an ontological status, a point well brought out by Lionel Trilling:

> Society is a concept that is readily hypostatized – the things that are said about it suggest that it has a life of its own and its own laws... and its being conceived... as having indeed a life of its own but not a human life, gives rise to the human desire to bring it into accord with humanity.[41]

How does this relate specifically to eighteenth-century novelists? Arnold Hauser claims that Defoe and Swift are preoccupied by the same basic problem:

> Namely the origin and validity of human culture. These problems could become so important... only in an age in which the social foundations of civilization had begun to totter, and it was only under the direct impact of the passing of leadership in cultural affairs from one class to another, that it was possible to formulate so pointedly the idea of the dependence of civilizations on social conditions.[42]

This is too sweeping in its detail as well as apocalyptic in its tone. It assumes a degree of self-consciousness on Defoe's part that is questionable and we might reasonably be puzzled by the conjunction of the Tory Swift and the Dissenting Defoe. Also, the tottering civilization of eighteenth-century aristocratic domination can now be seen to have had more vigour than Hauser supposed: leadership was not passing so easily from one class to another. But I would agree, more tentatively (or faint-heartedly), that Defoe, Smollett and the rest are responding to important developments in their world, above all the emergence of the concept, and so of the reality, of society. Raymond Williams posits a complex development of word, concept and reality here: 'the idea of society itself grew and developed. It changed first from the immediate "society of one's fellows" to the more general "system of common life," and changed later from reference to a particular system to abstraction of all such systems, the general state of "society"'[43] I would argue that the eighteenth century novelists are responding – some unconsciously, some with understanding – to the possibility of grasping society as an emergent reality. This development is the reverse of static, of course; indeed, as a process it may be said to be still continuing. But throughout the course of the eighteenth century we can see the movement from the faintly discernible notion of a world of relationships outside the personal to a point at which society can be accused as a cause of human suffering.

It might well be asked why eighteenth-century writers 'need' society in order to write novels. The answer seems to lie in the necessity for any story to embed its characters in a context that will dignify them beyond the merely personal. Story-telling itself may be regarded as a basic human necessity, as Barbara Hardy points out: 'Narrative...cannot be regarded as an aesthetic invention...but must be seen as a primary act of mind transferred to art from life.'[44] The primacy of narration is similarly stressed by Joan Rockwell:

> A selection of events on the basis of chronological logical sequence, causality, and value judgements has always been necessary; that is to say, information about reality has been presented to and by the human species in the forms of narrative fiction known to us as History, the Law, Religion, Epic Poetry, the Novel, the Drama, and the statements of politicians and journalists.[45]

This contains an element of fashionable sleight-of-hand – one may well be uneasy about the sense in which history and the novel are both fictional – but the stress on what might be called the narrative bias of the European mind seems entirely justified. The importance of context in relation to this is recognized by Edwin Muir when he states that Henryson's animal fables belong to an age of settlement where 'the life of man and of beasts turns naturally into a story because it is part of a greater story about which there is general consent.'[46] It is easy to find examples of this process in the literature of the past. The story of Ulysses' journey is embedded in its context of gods and supernatural intervention. And the Christian story – in itself a narrative of beginning, middle and promised end – is of incalculable influence in the history of European narrative forms. *The Pilgrim's Progress* is perhaps the last fully successful example in English literature of a work in which the context is purely spiritual. The notorious obscurities of Blake's prophetic books suggest the strains involved in invoking the spiritual in an increasingly secular world. Conversely, Wordsworth clearly feels the need to enrich the apparently private story of the growth of a poet's mind, in *The Prelude*, by seeing it in relation to the wider forces of nature. Indeed, the dignity of this relationship is inseparable from his sense of the personal story from his earliest childhood. Among the many formal discoveries made by the pioneers of the novel, the most important, I believe, was their realization of the possibility of achieving secular dignity for their characters, by embedding their lives in the wider life of human relationships that came to be known as society.

Further Reading

For this and subsequent chapters reference should be made to the thorough but manageable bibliographies contained in:

The English Novel: Select Bibliographical Guides edited by A. E. Dyson (London, 1974).

Amongst the more interesting works on Defoe are:

Daniel Defoe: Citizen of the Modern World by John Robert Moore (Chicago, 1958).

Economics and the Fiction of Defoe by M. E. Novak (Berkeley, 1962).

Defoe and the Nature of Man by M. E. Novak (London, 1963).

Daniel Defoe and Middle-Class Gentility by M. Shinagel (Cambridge, Mass., 1968).

Defoe by James Sutherland (London, 1950).

'*Robinson Crusoe* as a Myth,' by Ian Watt, *Essays in Criticism* 1 (1950) is an essay of particular interest to this study.

The following are some useful works on Smollett:

The Novels of Smollett by P. G. Boucé (London, 1976).

Tobias Smollett: A Study in Style by Damian Grant (Manchester, 1977).

Tobias Smollett, Traveler-Novelist by G. M. Kahrl (London, 1945).

3

Clarissa

The magnitude of Richardson's achievement in creating his great novel from such apparently inauspicious beginnings has tormented critics with the question of its origins. Some, whose interest is in the spiritual element of Richardson's work, have sought these in a fairly remote literary past. For David Daiches, *Pamela* and *Clarissa* are 'in some ways more closely related to mediaeval saints' lives than to the novel as we now know it...a kind of *Paradise Lost* and *Paradise Regained*, set not in Eden or the wilderness but in the mundane world of social convention and obligation.'[1] This is echoed by Mark Kinkead-Weekes, writing of the passage where Clarissa falls nearly naked at Lovelace's feet: 'It is...like a scene from a saint's life.'[2] These are interesting points, although they rely on the somewhat suspect phrases 'in some ways' and '*like* a scene.' Another suggestion by Kinkead-Weekes is perhaps more fruitful: 'Apart from *The Pilgrim's Progress*, Richardson's novels are the first really imaginative use of the habits of mind which produced the Puritan diaries of the seventeenth and eighteenth centuries.'[3] There is a stronger link of influences here and a recognition of Richardson's modernity which, on balance, is closer to his achievement than are any connections with the mediaeval world. But how central to the nature of Richardson's achievement are these influences? Making every allowance for vanity, there is no essential reason to quarrel with his claim that *Clarissa* is 'a Piece from first to last, that owes its Being to Invention.'[4] Richardson's statement also casts doubt on two of the central points advanced by Ira Konigsberg in his *Samuel Richardson and the Dramatic Novel*. While paying tribute to Watt's *The Rise of the Novel*, Konigsberg finds it unsatisfactory because 'it does not consider the writing of fiction as a craft requiring developed literary concepts and techniques. Watt does not account for the qualities that begin with Richardson and make the novel into an art form.'[5] The key word here is 'developed.' Of course, any 'total' attempt at an explanation of the novel's origins would have to deal with a host of factors, many of them literary: Elizabethan prose fiction, the Puritan diarists, the *Spectator*, earlier epistolatory writing. But do any of these, separately or together, constitute the 'developed literary concepts and techniques' that enabled Richardson to take off into his own work? Without discounting the presence of some, or all, as part of Richardson's inheritance, the famous story of his writing of *Pamela* points irresistibly towards an element of self-discovery in his creation of the psychological novel and also, incidentally, opens the way to extra-literary accounts of what made this discovery possible. Given the conviction that he could only have begun from a developed literary background, Konigsberg is driven to the somewhat desperate theory that 'Richardson brought to the English novel subject matter and techniques developed in the drama.'[6] The detail of Richardson's life makes this somewhat unlikely and the rather tenuous nature of Konigsberg's argument is summarized in the bibliographical chapter on Richardson in *The English Novel*: 'There are indeed similarities, but these similarities *remain* similarities and the influences *possible* influences. Richardson may not have been quite as original as he thought, but neither previous fiction nor drama explains how he produced these works.'[7]

Richardson's work can, though, be seen as theatrical in a sense not considered by Konigsberg, a sense that establishes his essential modernity and which throws some light on *Clarissa* as a work of art. This is the novel's strongly melodramatic aspect. We think of melodrama as a Victorian phenomenon, at least in its stage manifestation, and a passage in Chapter 1 of the present book argued for its immediate eruption in the turmoil of post-revolutionary Paris.[8] But historical explanation is a conveyor belt that recedes with extraordinary rapidity and leaping off at any particular point is bound to seem arbitrary. A full analysis of melodrama would need to consider eighteenth-century sentimentalism, the shift from the pre-Romantic to Romanticism proper and into the Victorian era, and the process whereby the English Gothic novel fed into French fiction and thence into popular drama only to reappear on the English stage by way of translation. In short, it is a movement of European dimensions and Richardson's originality is high-lighted by his being one of the first writers fully to deploy this new mode. Honesty compels the admission that Richardson himself made statements about his work which would qualify this claim. In a letter of 1741 to the labourer poet Stephen Duck, Richardson seems unequivocal in his hatred of 'the French marvellous and all unnatural Machinery. ... Nature is my whole view, and such a Conduct in such a Life [Pamela's married state], as may generally happen, and be of Use.'[9] Admittedly, Pamela is being referred to and above all her later, infinitely duller, married existence. But, as Ian Watt suggests, even *Pamela* can be seen in melodramatic terms if the novel is reduced to its skeletal outline of 'the rakish squire versus the humble but virtuous maid.'[10] And the example of *Clarissa* suggests that this is another case where we should trust the tale rather than the teller. Of course, there is a clear sense in which 'Nature' *is* its 'whole view', bearing in mind the novel's extraordinary psychological penetration. The form in which it is expressed is, however, a different matter. This is something profounder than the trappings of melodrama, although these are not difficult to find, as in Clarissa's brother's reported declaration that 'if ever my Sister Clary darkens these doors again, I never will' (IV, 282); the formal gesturing involved in the funeral arrangements which Clarissa makes on her own behalf which 'obtained their admiration, expressed by hands and eyes lifted up, and by falling tears' (IV, 428); and Lovelace's frenziedly joky reference to Satan clapping down the 'universal trapdoor' on Belford's 'grizzled' head (IV, 445).[11] More importantly. melodrama permeates the novel at a structural level, a fact demonstrated by comparing it with the extended outline of the characteristic melodramatic framework presented by Peter Brooks in *The Melodramatic Imagination*:

> ....a presentation of...virtue *as* innocence...we see this virtue, momentarily, in a state of taking pleasure in itself...mysteries and ambiguities hovering over the world, enigmas unresolved...there swiftly supervenes a threat to virtue.

The similarity is reinforced by considering the topoi related to this framework: the setting is frequently an 'enclosed garden... surrounded by walls', although an important alternative to the garden structure is 'that of the thwarted escape'; the villain erupts into this space and for a large part of the work 'evil appears to reign triumphant, controlling the structure of events' while virtue's 'tongue is often tied by the structure of familial relationships.'[12]

It would be tiresome to elaborate the point-by-point resemblances involved here, although it is worth noticing the particularly apt conjunction of virtue's 'tongue often being tied' with Anna Howe's outburst to Colonel Morden, 'But this *dumb* sorrow!' (IV, 402) What does seem genuinely remarkable is Richardson's anticipation of a formal configuration discerned by Brooks only after a detailed study of nineteenth-century plays. It is superfluous to anatomize the ingredients of this clearly elemental structure: a reference to the Paradisal nature of that 'enclosed garden ... surrounded by walls' is surely enough. If we ask what led Richardson himself to this formal arrangement, the answer lies surely in his imaginative recognition of the elemental aspects of his own story, the 'contention between... naked innocence and armed guilt.' (II, 483) The very universality of this theme, especially in relation to the Christian-European tradition, is such as to prompt the question: why melodrama? On this account, is not *Paradise Regained* melodramatic, *King Lear*, the New Testament itself? The vital distinction lies in the association made by specialist commentators between melodrama and realism, and it is here especially that we can grasp Richardson's truly astonishing originality. A fruitful tension exists between his claim that '*Nature* is my whole view' and his castigation of Fielding for basing his characters and situations on real life.[13] Indeed, Richardson's extreme insistence on his creative novelty is remarkable: *Pamela* 'might possibly introduce a new species of writing', '*Clarissa* is a Piece from first to last, that owes its Being to Invention', *Sir Charles Grandison* is 'entirely new and unborrowed, even of myself'.[14]

How can we explain this conjunction of Nature and Invention? The answer lies in Richardson's discovery of the possibility of combining the most basic themes of Western literature with a mundane particularity in what is essentially 'a new species of writing.' There is, of course, no conflict between the first claim and Richardson's relative lack of education. The basic themes of Western literature are, by definition, the staple of Western man's deepest personal experience and so accessible to introspection as much as inheritance. On the second point, there is ample evidence of that preoccupation with detail so hilariously indicated by one of Joyce's enquiries to an aunt concerning an incident in *Ulysses*:

> Two more questions. Is it possible for an ordinary person to climb over the area railings of no 7 Eccles Street, either from the path or the steps, lower himself from the lowest part of the railings till his feet are within 2 feet or 3 of the ground and drop unhurt. I saw it done myself but by a man of athletic build. I require this information in detail in order to determine the wording of a paragraph.[15]

Such apparent fussiness is liable to provoke the non-creative mind to the question: does it really matter? Indeed, how much of all this does even the careful reader notice? Chimneys in *Julius Caesar* presented no difficulty to Shakespeare, but Richardson's preoccupation with minutiae is evidence of a shift in the literary imagination. Much has rightly been made of the brilliance of Fielding's critical chapters in *Tom Jones*, but he was anticipated by Richardson at several points, as in a letter to Aaron Hill on *Clarissa's* chronological realism: 'The fixing of Dates has been a Task to me. I am afraid I make the writers do too much in the Time.'[16] Again, he seeks in the book to 'avoid hurting that kind of Historical Truth which Fiction itself is generally read with, tho' we know it to be Fiction'[17] This stress on time is characteristic of the shift just referred to. The time-scheme of Shakespeare's plays is notoriously flexible and so the movement towards 'getting it right' in Richardson and Fielding is yet another indication of the change from a quasi-magical to a scientific world. However difficult it may be for the literary man to swallow, and however explicitly anti-science many creative writers have been in the last two hundred and fifty years, it is undeniable that they, like everyone else, are influenced by the substitution of an objective for a subjective universe. In fact, it is an essential part of this book's argument that the novel was made possible by a division between subject and object. Only when the world 'out there', crystallized in its imaginative and practically graspable form as society, came into existence was the stage set for realistic prose fiction.

That realistic prose fiction was one of Richardson's central aims is also revealed by his preoccupation with detail, as evidenced by his complaint against careless readers:

> Ye World is not enough used to this way of writing, to the moment. It knows not that in the minutiae lie often the unfoldings of the Story, as well as of the heart; & judges of an action undecided, as if it were absolutely decided; Nor will it easily part with its first impressions. How few Lady Bs who will read it over once for Amusement, and a second time to examine into the unjustness or justness of its several parts, as they contribute to make one Whole.'[18]

A continuity between art and life on this point is established by a passage from his autobiographical letter to Stinstra: 'These, Sir, are little things to trouble you with: But my Circumstances were little, & your Enquiries are minute.'[19] *Clarissa* itself abounds in references to detail which serve both as justification for his artistic method and embodiment of his vision of the complexity of human experience, as can be seen from one of Clarissa's early letters to Miss Howe:

Excuse me, my dear, I never was thus particular before; no, not to you. .
Nor would I now have written thus freely of a sister, but that she makes a
merit to my brother of disowning that she ever liked him, as I shall
mention hereafter: and then you will always have me give you minute
descriptions, nor suffer me to pass by the air and manner in which things
are spoken that are to be taken notice of; rightly observing that air and
manner often express more than the accompanying words. (I, 5)

Turning to a full-scale example of Richardson's fusion of Nature
and Invention, the psychologically realistic and the universal,
Lovelace is surely the figure who claims our attention. Clarissa
herself is a powerfully moving character, but to the modern
sensibility she has a tenuousness of presentation which inhibits our
full involvement with such fictional characters. Of course, this is in
itself part of the point. Clarissa belongs in the line of figures such as
Cordelia, Fanny Price and Little Dorrit, and part of the demand
they make on us is a particularly taxing imaginative leap in order to
inhabit their spiritual universe. In each case, however, their creators
make serious attempts to humanize the allegorical. One thinks of the
debate concerning Cordelia's possible 'fault' in failing to confess her
love for Lear publicly. We are invited to smile at some of Fanny's
more ingenuously wide-eyed moments. And we note the 'ripening'
effect of the Italian sun on Little Dorrit, designed surely to make her
mature involvement with Arthur Clennam more acceptable. As for
Clarissa, she can say 'very cutting words in a cool manner' (I, 321) as
we notice for ourselves in her early comment to Anna, 'poor Bella
has, you know, a plump high-fed face.' (I, 30). Again, she is not so
attenuated as not to be able to refer to 'the marriage intimacies
(...what the purest, although with apprehension, must think of) so
very intimate.' (II, 167). And the fact that Richardson is not
infatuated with his heroine in art, whatever may have been the case
in life, is conclusively demonstrated by the quite extraordinary
passage where the prostitute Sally parodies Clarissa's manner for
Lovelace's entertainment:

But the little devil was not to be balked; but fell a crying, sobbing,
praying, begging, exclaiming, fainting, that I never saw my lovely girl so
well aped. Indeed I was almost taken in; for I could have fancied I had her
before me once more.

O this sex! this artful sex! There's no minding them. At first, indeed,
their grief and their concern may be real: but give way to the hurricane,
and it will soon die away in soft murmurs, trilling upon your ears like the
notes of a well-tuned viol. And, by Sally, one sees that art will generally so

well supply the place of nature that you shall not easily know the difference. (IV, 134-5).

This raises complex questions of appearance and reality, although it is crucial to our sense of Lovelace's discrimination that he should go on to say: 'Miss Clarissa Harlowe, indeed, is the only woman in the world, I believe, that can say, in the words of her favourite Job (for I can quote a text as well as she): *But it is not so with me.*' (IV, 135). Initially, when Sally offers to be 'virtuous for a quarter of an hour, and mimic your Clarissa to the life' Lovelace feels that he 'could not bear such an insult upon the dear creature.' (IV, 134). Despite himself, he is drawn in by the power of her performance and we, too, are forced to see Clarissa in a comic light through this degrading spectacle. Richardson's ability to do this without diminishing her purity is art of a high order.

At a deeper level, Clarissa is humanized by her vein of spiritual pride, what Lovelace calls the 'pride of setting an example to her sex.' (II, 36) but the presence of this quality, and her self-discovery of it, are the elements which push towards allegory rather than psychological complexity. The novel's 'contention between... naked innocence and armed guilt' (II, 483) can be seen as the opposition of spirit and world, and it is clearly central to its purpose that we should eventually be moved, and without irony, by Clarissa in 'the mantle of my own integrity.' (II, 168). In the very last analysis, the core of Clarissa's being is inviolable to speculative analysis, in a manner similar to her touching desire for ultimate physical inviolability:

> In the first place, I desire that my body may lie unburied three days after my decease, till the pleasure of my father be known concerning it. But the occasion of my death not admitting of doubt, I will not, on any account, that it be opened; and it is my desire that it shall not be touched but by those of my own sex. (IV, 416)

The passage is complex as well as moving. Clearly, Clarissa's body has already been 'opened' by someone not of 'my own sex', yet this does not render her desire to be untouched after death empty. Lovelace's penetration is real enough, but it leaves her essentially untouched because it was violation in the truest sense and did not result from a hidden desire to be raped, masked by a more or less suspect moral surface.

What, though, of Lovelace? One source of his power clearly lies in that melodramatic mode which is central to the artistry of *Clarissa*, as a passage from Eric Bentley suggests: 'Historically the villains in our tradition [melodrama] stem from the archvillain Lucifer.'[20] The association of Lovelace with the devil is conveyed by a texture of small details throughout the novel. At one point, Lovelace asks 'Was the devil in me!' as an explanation of the 'ecstatic nonsense' he 'no more intended' than 'flying in the air!' (II, 142). Later in the same book, this hardens into, 'Miss Howe will tell thee: she says, I am the *devil*' (II, 399), a judgement confirmed by Clarissa's 'O Lovelace, you are Satan himself.' (III, 210). Finally, we have his own admission:

> Pity me, Jack, for pity's sake, if thou dost not, nobody else will and yet never was there a man of my genius and lively temper that wanted it more. We are apt to attribute to the devil everything that happens to us which we would not *have* happen: but here, being (as perhaps thou'lt say) the devil myself, my plagues arise from an angel. I suppose all mankind is to be plagued by its *contrary*. (III, 231).

This prince of darkness is indeed a gentleman with whom, as with Clarissa, Richardson is working in a tradition too familiar to require elaboration. We may think backwards and forwards to the debonair evil of the Edmund of *King Lear* and the James Harthouse of *Hard Times* or the Grandcourt of *Daniel Deronda*, but there is infinitely more to Lovelace than any facile identification with the evil elements of the Christian story and to get at this it is, unfortunately, necessary to disagree with two distinguished critics.

It is difficult to know, firstly, what to make of this comment of Frank Bradbrook's: Richardson 'was incapable of writing a great "comic epic in prose"...since he was almost completely humourless.'[21] Nothing is more wayward than taste in humour, but it surely has to be argued that comedy is central to the novel, a fact recognized by Margaret Doody in her *'Natural Passion.'*[22] Richardson's letters are far from lively and socially he seems hardly to have been amusing, but this is only another example of the difference between art and life. Comedy is difficult to analyse without recourse to a series of examples, but the point at issue is important enough to make this necessary; also, risking the intentional fallacy, it is evident that Richardson himself intended Lovelace to create a partly comic impression. In a passage of linking commentary, he stresses the need to avoid repetition by giving only those passages which 'serve to embellish hers [Clarissa's]; to open his views; or to display the humorous talent he was noted for.' (II, 13). And this talent is embodied in a virtuoso range of effects. There is the mock coyness of

'Would it be *very* wicked, Jack, to knock her messenger o' the head as he is carrying my beloved's letters' (II, 97); the outrageous exclamation: 'I suppose she did not care to hear of so many children... *to be begotten upon the body of the said Clarissa Harlowe.* Charming matrimonial recitativoes!' (II, 47); the devastating aside: 'But though an acquaintance of no longer standing, and that commencing on the bowling-green (Uncle John is a great bowler, Belford).' (II, 449). There is something of the verbal dexterity of the Restoration rake in all this, as in the Mirabell-like references to Clarissa as a 'frost-piece' (II, 474) and 'the charming icicle.' (II, 473). A more sinister note is, however, struck in Lovelace's sexual effrontery:

> Let me perish, Belford, if I would not forgo the brightest diadem in the world for the pleasure of seeing a twin Lovelace at each charming breast, drawing from it his first sustenance. (II, 477).

The comic outrage of the picture this evokes is fused with the moral outrage we feel at such brutal masculine dominance over our image of Clarissa. Such passages could be multiplied almost indefinitely; an extended, and thematically significant, finale might be Lovelace's brilliant parody of bourgeois respectability:

> 'Tis true, this pretty little miss, being a *very* pretty little miss, being a *very much-admired* little miss, being a very *good* little miss, who always minded her book, and had passed through her sampler doctrine with high applause; had even stitched out in gaudy propriety of colours, an Abraham offering up Isaac, a Samson and the Philistines, and flowers, and knots, and trees, and the sun and the moon, and the seven stars, all hung up in frames with glasses before them, for the admiration of her future grandchildren: who likewise was entitled to a very pretty little estate: who was descended from a pretty little family upwards of one hundred years' gentility; which lived in a very pretty little manner, respected a very little on their own accounts, a great deal on hers. (III, 317)

This 'pretty little miss' had, according to Lovelace, 'formed pretty notions how charmingly it would look to have a penitent of her own making dangling at her side to church, through an applauding neighbourhood: and, as their family increased... boasting of the fruits of their *honest desires.*' (III, 316). The mingling of absurdity and penetration is, again, brilliantly handled. Through the verbal repetition which seems to anticipate the Dickensian bravura of such passages as the description of the 'decent' Bradley Headstone in *Our Mutual Friend,* Clarissa is reduced to the level of a Pamela who has got her man by way of characteristically middle-class techniques. And yet the desire to reform Lovelace is eventually seen by Clarissa herself as an element in her spiritual pride. Again, the fact that Richardson the novelist can be funny in himself, as it were, without the aid of Lovelace is shown in both that varied range of word coinings that are a continual delight ('newelty' (I, 17), for example) and, in another anticipatory passage, the effusions of the Rev. Elias Brand which seem to look forward to those of Mr Collins in *Pride and Prejudice*:

> I beseech you, let not this hint *go farther* than to *yourself,* your *spouse,* and *Mrs Barker.* I know I may trust my *life* in *your hands and theirs.* There have been (let me tell ye) *unlikelier* things come to pass, and that with *rich widows* (some of *quality* truly!), whose choice in their first marriages hath (perhaps) been guided by *motives of convenience,* or *mere corporalities,* as I may say; but who by their *second* have had for their view the *corporal* and *spiritual* mingled; which is the most eligible (no doubt) to *substances* composed of *both,* as *men* and *women* are. (IV, 312)

However, it remains true that the novel's comic strand is mainly connected with Lovelace and its relevance to the argument can be illustrated by my second critical disagreement, this time with David Daiches:

> Lovelace is a more interesting character than Mr B, though no more convincing. He is a mild and timid man's picture of the ideal rake, of Satan as gentleman...But he serves his purpose, which is after all little more than that of a catalyst.[23]

This is an amazing judgement to come from such a distinguished source, especially in relation to the first truly great character in English fiction. There is a genuine wildness in Lovelace's comic outbursts which is far removed from 'a mild and timid man's picture of the ideal rake.' Reference has already been made to the split between the man and the artist in Richardson which is, all in all, perhaps the most striking case of that not unusual phenomenon in the whole of English literature. Richardson was clearly gifted with one of the novelist's indispensable possessions, negative capability, a fact he seems to have recognized himself in a letter on *Sir Charles Grandison:*

> In short, this Part is one of those that I value myself most upon, having been as zealous a Catholic when I was to personate the Lady [Clementina] and her Catholic Friends, as a Protestant, when I was the Gentleman.[24]

81

This also provides an explanation of those aspects of *Clarissa* which have appeared to some disagreeably prurient. The novel's 'warm' episodes are powerful because of Richardson's total imaginative involvement in the situation rather than the distanced manipulation so characteristic of pornography. To paraphrase Richardson's letter, he is as zealously erotic in impersonating Lovelace as he is chastely spiritual in depicting Clarissa. But Richardson has a grasp of Lovelace's character as well as an involvement with it and this is highlighted by the second half of Professor Daiches's comment that Lovelace is 'after all little more than a catalyst.' Objective disproof of this can be found in the amount of space devoted to Lovelace's letters in the novel, a clear sign that he is of interest to Richardson in his own right. Again, one is forced to disagree with Walter Allen, appreciative though he is of Lovelace's force as a character:

> He is a most subtle creation, who, restless analyst of his own action though he is, scarcely knows any more than his creator does the true motives for his behaviour. [25]

The text itself provides evidence that Richardson understands the nature of his own creation as well as being dazzled by it, an insight that can be explored through Clarissa's own confusion about Lovelace:

> I am strangely at a loss what to think of this man. He is a perfect Proteus. I can but write according to the shape he assumes at the time. Don't think *me* the changeable person, I beseech you, if in one letter I contradict what I wrote in another: nay, if I seem to contradict what I said in the same letter; for he is a perfect chameleon; or rather more variable than the chameleon; for that, it is said, cannot assume the *red* and the *white*; but this man *can*. And though *black* seems to be his natural colour, yet has he taken great pains to make me think him nothing but *white*. (II, 82)

Part of the power of this remarkable passage lies in its manipulation of a traditional puzzlement of good in the face of evil. Cordelia may say she knows her sisters for what they are, but is she capable of understanding the depths they inhabit? In life as well as art, innocence is frequently at a loss to grasp the full range of evil possibilities. The most striking aspect of the passage is, however, Clarissa's sense that her own secure core of identity, 'the mantle of my own integrity', (II, 168), is being shaken by contact with Lovelace, so that she doubts something of what she herself is. How can this be otherwise when he is 'so light, so vain, so various, that there is no certainty that he will be next hour what he is this.'

(II, 95)? This feeling of complete changeability is well caught by John Preston:

> Lovelace lives a life of fantasy. He is divorced from reality, or would be so if his wealth did not allow him to consider giving substance to his fantasies. Fact is not stubborn for him... He can command not only his own appearance but the appearance of those around him.[26]

The accuracy of Preston's critical judgement is confirmed by the flood of examples that come readily to mind: Lovelace's use of disguises, especially as the old man at Hampstead; his forging of letters, a transposition of reality peculiarly disturbing in view of the epistolary nature of the novel itself; his endless schemes of sexual possession, enjoying Clarissa and Anna Howe as a kind of double mistress, kidnapping Anna and her mother, and so on. All of this is accompanied by his self-delight at his own exploits, real or imaginary:

> What an industrious spirit have I! Nobody can say that I eat the bread of idleness. I take true pains for all the pleasure I enjoy. I cannot but admire myself strangely; for certainly, with this active soul, I should have made a very great figure in whatever station I had filled. But had I been a prince! (III, 26)

Had he been a prince, indeed!

At this point we can start to feel our way into the heart of this remarkable being and, without any sense of strain, to grasp something of the social, as well as aesthetic, nature of Richardson's achievement. This is not to claim, however, that the novel's social aspects are reducible to the rise of the bourgeoisie or aristocratic-middle class antagonism. For an extreme, and non-Marxist, example of this viewpoint we can turn to Leslie Stephen:

> All his books are deliberate attempts to embody his ideal in model representatives of his society... Richardson was a typical tradesman of the period; he was the industrious apprentice who married his master's daughter.[27]

Literature and Society in the Eighteenth Century is of permanent value, but these comments are wildly beside the point. Richardson in life may have been 'a typical tradesman of the period,' but the chief interest of this is to highlight how utterly untypical a novel he created in *Clarissa*. In what sense can Lovelace and Clarissa be seen as 'model representatives'? In outline they may represent the rake and the lady, but their embodiment pushes completely beyond such a schema, to an evil at once devilishly complex and dazzling in its charm, and a spirituality closer to that of Plato's perfectly just man than a social ideal. The problem here is to grasp what is central to the novel, a problem similar to that experienced in *Wuthering Heights*. It would be absurd to argue that such works inhabit a closed world of personal confrontation, totally divorced from any social context. Some critics have suggested,[28] and it would be foolish to disagree, that the novel's characters inhabit an important social setting and the book itself provides evidence for going some way towards a socio-economic reading. When Clarissa remarks to Anna Howe, 'never was there a family more united in its different branches than ours' (I, 25) we soon realize that the basis of this unity is financial rather than emotional, an important aspect of this being the 'darling view...of *raising a family*', although this is social in its impetus rather than monetary: 'A view too frequently, it seems, entertained by families which having great substance, cannot be satisfied without rank and title.' (I, 53). We can see the outlines of class antagonism in Lovelace's description of one of his previous amours: 'Miss Betterton was but a tradesman's daughter. The family indeed were grown rich, and aimed at a new line of gentry; and were unreasonable enough to expect a man of my family would marry her.' (II, 147). The unfortunate lady's name indicates clearly enough the social aspect of the relationship, but can this legitimately be claimed of Lovelace and Clarissa? Lovelace himself is class-conscious; indeed, his harping on social upstarts is reminiscent of Iago's jealousy concerning Emilia: both protest a bit too much. Not content with his disparagement of the Harlowes – 'Everybody knows Harlowe Place; for, like Versailles, it is sprung up from a dunghill, within every elderly person's remembrance' (I, 170) – Lovelace has to find similar fault with Anna Howe: '*Young* families (Miss Howe's is not an ancient one) love ostentatious sealings.' (III, 89). But these aspects of the novel, important as they are, cannot finally be reduced to a materialist level.

Pamela and Mr B may be seen as 'model representatives' playing out a class as well as a personal game, but Richardson has moved beyond this in *Clarissa*. Leaving aside the intricacies of ideology, the final appeal is to a critical sense of what seems central in a novel. Lively and varied as the range of characters is in a book like *Bleak House*, for example, none has the commanding status to push the Court of Chancery from something close to a dominating position in the novel's economy. Conversely, fruitful discussion of a book largely given over to only two characters must start from this point. If there are important social elements in *Clarissa* they must be seen as emerging from character, and this involves a further stage in the argument about Lovelace, another aspect of his almost inexhaustibly interesting Protean quality.

In a way that, again, anticipates Fielding, Lovelace justifies himself in relation to the evil actions of 'great men', in the manner of Jonathan Wild:

> Caesar, we are told, had won, at the age of fifty-six, when he was assassinated, fifty pitched battles, had taken by assault above a thousand towns, and slain near 1,200,000 men; I suppose exlusive of those who fell on his own side in slaying them. Are not you and I, Jack, innocent men, and babes in swaddling-clothes, compared to Caesar, and to his predecessor in heroism, Alexander, dubbed for murders and depredation Magnus? (II, 424).

Lovelace clearly sees himself as a great man in his own line and, beneath the Protean surface, driven by a master impulse analagous to the hunger for power of Caesar and Alexander: 'Then there are so many stimulatives to such a spirit as mine in this affair, *besides* love: such a field for stratagem and contrivance, which thou knowest to be the delight of my heart.' (I, 150). Taking a hint from the marvellously suggestive discussion of Diderot's *Rameau's Nephew* in Lionel Trilling's *Sincerity and Authenticity*, this drive to power connects with one of the assertions of 'He' (the nephew):

> This is what I particularly value in men of genius. They are only good for one thing, and apart from that, nothing. They don't know what it means to be citizens, fathers, mothers, brothers, relations, friends.[29]

Remembering the enormous extent of Richardson's European influence, it is possible to see Lovelace as a link in the chain from Renaissance over-reaching to Byronic assertion. But qualifications are also necessary and they are pinpointed by contrasting a 'He' and 'I' passage from *Rameau's Nephew:*

> *He:* Devil take me if I really know what I am.
> *I:* It would be better to retire to one's garret, live on dry bread and water and discover one's real self.[30]

Lovelace is precisely in the He's state of confusion, as a confession to Belford reveals: 'So here I am in my dining-room, and have nothing to do but write...And what will be my subject...? Why, the old beaten one, to be sure; self-debate – through temporary remorse.'

(III, 155). The modernity of Richardson's insight is revealed by drawing a distinction between confusion and conflict. Marlowe's Faustus, say, is in a state of conflict between warring aspects of his character which are, in themselves, quite unproblematic. He is unable to resolve his conflict, through fear, but he could not say, with the Nephew *or* Lovelace, 'Devil take me if I really know what I am.' This is, surely, the psychological explanation of Lovelace's capacity to be so many different things and it connects with another of the central images which embody his complexity, his view that the theatre is 'the epitome of the world.' (IV, 35).

The world as 'this great stage' is a time-honoured convention, but it has a special force for *Clarissa* in the consistency with which Lovelace is presented in theatrical terms, as when Clarissa is utterly confused by his apparent blushing:

> But how was it possible that even that florid countenance of his should enable him to command a blush at his pleasure? For blush he did, more than once: and the blush, on this occasion, was a deep-dyed crimson, unstrained for, and natural, as I thought; but he is so much of the actor, that he seems able to enter into any character; and his muscles and features appear entirely under obedience to his wicked will. (III, 360).

We hardly need Clarissa's comment, of course, as one of the major experiences in reading the novel is a dramatic involvement with Lovelace's bewildering changes of role, a brilliance never more evident than in the striking scene where he plays shop-assistant in the business run by the Smiths, with whom Clarissa has been in hiding:

> I took a chair to Smith's, my heart bounding in almost audible thumps to my throat, with the assured expectation of seeing my beloved. I clasped my fingers, as I was danced along: I charged my eyes to languish and sparkle by turns: I talked to my knees, telling them how they must bend; and, in the language of a charming describer, acted my part in fancy, as well as spoke it to myself. (IV, 124).

On discovering that Clarissa has escaped him, Lovelace turns his spite against the Smiths:

> John and Joseph muttered and whispered together. [That is, Smith and his workman].
>
> No whispering, honest friends: 'tis not manners to whisper. Joseph, what said John to thee?
>
> JOHN, sir! disdainfully repeated the good woman.

I beg pardon, Mrs Smith: but you see the force of example. Had *you* showed your honest man more respect, *I* should. Let me give you a piece of advice: Women who treat their husbands irreverently teach strangers to use them with contempt. There, honest Master John; why dost not pull off thy hat to me? Oh, so thou wouldst, if thou hadst it on: but thou never wearest thy hat in thy wife's presence, I believe; dost thou?

None of your fleers and your jeers, sir, cried John.
I wish every married pair lived as happily as we do.

I wish so too, honest friend. But I'll be hanged if thou hast any children.

Why so, sir?

Hast thou? Answer me, man: has thou or not?

Perhaps not, sir. But what of that?

What of that? Why, I'll tell thee: the man who has no children by his wife must put up with plain John. Hadst thou a child or two, thou'dst be called Mr Smith, with a curtsy, or a smile at least, at every word...

A female customer, who had been gaping at the door, came in for some Scots snuff; and I would serve her. The wench was plaguy homely; and I told her so; or else, I said, I would have treated her. She in anger (no woman is homely in her own opinion) threw down her penny; and I put it in my pocket.

Just then, turning my eye to the door, I saw a pretty genteel lady, with a footman after her, peeping in... I ran to her from behind the counter, and, as she was making off, took her hand, and drew her into the shop, begging that she would be my customer; for that I had just begun trade.

What do you sell sir? said she, smiling; but a little surprised.

Tapes, ribbons, silk laces, pins, and needles; for I am a pedlar: powder, patches, washballs, stockings, garters, snuffs, and pincushions — don't we Goody Smith?... And so, flinging down a Portugal six-and-thirty, I took Mr Smith by the hand, telling him I was sorry we had not more time to be better acquainted; and bidding farewell to honest Joseph... and Mrs Smith adieu ... and, the chair being come, whipped into it; the people about the door seeming to be in good humour with me; one crying, A pleasant gentleman, I warrant him! And away I was carried to White's, according to direction. (IV, 127-8, 131-3).

It is difficult to maintain critical restraint in the face of imaginative power of this order, even distorted as it is by selective quotation. As with Hamlet, we do not need to be *told* of Lovelace's brilliance: it is enacted for us with total confidence. And the psychological strands woven together here are of great complexity. There is evidently an element of hysteria caused by Lovelace's disappointment at missing Clarissa, but also the fact that 'I, who had been so lately ill, was glad I was alive' (IV, 133), which makes it impossible not to respond to the outrageousness of his gaiety. However, a thread of implicit moral judgement is also present which makes the passage a touchstone for a total view of Lovelace. Class privilege is devastatingly revealed in 'the proud man's contumely' with which he treats the Smiths and, on a more personal level, the nastiest side of his character in his jeering at their childlessness. Sexually and socially Lovelace is master of the situation, and subtleties of personal and social antagonism are registered in the dialogue with a precision reminiscent of the suggestive exchanges between Eugene Wrayburn and Bradley Headstone in *Our Mutual Friend.*

I referred a moment ago to the similarities between Lovelace and *Rameau's Nephew.* Diderot's idolatry of Richardson is well known, but there are aspects of their literary relationship which have not been fully brought out. What follows on Diderot relies greatly on Professor Trilling's *Sincerity and Authenticity,* whose argument, to use his own words, it 'is scarcely possible to describe...in a way that will be both summary and accurate.'[31] Trilling is at pains to emphasize the Nephew's modernity which he finds illustrated by the admiration felt for the work by some of the key thinkers of the modern period, including Marx and Freud. In Trilling's view, Hegel, for example, saw *Rameau's Nephew* as the 'paradigm of the modern cultural and spiritual situation' and the Nephew himself as the 'exemplary figure of the modern phase of developing Spirit.' Despite his great talents, the Nephew 'must endure the peculiar bitterness of modern man, the knowledge that he is not a genius', and 'Diderot's dialogue continues and further particularizes Pascal's sense of the human contradiction, of man as the opposite of himself.' The concrete result of all this is the 'extravagant histrionicism of *Rameau's Nephew,* as he assumes an endless succession of roles.' The resemblances to Lovelace seem clear, but an extended example from each work may serve to put the point beyond doubt. The most famous passage in *Rameau's Nephew,* in Trilling's words 'the great climax of the dialogue', is the 'Nephew's astonishing operatic performance, his momentous abandonment of individuated selfhood to become all the voices of human existence, of all existence'[32]:

> Here we have a young girl weeping, and he mimes all her simpering ways, there a priest, king, tyrant, threatening, commanding, flying into a rage or a slave obeying. He relents, wails, complains, laughs, never losing sight of tone, proportion, meaning of words and character of music...But you would have gone off into roars of laughter at the way he mimicked the

various instruments. With cheeks puffed out and a hoarse, dark tone he did the horns and bassoons, a bright, nasal tone for the oboes...he whistled the recorders and cooed the flutes, shouting, singing and throwing himself about like a mad thing: a one-man show featuring dancers, male and female, singers of both sexes, a whole orchestra, a complete opera house, dividing himself into twenty different stage parts, tearing up and down, stopping, like one possessed, with flashing eyes and foaming mouth...What didn't he do? He wept, laughed, sighed, his gaze was tender, soft or furious: a woman swooning with grief, a poor wretch abandoned in the depth of his despair, a temple rising into view, birds falling silent at eventide...By now he was quite beside himself.[33]

Perhaps the most apt comparison is Lovelace's assumption of his old man's disguise, not least because it is cast in a directly theatrical form, 'ACT II Scene. – *Hampstead Heath, continued. Enter my Rascal*':

All this time I was adjusting my horseman's coat, and Will was putting in the ties of my wig, and buttoning the cape over my chin.

I asked the gentlewoman for a little powder. She brought me a powder-box and I lightly shook the puff over my hat, and flapped one side of it, though the lace looked a little too gay for my covering; and slouching it over my eyes, Shall I be known, think you, madam?

Your honour is so expert, sir!...except they find you out by your clocked stockings.

Well observed. Can't you, landlord, lend or sell me a pair?...

He could let me have a pair of coarse, but clean, stirrup-stockings, if I pleased. The best in the world for the purpose.

He fetched them. Will drew them on; and my legs then made a good gouty appearance...

And as thou knowest that I am not a bad mimic, I took a cane, which I borrowed of the landlord, and stooped in the shoulders to a quarter of a foot of less height, and stumped away across the bowling-green, to practise a little the bobbling gait of a gouty man...

I can suit myself to any condition, that's my comfort...

The maid came to the door. I asked for her mistress. She showed me into one of the parlours; and I sat down with a gouty Oh!

Enter Goody Moore
Your servant madam—but you must excuse me; I cannot well stand. I find by the bill at the door, that you have lodgings to let (mumbling my words as if, like my man Will, I had lost some of my fore-teeth)...

She [Clarissa] started, and looked at me with terror..

I saw it was impossible to conceal myself longer from her, any more than (from the violent impulses of my passion) to forbear manifesting myself. I unbuttoned therefore my cape, I pulled off my flapped, slouched hat; I threw open my greatcoat, and, like the devil in Milton (an odd comparison though!)

> I started up in my own form divine,
> Touched by the beam of her celestial eye,
> More potent than Ithuriel's spear. (III, 30-41)

Comparison rather than analysis is the issue here, although analysis is hardly necessary to grasp Lovelace's self-presentation as Lucifer and, whether fully conscious on Richardson's part or not, the sexual appropriateness of Milton's lines.

The element of drama in all this is unmistakably powerful. Possibly the most theatrical aspect of both, and one of their most striking similarities, is the sense that Lovelace and the Nephew are spectators of their own lives, that self-divided as they are, they lose themselves not in an authentic unity of soul, but in the momentary absorption of a role of which they are always ultimately aware. The nature of the claim being advanced is, again, clarified by Trilling in a comment on the literary relationship of Jane Austen to Rousseau:

> Jane Austen never mentions Rousseau in her letters, and although there is ground for believing that she read *La Nouvelle Héloïse*, it is unlikely that her acquaintance with him went beyond this one work. It is not, however, an influence that I would propose, but, rather, an affinity.[34]

Similarly, there is no suggestion that Richardson's creation of Lovelace was a direct influence on Diderot's of the Nephew. But that there is an affinity seems clear and that in preceding Diderot in this way, Richardson steps forward with an indisputable modernity, that he anticipates (to put it no more strongly) the 'modern cultural and spiritual situation.' Lovelace is, then, a creature of the modern world and it is in this sense that *Clarissa* is a significantly social as well as spiritual work of art. Richardson is clearly not interested in the social panorama to be found in Fielding, but the controlled vision of *Clarissa* embodies an image of society nonetheless. Unlike Defoe and earlier Smollett, his novel does not simply go on and on until it reaches an arbitrary conclusion. And although the weight of his interest falls on the spiritual conflict between Clarissa and Lovelace, this is embodied in a context of social manners, Lionel Trilling's 'hum and buzz of implication...that part of a culture which is made up of half-uttered or unuttered or unutterable expressions of value.'[35] His image of society is a stage on which an elemental opposition is played out, but this setting has some radical differences from the 'great stage of fools' of an earlier tradition. For Lovelace especially it is a modern arena which permits a degree of role-playing which exceeds even the complexities of Iago. Iago's inner core of evil is impenetrable, but the core does exist and acts as a touchstone of comparison for his part of the genially rough soldier. Lovelace is nothing but his roles, and the rapidity of his movement from one to the other dissolves the possibility of his having a central core of personality. This degree of psychological richness is not to be found in Fielding; richness of another kind may, however, exist in the wider scope of his view of the social world.

Further Reading

The major modern study of Richardson is:

Samuel Richardson: Dramatic Novelist by Mark Kinkead-Weekes (London, 1973).

Also of importance is:

'Natural Passion': A Study of the Novels of Samuel Richardson by M. A. Doody (London, 1974).

A provocative, Marxist viewpoint is provided by:

The Rape of Clarissa: Writing, Sexuality and Class Struggle in Samuel Richardson by Terry Eagleton (Blackwell, Oxford, 1982).

The following are generally useful:

Samuel Richardson by R. F. Brissenden (London, 1958).

Samuel Richardson: Printer and Novelist by A. D. McKillop (North Carolina, 1936).

The Early Masters of English Fiction by A. D. McKillop (London, 1956).

Some interesting critical judgements will be found in:

Samuel Richardson: A Collection of Critical Essays edited by John Carroll (London, 1969).

4

Tom Jones

Criticism is a never-ending, and never fully won, battle to establish a balance between order and spontaneity. Better to view the bird on the wing, however imperfectly, than to shoot it for dissection. That this flexibility is fully demanded by *Tom Jones* is illustrated by its reference to critics as 'in most...parts of our work...every reader in the world' (VIII, 1), only to offer (a hundred pages later) a swipe at the 'little reptile of a critic.' (X, 1)[1] The reptile must move warily, then, but with sufficient courage to risk his own view. The earlier crudities of the biographical fallacy, whereby Fielding's supposed moral lapses were said to have infected his work, are past, though the longevity of this nonsense is revealed in the Everyman *Short Biographical Dictionary of English Literature* of 1910 with its routine gesture towards Fielding's 'many weaknesses and serious faults.'[2] The pendulum has now swung in a more interesting direction, but one still in danger of imposing its own kind of schematic rigidity on the work. Martin C. Battestin makes the general point with magisterial force:

> *Tom Jones* (1749) is at once the last and the consummate literary
> achievement of England's Augustan Age: an age whose cast of mind saw
> the moral drama of individual life enacted within a frame of cosmic and
> social order, conceived in the then still compatible terms of Christian
> humanism and Newtonian science, and whose view of art, conditioned by
> the principles of neo-Aristotelian aesthetics, saw the poem as
> fundamentally mimetic of this universal design.[3]

But when he goes on to remark that the 'author-narrator of *Tom Jones* stands in relation to the world of his novel as the divine Author and his Providence to the "Book of Creation" '[4] we may jib a little, if only at the memory of that inconsistency towards critics just referred to. There is something too playful about this 'author-narrator' for him to be entirely God-like. Henry Knight Miller stresses a related, but this time linguistic, conservatism:

> By Fielding's time...the whole tradition of literary 'decorum' was
> becoming...somewhat old-fashioned...and it is one of the measures of
> the separation from his own age...that he should have held so tenaciously
> to the tradition.[5]

But how does this square with Fielding's mockery of these standards,
their sudden abandonment in favour of the down-to-earth and
direct? The reductiveness of such a monolithic reading of a writer, or
period, is crystallized in A. R. Humphreys's assertion that Fielding is
'less an individual artist than the voice of his time.'[6] This is reflection
theory with a vengeance and needs to be countered by Wolfgang
Iser's sense that Fielding's relationship to his readers was not totally
unlike that of Dickens: 'Fielding was not only concerned with
catering for a varied public; he was also at pains to transcend the
social or educatonal limitations of the individual'.[7] In other words,
however massively Augustan, Fielding is not simply writing for an
élite in the way possible for Pope. Again, if Fielding belongs so
centrally to his period, he could hardly pose the problem seen by the
editors of the *Critical Heritage* volume, whose collection of
contemporary views of Fielding 'presents from all angles the
problem of how to fit Fielding's transitional works into the critical
categories available at the time.'[8] There is a biographical trap on the
other side of the question, of course; life and art are never the same
thing, although as Miller wisely observes a 'work of literature is *both*
continuous with life *and* an object of aesthetic concern, not either/
or.'[9] But some corrective to the Fielding of order and decorum is
suggested by the fact that he married his first wife's maid and by
Lady Mary Wortley Montagu's wonderful evocation:

> No man enjoyed life more than he did...His happy constitution...made
> him forget everything when he was before a venison pasty, or over a flask
> of champagne; and I am persuaded he has known more happy moments
> than any prince upon earth. His natural spirits gave him rapture with his
> cook-maid, and cheerfulness when he was fluxing in a garret...each
> [Fielding and Sir Richard Steele] of them [was] so formed for happiness, it
> is pity he was not immortal.[10]

In the light of this, Tom Jones can hardly seem entirely a product of
the imagination.

Another trap waits, however, if this evidence is pushed too far.
Fielding is *the* central problem for the view that the rise of the novel
is intimately connected with the rise of the bourgeoisie. The whole
argument has been met head on by Diana Spearman in *The Novel and*

Society, although with a degree of exaggeration and special pleading that weakens her own case: 'Tom Jones is like a mediaeval hero in his courage, recklessness and generosity, these qualities merely being adjusted to eighteenth century conditions.'[11] That 'merely' surely leaves too many questions unanswered. What is certain, though, is the extreme difficulty of assimilating Fielding to a bourgeois standpoint in any convincing way. Again, the extreme position is useful and it can be found in Arnold Kettle's statement that 'Tom and Sophia fight conventional society, embodied in the character of Blifil.'[12] Professor Kettle's argument hinges on the point that 'for the purposes of the plot (and to placate conventional taste) Fielding makes Tom a gentleman after all; but that is not really important.'[13] Part of the point of what follows is to show that Tom's ultimate gentility is central to Fielding's purpose. Also, Kettle seems to regard plot with almost the airy dismissiveness of E.M. Forster in *Aspects of the Novel*, whereas Ian Watt is surely correct in seeing Fielding's handling of his plot as central, 'for it reflects the whole of his social, moral and literary outlook.'[14] A full examination of the novel's plot reinforces the judgement advanced in the best chapter of an otherwise indifferent work on the sociology of literature by Laurenson and Swingewood:

> He seems finally to assert the virtues of a traditional rural England over the secular, advancing urban capitalist areas. It is hard to see how Fielding can be situated in the history of the novel as a bourgeois writer.[15]

They continue by saying that for Fielding to have depicted Tom in 'a "bourgeois manner" would have created obvious difficulties... leading him into criticism of a system of social stratification and inequality which he saw as essentially natural and necessary.'[16]

Where, then, do these contrary views leave us? Perhaps with Neil Compton's formulation of Fielding as a conservative innovator:

> Another way of putting it might be to say that *Tom Jones* represents a kind of counter-revolution, an attempt to use the new radical form of prose fiction in defence of established Augustan values. Like all counter-revolutionary enterprises it ends by bearing a closer resemblance to its rivals than the instigator probably intended.[17]

This position answers to one's sense of the novel as a living text and also to its place in history. Fielding *is* Augustan in many important ways, the book resolving ultimately into a not uncritical celebration of an idealized version of the *status quo*. But he is, simultaneously, innovatory in writing a novel at all and this is perhaps most clear in his self-consciousness about artistic form. At this point, if no other, there is an essential similarity between Fielding and Richardson. Both were aware of doing something new in literature and both thought about the nature of this new literary activity. Like Richardson, Fielding has his own 'kind of writing, of which we have set ourselves at the head.' (V, 1) Although claiming that, except for Boswell, Fielding is the writer who most 'fairly and comprehensively transports us to Hanoverian England', A. R. Humphreys sees the limitations of a mechanical externality in the depiction of society in his comparison of Smollett with Fielding:

> Fielding's is the higher and more philosophical truth which epitomizes the spirit, the ethos, as well as the body, of the time, which deals primarily not in externals but in the nature of man and in an intellectual and moral code.[18]

It is through complexity of form that Fielding is able to embody this wider perspective. In so far as, say, *Moll Flanders* and *Roderick Random* have any sense of form it is of a rudimentary kind, the movement involved in following what might be called the trajectory of a life. Fielding is clearly dependent to some extent, not surprisingly, on existing fictional conventions and the trajectory of Tom's life is of great importance to the novel, but as something more than a device on which to hang narrative events. Tom's adventures are placed within a series of contexts, an application of what Pat Rogers sees as an essential aspect of Augustan literary practice: 'The whole "layered" technique of a poem like *The Dunciad*...with its elaborate series of parallel undertakings, may be plausibly linked to a habit of mind which encouraged reading on several different levels.'[19] But there is more than just a matter of inheritance here; Fielding is seizing a method which has implications for the kind of prose fiction he wishes to create, with its rich sense of social complexity. In any event, these contexts are worth examining in some detail. An obvious one is the novel's critical machinery, the paraphernalia of chapters that introduce each Book, and the obvious question that presents itself is: what is Fielding up to in them? One explanation that should not be overlooked is that he is simply having fun, rather in the manner of Sterne, with chapter headings such as 'Containing Little or Nothing' (III, 1) and 'Containing Five Pages of Paper' (IV, 1). A move to more serious explanation can follow from asking what Fielding himself thinks of the whole enterprise of writing *Tom Jones*, a clue to which can be found in an often-quoted passage:

> For as I am, in reality, the founder of a new province of writing, so I am at liberty to make what laws I please therein. And these laws, my readers, whom I consider my subjects, are bound to believe in and obey; with which that they may readily and chearfully comply. I do hereby assure them, that I shall principally regard their ease and advantage in all such institutions. (II, 1).

It is typical of Fielding that he should present himself as merely perverse, again like Sterne, in the disposition of his material, but there are clear differences between Sterne's genuine wilfulness which often creates effects simply for their own sake, and the mockery of Fielding's ironic manner. Considering the novel as a whole, especially what Dorothy Van Ghent calls the 'seriousness and depth of significance' in its 'broad social panorama of comedy',[20] there is no reason to doubt that Fielding took his own claim, of founding a new province of writing, quite seriously, as did Richardson in his more portentous way. The same mixture of banter and underlying seriousness is to be found when he tackles directly the question of his reader's response to the book's critical machinery:

> Peradventure there may be no parts in this prodigious work which will give the reader less pleasure in the perusing, than those which have given the author the greatest pains in composing. Among these, probably, may be reckoned those initial essays which we have prefixed to the historical matter contained in every book; and which we have determined to be essentially necessary to this kind of writing, of which we have set ourselves at the head.
>
> For this our determination we do not hold ourselves strictly bound to assign any reason; it being abundantly sufficient that we have laid it down as a rule, necessary to be observed in all prosai-comi-epic writing. (V, 1)

This shows that Fielding is both aware of the originality of his own undertaking and also that sheer unfamiliarity may cause problems for his readers. The second point relates to a distinctively modern aspect of his enterprise, the heterogeneous nature of his audience. As he himself remarks, 'Reader, it is impossible we should know what sort of person thou wilt be.' (X, 1) This sense of the variety of his readership is surely a factor in Fielding's repeated stress on leaving things to 'the judgement of the sagacious reader.' (V, II) There is, again, a playful element in this; on occasion, Fielding indicates clearly enough what we are to think. But it is plain that he also recognizes that he cannot look for the community of response assumed, for different reasons, by Shakespeare or Pope. With an expansiveness that can now seem curiously modern in view of recent developments in the novel, although with a geniality all his own, Fielding clearly feels that the best place for this material is within the body of the work itself. Again, there is a relation to tradition here, by way of, for example, the endless prefaces and introductions of Swift's *Tale of a Tub*. But the specific use to which Fielding puts his chapters may lead us to question a statement of Ian Watt's which bears more obviously on Richardson than on his great contemporary: 'Reading *Tom Jones* we do not imagine that we are eavesdropping on a new exploration of reality; the prose immediately informs us that exploratory operations have long since been accomplished, that we are to be spared that labour, and presented instead with a sifted and clarified report of the findings'.[21] Fielding's introductory chapters cannot be called experimental, but they do surely contain an exploratory element in their attempt to discover the 'laws' of this 'new province of writing', a genuine discovery rather than what Fielding jokingly calls his 'liberty to make what laws I please.'

That this is so emerges from a certain conflict between the inherited and what is genuinely new in the book. It is worth noticing the novel's full title, *The History of Tom Jones*, which suggests a relationship to the documentary impulse which is an important aspect of the growth of the eighteenth-century novel. Relevant here are the subtitle of *Moll Flanders* and the detailed, sometimes too detailed, evocation of contemporary life in *Roderick Random*. Fielding's documentary impulse is evident in his only partly ironic claim that 'our province is to relate facts, and we shall leave causes to persons of much higher genius.' (II, 4) A related point that becomes almost traditional in later fiction (in Thackeray, for one) is the risk of moral misunderstanding Fielding must run in his presentation of Thwackum and Square, because of his duty to protect religion and virtue by taking upon himself to 'record the lives and actions of two of their false and pretended champions.' (III, 4) This is part of the tradition of satire in its assurance that the evoking of laughter must not be taken as a sign of moral complaisance. But the use of the word 'record' registers a more modern awareness, one that is particularly associated with the novel, the moral imperative to set down the truth of human lives no matter how reprehensible. Ronald Paulson recognizes this as a decisive break with Augustan literary conventions: 'A form interested in human experience for its own sake replaced one that advocated strict moral judgement.'[22] That this was not without its contemporary critics is shown by a comment of Sir John Hawkins:

> His morality in respect that it resolves virtue into good affections in contradiction to moral obligations and a sense of duty, is that of Lord Shaftesbury vulgarized, and is a system of excellent use in palliating the vices most injurious to society. He was the inventor of the cant phrase, goodness of heart, which is every day used as a substitute for probity...in short, he has done more towards corrupting the rising generation than any writer we know of.[23]

There is a clear resemblance between this apparent amorality and Defoe's delight, in the Preface to *Moll Flanders*, in the 'incredible variety of human life', a delight that is fully validated by his novel's fascinated interest in the details of how a particular life is lived, and which is echoed by Fielding in his complaint about the 'variety of matter...which I shall be obliged to cram into' (XVIII, 1) his final book of *Tom Jones*.

But Fielding is not bound by his fictional inheritance – 'less an individual artist than the voice of his time' – and if we go on to examine his introductory chapters in detail, it becomes clear that he realizes the novel can be more than simply a factual record of events. The laws that govern his new province of writing may by now seem somewhat banal, but this is only because, far from being Fielding's whims, they are part of the very nature of classic fiction. For example, again in comparison with Defoe, we can note Fielding's firm grasp of the concept of fictional time:

> Now it is our purpose in the ensuing pages, to pursue a contrary method. When any extraordinary scene presents itself, (as we trust will often be the case) we shall spare no pains nor paper to open it at large to our reader; but if whole y ars should pass without producing anything worthy his notice, we shall not be afraid of a chasm in our history; but shall hasten on to matters of consequence, and leave such periods of time totally unobserved. (II, 1)

If this seems obvious, we have only to remember the handling of time in, say, *Moll Flanders* with its lack of discretion and proportion in the allotting of space to its various narrative events. Fielding is also theoretically aware of the possibility of inside views, although he does not make very much use of them:

The reader is greatly mistaken, if he conceives that Thwackum appeared to Mr Allworthy in the same light as he doth to him in this history; and he is as much deceived, if he imagines, that the most intimate acquaintance which he himself could have had with that divine, would have informed him of those things which we, from our inspiration, are enabled to open and discover. (III, 5)

Perhaps the most important of all Fielding's fictional laws is one that occurs outside the introductory chapters, after the incident when Squire Western throws Sophia's muff on the fire and she retrieves it:

Though this incident will probably appear of little consequence to many of our readers, yet, trifling as it was, it had so violent an effect on poor Jones, that we thought it our duty to relate it. In reality, there are many little circumstances too often omitted by injudicious historians, from which events of the utmost importance arise. The world may indeed be considered as a vast machine, in which the great wheels are originally set in motion by those which are very minute, and almost imperceptible to any but the strongest eyes. (V, 4)

The novel's combination of inheritance and originality is obviously at work in this passage also. The mechanistic image of the universe is a favourite Augustan conceit, but the 'duty to relate' details, however small and apparently insignificant, is an important break-through in the novel's development. In fact, it might be said that the distinctive mark of the true novelist is his ability to flesh out the skeleton of plot and theme in an embodying mass of detail, a fact which makes the novel radically unlike other literary kinds.

Fielding is a master of these laws at a concrete as well as a theoretical level, as an extended example makes clear, a scene touched on by Ian Watt, but not fully developed by him,[24] in which Tom has sexual intercourse with Mollie after he has already fallen in love with Sophia. As the scene gains its effect in what might be called a contextual manner, it is important to have a grasp of all the elements which make it up. Tom has moved from despair at Allworthy's apparently imminent death to joy at his recovery; a celebratory dinner has made him drunk, he has quarrelled with Blifil, and it is at this point that we join him in 'the fields...where he intended to cool himself by a walk in the open air':

Jones retired from the company, in which we have seen him engaged, into the fields, where he intended to cool himself by a walk in the open air, before he attended Mr Allworthy. There, whilst he renewed those meditations on his dear Sophia, which the dangerous illness of his friend and benefactor had for some time interrupted, an accident happened, which with sorrow we relate, and with sorrow, doubtless, will it be read; however, that historic truth to which we profess so inviolable an attachment, obliges us to communicate it to posterity.

It was now a pleasant evening in the latter end of June, when our heroe was walking in a most delicious grove, where the gentle breezes fanning the leaves, together with the sweet trilling of a murmuring stream, and the melodious notes of nightingales, formed all together the most enchanting harmony. In this scene, so sweetly accommodated to love, he meditated on his dear Sophia. While his wanton fancy roved unbounded over all her beauties, and his lively imagination painted the charming maid in various ravishing forms, his warm heart melted with tenderness, and at length throwing himself on the ground, by the side of a gently murmuring brook, he broke forth into the following ejaculation.

'Oh Sophia, would Heaven give thee to my arms, how blest would be my condition! Curst be that fortune which sets a distance between us. Was I but possessed of thee, one only suit of rags thy whole estate, is there a man on earth whom I would envy! How contemptible would the brightest Circassian beauty, drest in all the jewels of the Indies, appear to my eyes! But why do I mention another woman? Could I think my eyes capable of looking at any other with tenderness, these hands should tear them from my head. No, my Sophia, if cruel fortune separates us for ever, my soul shall doat on thee alone. The chastest constancy will I ever preserve to thy image. Though I should never have possession of thy charming person, still shalt thou alone have possession of my thoughts, my love, my soul. Oh! my fond heart is so wrapt in that tender bosom, that the brightest beauties would for me have no charms, nor would a hermit be colder in their embraces. Sophia, Sophia alone shall be mine. What raptures are in that name! I will engrave it on every tree.'

At these words he started up, and beheld – not his Sophia – no, nor a Circassian maid richly and elegantly attired for the Grand Signior's seraglio. No; without a gown, in a shift that was somewhat of the coarsest, and none of the cleanest, bedewed likewise with some odoriferous effluvia, the produce of the day's labour, with a pitch-fork in her hand, Molly Seagrim approached. Our heroe had his penknife in his hand, which he had drawn for the before-mentioned purpose, of carving on the bark; when the girl coming near him, cry'd out with a smile, 'You don't intend to kill me, squire, I hope!' 'Why should you think I would kill you?' answered Jones. 'Nay,' replied she, 'after your cruel usage of me when I saw you last, killing me would, perhaps, be too great kindness for me to expect.'

Here ensued a parly, which, as I do not think myself obliged to relate, I shall omit. It is sufficient that it lasted a full quarter of an hour, at the conclusion of which they retired into the thickest part of the grove.
(V, 10)

This truly wonderful little scene gives the lie to Dr Johnson's claim that Fielding could not 'dive into the recesses of the human heart.'[25] It clearly exemplifies most of Fielding's fictional laws: the moral imperative to tell the truth, however unpleasant, by relating the facts of a particular human situation; the ironic suggestion that Fielding would prefer to hide from wrong-doing: 'However, that historic truth to which we profess so inviolable an attachment, obliges us to communicate to posterity.' He presents these 'facts' without any explicit analysis of causes; time is cleverly manipulated in the omission of the parley that 'lasted full quarter of an hour'; and the scene is rich in detail, as in Mollie's amorous response to Tom's phallic pen-knife: 'You don't intend to kill me squire, I hope!' What is conspicuously missing is any inside view of Tom himself, but the scene's richness makes this no deprivation. Defoe and Smollett may omit psychological detail because they are unaware of it, or are unable to present it in fictional terms; Fielding himself is frequently weak in this area. We remember the unconvincing gratitude of Mrs Miller who 'seeing Jones in the arms of his uncle... in an agony of joy, fell upon her knees, and burst forth into the most ecstatic thanksgivings to Heaven. ... The running to Jones, she embraced him eagerly' (XVIII, 11) and so on. This is similar to the floods of tears and mad caperings that do duty for grief and happiness in Smollett. But a perfectly satisfying explanation for Tom's behaviour is presented in the way all the elements of the scene are made to work together. Our hero begins the chapter heated by food, drink and anger, is cooled by the 'gentle breezes' of a 'pleasant evening in the latter end of June' and thinks, naturally enough, of the girl he loves. In the circumstances, it is hardly surprising that he should do so in an intimate way, his 'wanton fancy' roving 'unbounded over all her beauties... in various ravishing forms.' There follows one of those modulations into a high style, often tiresome, but in this case entirely appropriate as the callow expression of a young man's sexual excitement veiled from himself by a strained idealism: 'How contemptible would the brightest Circassian Beauty, drest in all the jewels of the Indies, appear to my eyes!' But all that Tom requires is availability and when this turns up in the form of the 'odoriferous' but already enjoyed Mollie his downfall is complete. The scene is a perfect embodiment of Fielding's concern to present a general insight into human behaviour through the character of a likeable but in no sense idiosyncratically delineated young man. And the perfection of the moment can be felt in its balancing of comedy and pathos, for there *is* pain as well as laughter, both in the memory of the delightful Sophia's sexual purity and in the spectacle of erring humanity. Fielding's famous geniality is more than a matter of belching acquiescence in the fact that boys will be boys. The warmth of his forgiveness is matched by a real concern for moral worth. The more romantic of Fielding's readers 'may be inclined to think this event unnatural. However, the fact is true' (V, 10) and our recognition of this truth is a small example of what A. R. Humphreys may have in mind when he says that Fielding's new province of writing is 'the prose tale so intelligently organized that everything contributes to a pattern and the whole is life intellectually disposed and clarified.'[26]

If we ask how Fielding is able intellectually to dispose and clarify life into a pattern, then the answer must be that his novel has a unity that stems from some vision of human life. His major subject is, in fact, clearly stated on the novel's first page: 'The provision then which we have here made is no other than HUMAN NATURE.' (I, 1) But the question remains of how this very broad area of interest is limited and focused and, once again, the best way to answer this is through an examination of the novel's artistry. Clearly, the most striking aesthetic feature of *Tom Jones*, or at least that aspect of it which has claimed most praise, is its plot. Some adjustment to this degree of praise is in order when we notice how often critics find it useful, or even necessary, to summarize the book's events, as is done to the extent of a full page in the Penguin edition. Memorability is surely an important index of quality in this area of technique: Dickens's plots are notoriously involved but, assuming that the reader has actually read the book in question, it does not seem to be indispensable to preface a critical reading of *Bleak House*, say, with a summary. At any rate, with a plot of this kind it is important not to fall into the error of the Penguin editor who begins his synopsis by talking of 'complexity' which by the end has become 'complicated.'[27] It is a pity to blur the usefulness of these words for critical discussion when a crucial distinction can be made between them so easily. They are distinguishable, surely, by their range of meaning. The complications of the detective story exist in and for themselves; a pleasurable confusion in the reader's mind is their only reason for existence. The twists and turns of a complex plot are designed to bear the weight of significance for the work as a whole. Lionel Trilling long ago pointed out an example that has since become well known, from *Great Expectations:* the fact that Magwitch, and not

Miss Havisham, turns out to be Pip's benefactor, gives the novel a meaning beyond the literal level of the events of which it is composed. If we apply this analysis to the plot of *Tom Jones* the results can be rewarding, although it would be foolish, and historically inaccurate, to claim too much for Fielding, an error of the otherwise often brilliant Dorothy Van Ghent:

> Structurally, it is characterized, like *Don Quixote*, by a systematic organization of contrasts, a playing off of one attitude and one way of life against another attitude and way of life, with a constant detail of contrast in the character relationships, scene relationships, and even verbal relationships.[28]

She gives as an example the necessity of Blifil to the novel's structure: 'Tom's "opposite", chief cause of his sorrows, and affording the chief character contrast in the book.'[29] Fielding may have intended this effect, but it is surely weakened, in our actual experience of reading, by the fact that Blifil is missing from the novel for hundreds of pages.

It is more fruitful to think of Fielding's unambiguous successes. Beginning at a fairly mechanical level, he is able to impose quite flexible patterns on the actual events that make up the story. For example, he seeks escape from the monotony of simple linear development by a neat reversal introduced into the novel's basic pattern of pursuit. The book moves from Paradise Hall to Upton and from Upton to London, and involved in this is an amusing inversion of the conventions of erotic pursuit. For the first half of the novel Sophia is chasing Tom and it is only after Upton that he turns into the pursuer. There is aesthetic pleasure to be gained from this change of direction (it is a technically skilful avoidance of the dangers of repetition) but to grasp its full significance, and to see how *Tom Jones* embodies a relationship to society, we need to think about the place where this change occurs, the inn at Upton. The point is that Fielding uses his inn significantly rather than simply making it a place where chamber-pots whizz about. In other words, he builds on the tradition of horse-play used by Smollett (at a later stage of course) and others. The use of the inn in eighteenth-century fiction is a clear example of a very simple relation between life and literature. As a crucial link in the pre-industrial transport system, it forms a highly stratified image of society where almost all sorts and conditions of men could mix, and was early seized on by the novelists of the road as a natural setting to break the unvarying pattern of movement that made up their works' only form. In Smollett's hands, however, it develops its own kind of monotony because each inn becomes the scene of basically the same crudely violent actions. *Tom Jones* is by no means exempt from this kind of thing, as in the fight that occurs when Tom and Partridge arrive at the inn, a mêlée brought to an end by a Smollett-like chambermaid:

> This Susan was as two-handed a wench...as any in the country...for her form was robust and manlike ... her face as well contrived to receive blows without any great injury to herself: her nose being already flat to her face; her lips were so large, that no swelling could be perceived in them, and moreover they were so hard, that a fist could hardly make any impression on them. (IX, 3)

But there are many signs that this part of the novel is working on a much higher plane than that of a dreary preoccupation with obvious physical action.

On one level, the inn's role in the novel's general pattern of movement can be seen as an example of the innovatory-conservative tension in Fielding, the tension between stasis and movement. One historian sees stasis as central to the understanding of eighteenth-century society: 'But...it must still be said that relationships were treated almost as if they were static structures; there was little that was mobile, fluctuating or processual about them; pattern, rather than action, received the emphasis.'[30] And Pat Rogers extends this idea in his comments on the influence of the eighteenth-century assembly room, which is for him 'the characteristic unit of Georgian social living. It carries over to the public sphere some of the amenity of a substantial private house, but it obviously made for gregariousness. ... The setting enjoins a sort of public intimacy, exactly the mode of contact Augustan mores found most congenial.'[31] A similar point can be suggested about the inn with the addition of a claim for its greater centrality in the socio-economic life of the time. Indeed, the frequency of its use in fiction might suggest a role analogous to the image of 'this great stage', the Elizabethan theatre, as a microcosm of human life, and of the world ('the great Globe') itself. Just as the physical layers of the Elizabethan playhouse could accommodate the heavenly, the sublunary and the nether regions, so the ascending scale of kitchens (servants), living rooms (a wide range of social groups) and bedrooms might suggest that the eighteenth-century inn could be a microcosmic image of its society. This possibility is reinforced by Fielding's self-conscious awareness of his own achievement in the words that end the chapter immediately before this episode, Tom and Mrs Waters entering 'safe into the famous town of Upton' (IX, 2); famous, of course, in the light of the events that are to follow. Fielding's imaginative engagement is revealed, too, by the way in which his energetic style rises into a wit that is not frequently to be observed in the novel; for example, the inn is a place 'whither Irish ladies of strict virtue, and many northern lasses of the same predicament, were accustomed to resort in their way to Bath.' (IX, 3) This creative energy is an index of the importance of these scenes in the scheme of the book as a whole, and what this is may be discerned by looking at a paragraph that begins the chapter immediately after the one in which Tom has capitulated to Mrs Waters:

> While our lovers were entertaining themselves in the manner which is partly described in the foregoing chapter; they were likewise furnishing out an entertainment for their good friends in the kitchen. And this in a double sense, by affording them matter for their conversation, and, at the same time, drink to enliven their spirits. (IX, 6)

More than one kind of connection is suggested by this passage! It creates the sense that the inn is a place full of vitality and activity, some of it reprehensible, but all charged with the pulse of life. This interconnection is what differentiates the book's farcical episodes – Tom discovered in bed with Mrs Waters, the fracas with Fitzpatrick – from similar activities in most early novels of the road. And so it is perhaps not fanciful to see in all of this an image of the world itself: at one moment the kitchen is 'a scene of universal confusion' (X, 7) as Western, Fitzpatrick and Tom all suddenly meet; there is love-making in the bedrooms; eating, sleeping and arguing; and poor Sophia, declaring to Honour that she is 'easy' (X, 5) after the discovery of Tom's infidelity. In short, this is yet another example of one of Fielding's laws of fiction, the principle of contrast,

> which runs through all the works of the creation, and may, probably, have a large share in constituting in us the idea of all beauty, as well natural as artificial: for what demonstrates the beauty and excellence of anything, but its reverse? Thus the beauty of day, and that of summer, is set off by the horrors of night and winter. (V, 1)

This suggests that for Fielding contrast is something more than a slice of life, the random display of multiplicity. These different activities constantly come into relation with each other, if only as topics of conversation or through physical collision. Underlying this accidental quality, however, is the sense that connections are being established at more fundamental levels. One of these is a critical scrutiny of the very variety that, in one way, this episode is designed to display. This scrutiny exists partly in the abstract, as in a generalized examination of human nature:

> Heroes...have certainly more of mortal than divine about them. However elevated their minds may be, their bodies at least...are liable to the worst infirmities, and subject to the vilest offices of human nature. Among these latter the act of eating...must be in some measure performed by the greatest prince, heroe, or philosopher upon earth...To say the truth, as no known inhabitant of this globe is really more than man, so none need be ashamed of submitting to what the necessities of man demand. (IX, 5)

But generalization is rooted in the concrete actions, relationships and people of the Upton episode, and the imagery of eating is extended, famously, in the preliminaries to Mrs Waters's triumph over Tom, and also in this devastating comment on her intuition that Tom is in love:

> She was not nice enough in her amours to be greatly concerned at the discovery. The beauty of Jones highly charmed her eye; but, as she could not see his heart, she gave herself no concern about it. She could feast heartily at the table of love, without reflecting that some other already had been, or hereafter might be, feasted with the same repast. (IX, 6)

However, it would clearly be a mistake to accept this as Fielding's last word on the subject of the female attitude to love, for the inn contains simultaneously a very different woman, Sophia.

The delightful Sophia, humanized as she is by many little touches of weakness, obviously presents us with another dimension of what it means to be no 'more than man' and, at the same time, suggests a different way in which relationship is created within the Upton episode. The episode contains an unusually concentrated number of references to station and hierarchy, a useful example occurring when the sergeant 'mistakes' Partridge for Tom's servant:

> 'None of your magisters,' answered Partridge; 'I am no man's servant...for tho' I have had misfortunes in the world, I write gentleman after my name; and as poor and simple as I may appear now, I have taught grammar-school in my time'...'No offence, I hope, sir,' said the sergeant. (IX, 6)

This is followed immediately by a mention of Tom's being liable to 'have a swinging great estate hereafter' as the heir to Squire

Allworthy who 'doth so much good all over the country,' That hierarchy is a complex matter for Fielding is suggested by the landlady's determination to 'drive all whores in rags from within the walls' which her 'virtuous guests, who did not travel in rags, would very reasonably have expected of her.' (IX, 3) And this irony is sharpened by the abrupt about-face in her treatment of Mrs Waters: '"I am sure, madam, if I had once suspected that your ladyship was your ladyship, I would sooner have burnt my tongue out, than have said what I have said."' (IX, 4) The landlady is just as ready with her 'curt'sies, and her ladyships' (X, 3) on Sophia's first appearance, but even she is constrained to join the chorus of praise that greets Sophia's considerate and delicate behaviour:

> When that good woman returned, the conversation in the kitchen was all upon the charms of the young lady. There is indeed in perfect beauty a power which none almost can withstand: for my landlady, though she was not pleased at the negative given to the supper, declared she had never seen so lovely a creature. Partridge ran out into the most extravagant encomiums on her face, though he could not refrain from paying some compliments to the gold lace on her habit: the postboy sung forth the praises of her goodness, which were likewise echoed by the other postboy, who was now come in. 'She's a true good lady, I warrant her,' says he: 'for she hath mercy upon dumb creatures; for she asked me every now and tan upon the journey if I did not think she should hurt the horses by riding too fast; and when she came in, she charged me to give them as much corn as ever they would eat'.
>
> Such charms are there in affability, and so sure is it to attract the praises of all kinds of people. (X, 3)

For a moment the kitchen is unified not by gossip, booze or fighting, but by a wholehearted response to the beauty and goodness of a true lady; the landlady, Partridge, the post-boys, Susan, are all enraptured by Sophia's courtesy. The point must not be exaggerated; indeed, it is part of Fielding's skill to make exaggeration impossible. As we have seen, the inn is full of sordid and violent behaviour, an accurate reflection of human life as Fielding knows it. But it is not impossible to see in the response to Sophia, however momentary, the glimpse of an ordering of society based on a hierarchy of goodness, not social position. Of course, Sophia does *have* social position. Fielding recognized the possibility of goodness in all classes of society, but for him Sophia's purity is an apex in a social as well as a moral sense. Yet the complexity of his vision of hierarchy is clear when we consider the implicit contrast between Sophia, the true lady, who creates a positive human response in all levels of the society around her, and Lady Bellaston, who is the apex of her social group in a purely mechanical and materialistic sense.

If it has done nothing else, the foregoing analysis substantiates George Sherburn's modest claims that Fielding 'shows a curiosity as to the organization of society' and an 'interest in society as an organic whole.'[32] The point can, of course, be made more elaborately, and we begin to move on to a slippery slope with Lukács:

> Fielding is to some extent aware of this... increasing concreteness of the novel in its grasp of the historical peculiarity of characters and events. His definition of himself as a writer is that of an historian of bourgeois society[33]

Some sleight-of-hand is at work here. Fielding does frequently refer to himself as an historian and it is clearly central to his purposes for the novel to depict, as Mrs Western says, 'a true idea of the several relations in which a human creature stands in society.' (VII, 3) But the word 'bourgeois' is, in this instance, an ideological intrusion. The plot of *Tom Jones* is a celebration of the idea of structure in all its manifestations; indeed, the point is that its elaborations are at least partly in the service of creating an image of society, above all in the 'adventures at Upton' which, in Battestin's words, 'stand as the keys of the arch in the mathematical centre of the novel.'[34] This centrality reinforces, at the formal level, the structural complexity of the social microcosm presented through the inn, a vision of order and hierarchy complemented, but not seriously weakened, by an awareness of the chaos of ordinary life. In other words, although the opposite assumption is often made, it is perfectly possible to have an analytical interest in the formation of society which is essentially conservative. The view of the world created by Upton is a conclusive demonstration of this on the large scale and can be substantiated by a series of reinforcing details. There are elements of social modernity in *Tom Jones* (Fielding's uncertainty about the precise nature of his readership, for example) but they are more than balanced by, say, his traditional use of the word 'family'. When Mr Allworthy is supposedly dying, the 'whole family' is 'assembled round his bed', 'namely Mr Blifil, Mr Jones, Mr Thwackum, Mr Square, and some of the servants.' (V, 7). This extension of family to include servants is seen even more clearly in a passage concerning Mrs Fitzpatrick:

> Now this lady had departed from the inn much about at the same time with Sophia: for having been waked by the voice of her husband, she had

sent up for the landlady, and being by her apprized of the matter, had
bribed the good woman, at an extravagant price, to furnish her with
horses for her escape. Such prevalence had money in this family; and tho'
the mistress would have turned away her maid for a corrupt hussy, if she
had known as much as the reader, yet she was no more proof against
corruption herself than poor Susan had been. (X, 7)

Again, when menaced with rape by Lord Fellamar Sophia threatens
to 'raise the family.' (XV, 5).

Fielding's essentially 'unprogressive' viewpoint is perfectly
compatible, of course, with sympathy for the poor:

Those members of the society, who are born to furnish the blessings of
life, now began to light their candles, in order to pursue their daily
labours, for the use of those who are born to enjoy these blessings. The
sturdy hind now attends the levee of his fellow labourer the ox; the
cunning artificer, the diligent mechanic spring from their hard matress;
and now the bonny housemaid begins to repair the disordered
drum-room, while the riotous authors of that disorder, in broken
interrupted slumbers tumble and toss, as if the hardness of down
disquieted their repose. (XI, 9)

This apparent paradox is illuminated by Zirker's study of Fielding's
social pamphlets which amply justifies his aim 'to show specifically
that Fielding's *feeling* about the poor as a class...in his language as
well as in his specific proposals, is congruent with that of many of his
contemporaries.'[35] But Zirker is responsible enough as a critic to see
the limitations of this in relation to the fiction:

Yet no one would deny that Fielding's novels imply a far richer and more
complex sense of the individual in society that one finds in the
pamphlets...The disparity...is in fact part of a larger conflict reflected in
Fielding's career. Fielding inherited and believed most fully in the older
classical values at a time when these values were becoming increasingly
hard to maintain...Fielding, well born, well educated, ready to take his
place in polite society...was obliged for his livelihood to write plays...
and...achieve fame...in the most bourgeois and least prestigious of all
literary forms, the novel....Fielding was able to maintain the serenity
and ideality of the classical Christian virtues only by recourse to the
manipulation available in fiction.[36]

In other words, Fielding's imaginative grasp of society possesses a
richness lacking when he is working purely cerebrally. The range of
sympathies possible within the essentially non-bourgeois framework
of the novel is nowhere more apparent than in the vivid sketch of
Partridge's wandering life on the fringes of established society:

'The first place I came to was Salisbury, where I got into the service of a gentleman belonging to the law, and one of the best gentlemen that ever I knew; for he was not only good to me, but I know a thousand good and charitable acts which he did while I staid with him; and I have known him often refuse business because it was paultry and oppressive.' – 'You need not be so particular,' said Allworthy; 'I know this gentleman, and a very worthy man he is, and an honour to his profession.' – 'Well, sir,' continued Partridge, 'from hence I removed to Lymmington, where I was above three years in the service of another lawyer, who was likewise a very good sort of a man, and to be sure one of the merriest gentlemen in England. Well, sir, at the end of the three years I set up a little school, and was likely to do well again, had it not been for a most unlucky accident. Here I kept a pig; and one day, as ill fortune would have it, this pig broke out, and did a trespass I think they call it, in a garden belonging to one of my neighbours, who was a proud, revengeful man, and employed a lawyer, one – one – I can't think of his name; but he sent for a writ against me, and had me to Size. When I came there, Lord have mercy upon me – to hear what the counsellors said. There was one that told my lord a parcel of the confoundedst lies about me; he said, that I used to drive my hogs into other folks gardens, and a great deal more; and at last he said, he hoped I had at last brought my hogs to a fair market. To be sure, one would have thought, that instead of being owner only of one poor little pig, I had been the greatest hog-merchant in England. Well,' – 'Pray,' said Allworthy, 'do not be so particular. I have heard nothing of your son yet.' 'O it was a great many years,' answered Partridge, 'before I saw my son, as you are pleased to call him. – I went over to Ireland after this, and taught school at Cork, (for that one suit ruined me again, and I lay seven years in Winchester gaol.)' – 'Well,' said Allworthy, 'pass that over till your return to England.' – 'Then, sir,' said he, 'it was about half a year ago that I landed at Bristol, where I stayed some time, and not finding it do there, and hearing of a place between that and Gloucester, where the barber was just dead, I went thither, and there I had been about two months, when Mr Jones came thither.' He then gave Allworthy a very particular account of their first meeting, and of everything as well as he could remember, which had happened from that day to this; frequently interlarding his story with panegyricks on Jones, and not forgetting to insinuate the great love and respect which he had for Allworthy. He concluded with saying, 'Now, sir, I have told your honour the whole truth,' And then repeated a most solemn protestation, 'that he was no more the father of Jones than of the Pope of Rome;' and imprecated the most bitter curses on his head if he did not speak truth. (XVIII, 6)

The particularity of which Allworthy complains is the very quality which touches this little autobiography into vividness in a way that anticipates Magwitch's great evocation of his life in Chapter 42 of

Great Expectations, where one life story takes on the force of a representative image of human suffering.

Returning to the fact that Upton marks a turning point in Tom's pursuit of Sophia, can we not see a fitness in this reversal of roles deeper than mere formal neatness? The point can be crystallized in a question: why is Tom now the pursuer? This surely marks a genuinely guilty element in his behaviour with Mrs Waters, however much we may be led to condone it by Fielding's tone: 'To confess the truth, I am afraid Mr Jones maintained a kind of Dutch defence, and treacherously delivered up the garrison, without duly weighing his allegiance to the fair Sophia.' (IX, 5) This lightness of touch might well be set against the later actions of the temporary 'lovers':

> Jones likewise . . . set forward the moment he had paid his reckoning, in quest of his lovely Sophia. . . . Nor could he bring himself even to take leave of Mrs Waters; of whom he detested the very thoughts. . . . As for Mrs Waters. . . . Upon the road she was perfectly reconciled with Mr Fitzpatrick, who was a very handsome fellow, and indeed did all she could to console him in the absence of his wife. (X, 7)

The fact that there is a guilty aspect to Tom's behaviour, however pardonable, lifts the novel to a plane of moral seriousness which helps to make it, to take up the quotation's hint, one of the staple forms of narrative fiction, the quest. In this case, the object of the quest is Sophia which, given her nature (to say nothing of her name), is the same as saying that the object is goodness and beauty.

At this point, however, one needs to draw an important distinction between the form taken by the quest in *Tom Jones* and in many later novels. In Dickens's *Great Expectations*, for example, the quest is realized by, and embodied in, a profound development and change in the character of the hero, Pip. Quite obviously, this kind of character development does not occur in Fielding, a gap which raises the problem of how the quest is realized. Its realization, the saving of Tom, does in fact occur in two major ways. There is, first, the given and unchanging element in Tom's own character, to which we are afforded a clue by a comment on Thwackum and Square:

> Upon the whole, it is not religion or virtue, but the want of them which is here exposed. Had not Thwackum too much neglected virtue, and Square religion, in the composition of their several systems; and had not both utterly discarded all natural goodness of heart, they had never been represented as the objects of derision in this history. (III, 4)

Goodness of heart is, then, both 'natural' and something that may be discarded voluntarily. Tom's retention of this universal human possession is one guarantee that he will never go completely astray. And the maintenance of this quality is aided by another important strand in Tom's character:

> Mr Jones had somewhat about him, which, though I think writers are not thoroughly agreed in its name, doth certainly inhabit some human breasts; whose use is not so properly to distinguish right from wrong, as to prompt and incite them to the former, and to restrain and with-hold them from the latter. . . . Our heroe, whether he derived it from Thwackum or Square I will not determine, was very strongly under the guidance of this principle: for though he did not always act rightly, yet he never did otherwise without feeling and suffering for it. (IV, 6)

But Tom's character in itself would not be enough to bring him triumphantly to the possession of Sophia; if this were so, one might be inclined to agree with this fundamental misconception of Ioan Williams:

> The closing chapters of *Tom Jones* are clearly its weakest part. As the elements of tension in our relationship with the narrator becomes relaxed, so we are left in more and more direct contemplation of the situation of Tom Jones, whose complete and quite undeserved prosperity together with Fielding's evident satisfaction in narrating it, give us serious doubts as to his sensitivity.[37]

What is needed for this is the collaboration of Tom's natural goodness with luck, chance or what the eighteenth century would have called Fortune. As Sophia says to Tom near the end of the novel, '"Sure, sir, you are the most fortunate man in the world in this discovery"' (XVIII, 12), a concluding reinforcement of its role as a key word throughout the book, a role which helps to justify Battestin's view that the 'idea of Fortune is, indeed, a controlling theme in *Tom Jones*.'[38] The fact that for Fielding – and it is here that we can see him as Augustan in a profound sense – the idea of Fortune has a metaphysical force, is clearly implied by the following:

> Notwithstanding the sentiment of the Roman satyrist, which denies the divinity of Fortune; and the opinion of Seneca to the same purpose; Cicero, who was, I believe, a wiser man than either of them, expressly holds the contrary; and certain it is, there are some incidents in life so very strange and unaccountable, that it seems to require more than human skill and foresight in producing them. (XIV, 8)

It is at this stage that we can grasp the real justification of Fielding's plot, as the crucial embodiment of Tom's Fortune, a plot whose clarity and absence of sentimentality are highlighted by comparison with another richly plotted book, *Bleak House*. Although the central human mysteries of that novel are cleared up, it generates such a pervasive miasma of doubt and confusion that it is impossible for us not to feel that these are qualities that belong to the very nature of the world depicted by Dickens. And by the same token, the happiness gained in the book is both precarious and limited. One drop from the ocean of suffering may be saved in the person of Esther Summerson's little maid, Charley, but what of the thousands who are left to their fate? In contrast, there is, finally, an explanation for every twist and turn in Fielding's story, a fact which contributes to the novel's general atmosphere as described by Dorothy Van Ghent: 'A world conceived as fundamentally intelligible and tending in all its phenomena towards the general highest good of total intelligibility.'[39] On the other hand, and here there is a similarity with Dickens, just as we saw the realism of Fielding's view of human nature in his implicit contrasting of Sophia and Mrs Waters, so it is evident that he does not think, in any simple way, that all is for the best in the best of all possible worlds, a recognition succinctly expressed by R. S. Crane:

> We are not disposed to feel, when we are done laughing at Tom, that all is right with the world or that we can count on Fortune always intervening in the same gratifying way, on behalf of the good.[40]

We *can* see the complications of the novel's plot as designed to create a world in which goodness is rewarded, if that goodness is sufficiently frank and consistent, but we must be made to feel that this does not happen automatically, and the only guarantee of this is the presence of real feeling.

In the end, though, *Tom Jones* is a product of the comic imagination; any excess of grief or remorse would clearly be out of place. The novel's fundamental direction is positive, an intention furthered by an important ambiguity in the word 'Fortune' itself. It may signify luck, fate or chance, but also what is stated in this passage on Allworthy:

> In that part of the western division of this kingdom, which is commonly called Somersetshire, there lately lived (and perhaps lives still) a gentleman whose name was Allworthy, and who might well be called the favourite of both Nature and Fortune; for both of these seemed to have contended which should bless and enrich him most. In this contention, Nature may seem to some to have come off victorious, as she bestowed on

113

him many gifts; while Fortune had only one gift in her power; but in pouring forth this, she was so very profuse, that others perhaps may think this single endowment to have been more than equivalent to all the various blessings which he enjoyed from Nature. From the former of these, he derived an agreeable person, a sound constitution, a solid understanding, and a benevolent heart; by the latter, he was decreed to the inheritance of one of the largest estates in the county. (I, 2)

This suggests a remarkable change in the hundred years between Fielding and Dickens, a transformation that has as much to do with the movement of history as the difference between the writers. For Fielding there is absolutely no contradiction between the possession of a 'benevolent heart' and 'one of the largest estates in the country': in A. R. Humphreys's words, 'the idea of prosperity kindles the imagination.' Dickens's benefactors must be, by definition, wealthy men, but after Mr Pickwick's unique innocence this wealth is attended by the contradictions of personality, present willy-nilly in the Cheeryble Brothers, consciously created in the case of Mr Jarndyce. And these differences are related to opposing images of society that are rooted in real differences between the eighteenth and the nineteenth century. What I am suggesting is that *Tom Jones* presents an image of the best possibilities of eighteenth-century society, an idealized vision of a world of decently arranged hierarchical values in which goodness and beauty triumph despite the very real presence of evil, a complexity finely stated by Henry Knight Miller:

It is the vein of iron that gives validity to his ultimate optimism; because it provides a context in which that optimism can be seen as fully earned, in confrontation with and in total recognition of the contrary evidence that must press itself upon any intelligent observer.[41]

Further Reading

Two general works which contain interesting essays on Fielding (and which can be read with profit on many of the novels considered in this study) are also useful as representing alternative critical positions. The first examines the novel from a standpoint which is both Marxist and critically sensitive; the second is a brilliant example of the application of the techniques of New Criticism to the reading of fiction:

An Introduction to the English Novel by Arnold Kettle (London, 1951).

The English Novel: Form and Function by Dorothy Van Ghent (New York, 1961).

An interesting general study of Fielding will be found in:

Henry Fielding: Mask and Feast by Andrew Wright (London, 1968).

A variety of viewpoints is illustrated by a volume in the Twentieth Century Views series:

Fielding: A Collection of Critical Essays edited by Ronald Paulson (1962).

A good general introduction to *Tom Jones* is provided by:

Fielding: Tom Jones by Irvin Ehrenpreis (London, 1964).

Two famous essays on the novel are:

'The Plot of *Tom Jones*,' by R. S. Crane in *Critics and Criticism: Ancient and Modern* (Chicago, 1952).

'*Tom Jones*,' by William Empson in *Kenyon Review* XX (1958).

Two works of particular interest to this study are:

'Fielding's Social Outlook,' by George Sherburn in *Philological Quarterly* Vol. XXXV No. 1 (1956).

Fielding's Social Pamphlets by Malvin R. Zirker (Berkeley, 1966).

5

Persuasion

There is a peculiar beauty and a peculiar dullness in *Persuasion*. The
dullness is that which so often marks the transitional stage between two
different periods. The writer is a little bored. She has grown too familiar
with the ways of her world; she no longer notes them freshly. There is an
asperity in her comedy which suggests that she has almost ceased to be
amused by the vanities of a Sir Walter or the snobbery of a Miss Elliot.
The satire is harsh, and the comedy crude. She is no longer so freshly
aware of the amusements of daily life. ... But, while we feel that Jane
Austen has done this before, and done it better, we also feel that she is
trying to do something which she has never yet attempted. There is a new
element in *Persuasion*. ... She is beginning to discover that the world is
larger, more mysterious, and more romantic than she had supposed. ...
But it is not only in a new sensibility to nature that we detect the change.
Her attitude to life itself is altered...the observation is less of facts and
more of feelings than is usual.[1]

As so often, the academic critic is forced to hobble after the insight
inspired by the meeting of creative minds. The passage enforces
Virginia Woolf's brilliance as a critic even when, as in this case, there
is an element of self-consciousness in the bravura yoking of beauty
and dullness. Her reading of *Persuasion* is too personal to be
generally useful, but the depth as well as the intelligence of her
overall view of the novel has left to others the task of filling out
inspiration with argument. Critics have dealt skilfully with different
facets of Jane Austen's originality in *Persuasion*,[2] making specific a
sense of new departures that must be experienced by most readers. It
is richly characteristic of Jane Austen that an element of paradox
should pervade this originality, a fruitful tension between what in
other hands might be opposites. We may wish to qualify Marilyn
Butler's judgement in favour of Richardson, but it is perfectly
acceptable in relation to Jane Austen's own career: 'There is nothing
in subjective writing in any earlier English novel to compare in
subtlety of insight or depth of feeling with the sequence of nervous

116

scenes between the hero and heroine in *Persuasion*.'[3] On the other hand, this is in no way negated by Alastair Duckworth: 'Jane Austen's serious concern over the state and continuity of the social structure is not, I think, to be doubted.'[4] Indeed, a major purpose in what follows is to demonstrate a heightened richness in the novel's social elements while acknowledging the depth and poignancy of its 'little history of sorrowful interest'. (4)[5]

Paradox, and the fusion of opposites, are as evident in Jane Austen's place in literary history as within the detail of her work. She is important to the argument of this book not merely because her apparent stress on the private poses a threat to its method, but also because of her position at the cross-roads of eighteenth and nineteenth-century fiction. Like all great writers, Jane Austen is peculiarly herself, but she also stands in an unusually rich network of relations to past and future. For example, one important way in which she differs from most Victorian novelists is in what might be called her belief in the world. In *Pride and Prejudice*, Elizabeth's mortifying reassessment of Wickham is clinched in these terms:

> That had his actions been what Wickham represented them, so gross a violation of everything right could hardly have been concealed from the world; and that friendship between a person capable of it, [Darcy] and such an amiable man as Mr. Bingley, was incomprehensible. (36)

This displays a confidence in the right judgement of right-thinking people not easily found in Thackeray, Dickens, George Eliot or, even, Trollope. The possibility of a socially objective assessment of good and evil is connected with a key word in Jane Austen's fictional vocabulary, her use of 'friends', some illustrations of which can come from the same book: '"My youngest sister has left all her friends – has eloped; – has thrown herself into the power of – of Mr. Wickham."' (46); '"Could he expect that her friends would not step forward? Could he expect to be noticed again by the regiment, after such an affront to Colonel Forster?"' (47); 'His first object with her, he acknowledged, had been to persuade her to quit her present disgraceful situation, and return to her friends as soon as they could be prevailed on to receive her.' (52) This connects with the eighteenth century use of 'family' exemplified with particular clarity in Richardson's *Pamela*, to mean all the members of a household, including servants. Clearly, Jane Austen does not imply by friends the limitations of intimate contact. Both family and friends carry the weight of extension and connection, the feeling of an individual enmeshed in, and supported by if he chooses to be, a web of relationships that are social as well as personal.

But if this shows a strong elements of continuity with the eighteenth century, it is obviously a mistake to overstress Jane Austen's Augustan affiliations in the manner of Lord David Cecil:

> Jane Austen lived at a period of intellectual revolution. The standards of reason and common sense which had guided the larger part of educated opinion during the eighteenth century were being overthrown.... On the revolutionary side were ranged almost all the distinguished writers of the day... against them stood only one, Jane Austen.[6]

In fact, more usually her work displays the co-existence of eighteenth and nineteenth century elements, as in two contrasting passages from *Persuasion*. First, Anne Elliot's thoughts on her home being occupied by relative strangers:

> She could have said more on the subject; for she had in fact so high an opinion of the Crofts, and considered her father so very fortunate in his tenants, felt the parish to be so sure of a good example, and the poor of the best attention and relief, that however sorry and ashamed for the necessity of the removal, she could not but in conscience feel that they were gone who deserved not to stay, and that Kellynch Hall had passed into better hands than its owners'. (13)

Behind this can be felt the force of the eighteenth-century country house as something more than the habitation of the fortunate wealthy: as the focal point of moral concern as well as material comfort. This is only a short distance from the world of *Tom Jones* where Allworthy stands at the centre of a network of relationships based on duty and obligation. It contrasts, secondly, with a piece of natural description:

> The scenes in its neighbourhood, Charmouth, with its high grounds and extensive sweeps of country, and still more its sweet retired bay, backed by dark cliffs, where fragments of low rock among the sands make it the happiest spot for watching the flow of the tide, for sitting in unwearied contemplation; – the woody varieties of the cheerful village of Up Lyme, and, above all, Pinny, with its green chasms between romantic rocks, where the scattered forest trees and orchards of luxuriant growth declare that many a generation must have passed away since the first partial falling of the cliff prepared the ground for such a state... these places must be visited, and visited again, to make the worth of Lyme understood. (11)

The change into the present tense gives a personal note to a passage whose imaginative commitment is sufficiently clear not to need the additional clue of the word 'romantic' itself. Indeed, there is something positively Wordsworthian in the idea of 'sitting in unwearied contemplation'.

Such passages reveal more than simple co-existence. The opposition here, the lifelong preoccupation crystallized in the title of *Sense and Sensibility*, is a creative tension that operates at every level in *Persuasion*, of style and of moral insight into character and behaviour. An example of the latter illuminates the tension at work in a single page of the novel:

> Though they had now been acquainted a month, she could not be satisfied that she really knew his character. That he was a sensible man, an agreeable man... this was all clear enough... but yet she would have been afraid to answer for his conduct. She distrusted the past, if not the present.... She saw that there had been bad habits; that Sunday-travelling had been a common thing.... Mr. Elliot was rational, discreet, polished, – but he was not open. There was never any burst of feeling, any warmth of indignation or delight, at the evil or good of others. This, to Anne, was a decided imperfection. Her early impressions were incurable. She prized the frank, the open-hearted, the eager character beyond all others. Warmth and enthusiasm did captivate her still. She felt that she could so much more depend upon the sincerity of those who sometimes looked or said a careless or a hasty thing, than of those whose presence of mind never varied, whose tongue never slipped. (17)

The complexity here is, of course, wonderfully representative. The opening discloses an almost Addisonian fusion of moral and social propriety. And yet this modulates – by way of 'rational, discreet, polished', quite the *Spectator* gentleman, we might feel – into 'he was not open' and Anne's delight in 'the frank, the open-hearted, the eager character beyond all others.' We note the psychological accuracy of the origin of this incurable early impression and the writer's endorsement of her heroine's love of 'enthusiasm' (despite her admiration for Dr. Johnson). In short, the passage contains a fine balancing of Augustan restraint and Romantic self-expression as twin sources of value. And it is possible to penetrate a little more deeply than this. In the delicious mockery of Anne's combination of insight and naiveté – 'Sunday-travelling' must surely be measured against the kind of thing we can guess Elliot was really up to – we are assured that even this most touchingly lovely of heroines is another proof of Jane Austen's claim that 'pictures of perfection... make me sick & wicked.'[7] This ironic stance is a sure guard against the solemnity that is one of Romanticism's besetting dangers.

However, in opposition to that stance must be placed her celebration of an intensely felt Romantic virtue, that reliance on the self in developing, through maturity of judgement, an authentically individual character. The central importance of this self-reliance for Jane Austen is easily demonstrated. We see it in Anne's response to her oldest and best friend: 'It was now some years since Anne had begun to learn that she and her excellent friend could sometimes think differently.' (16). The ability to mature in a direction away from the older and, according to the dictates of society, the wiser woman could be paralleled in all Jane Austen's novels; the strength of individual judgement in the apparently feeble and defenceless Fanny Price is only the most obvious example of a continuing preoccupation. And the importance of this value in life can be shown from the novelist's letter of advice to her favourite niece, Fanny Knight: 'Your affection gives me the highest pleasure, but indeed you must not let anything depend on my opinion. Your own feelings & none but your own, should determine such an important point.'[8] There is no question here of the deference due to parents, friends or society at large. In fact, Jane Austen's work can be seen as an important stage on the road towards the celebration of youth and the almost total rejection of parental wisdom characteristic of Dickens. On this point, Dorothy Van Ghent's view of the role of fathers in eighteenth and nineteenth-century fiction requires some qualification: 'We see, in the notion of the father in eighteenth century literature, a reflection of social trust.'[9] Richardson is clearly an exception: Clarissa is at least partly the victim of the unwise authority of a tyrannical father. But there remains an important line of development here. For Dickens the evasions of a Mr Dorrit or the ultimate powerlessness of John Jarndyce are failures of society itself in its role of father-figure. Jane Austen does not go as far as this, but Mr Bennet is a sobering, as well as comic, portrayal of irresponsible wit.

This theme of the creative tension between conflicting value systems could be pursued in many directions, but perhaps one small example is enough, the richness of *Persuasion* on the subject of marriage and money, a subject which amply makes J. P. Stern's point that 'Money is one of the elements that anchors Jane Austen's fiction in a reality we can place and date'.[10] A relevant passage concerns Lady Russell's reaction to Wentworth:

Captain Wentworth had no fortune. He had been lucky in his profession, but spending freely, what had come freely, had realized nothing. But, he was confident he should soon be rich: – full of life and ardour, he knew that he should soon have a ship, and soon be on a station that would lead to every thing he wanted. He had always been lucky; he knew he should be so still. – Such confidence, powerful in its own warmth, and bewitching in the wit which often expressed it, must have been enough for Anne; but Lady Russell saw it very differently. – His sanguine temper, and fearlessness of mind, operated very differently on her. She saw in it but an aggravation of the evil. It only added a dangerous character to himself. He was brilliant, he was headstrong. – Lady Russell had little taste for wit; and of anything approaching imprudence a horror. (4)

The passage clearly works against Lady Russell – a contest between prudence and 'life and ardour' is easily settled – and we read on in the relief of confirmation when we find:

How eloquent could Anne Elliot have been – how eloquent, at least, were her wishes on the side of early warm attachment, and a cheerful confidence in futurity, against the over-anxious caution which seems to insult exertion and distrust Providence! She had been forced into prudence in her youth, she learned romance as she grew older – the natural sequel of an unnatural beginning. (4)

The 'unnatural' seems to make the whole matter straightforward until, of course, we consider the scheme of the novel as a whole and not simply isolated passages. When we do, we remember that Wentworth is, in fact, rich when he wins Anne the second time. Mr Elliot is a clear example of naked self-seeking in marriage – '"Money, money, was all that he wanted."' (21) – and for this he is condemned to a fate worse than death, to have Mrs. Clay for a mistress. But affluence is the indispensable and fitting context for those who can love without seeking it. What Dorothy Van Ghent says of Fielding is equally true of Jane Austen: 'The signature of Fortune's favour is wealth.'[11] This is yet another way in which Jane Austen can be seen as transitional. We notice that for Captain Wentworth 'fortune' has lost the capital letter which gives it the resonance of double meaning in Fielding: luck *and* money. Some critics have, in fact, suggested that in *Persuasion* Jane Austen is creating a world of chance, of pure fortuitousness, which anticipates later fiction in its rejection of a traditional faith in Providence. Chance does undoubtedly play an important part in the novel, in Anne's overhearing Louisa's conversation with Wentworth, for example, and in the detail, important in its consequences, of Mr Elliot's glance of approval at Anne's attractiveness. As for Wentworth, he 'had always been lucky; he knew he should be so still'

(4) and, of course, he is. But this stress must be set against Anne's disapproval of her own earlier 'over-anxious caution which seems to insult exertion and distrust Providence.' (4) Here is a case where co-existence is perhaps a better word than fusion. Jane Austen seems genuinely, and uncharacteristically, unsure of her view of the world on this point. Providence, with its capital letter, is present in the novel, and is insulted and distrusted at one's peril, but luck plays too large a part in its structure of events for the book's scheme to be confidently asserted to be one or the other. One might guess that with the unfinished *Sanditon* Jane Austen was beginning to move into a world where chance would have predominated firmly over Providence.

As a novelist, then, Jane Austen exists within a rich context, but can the same be said of the heroine of *Persuasion*? The question may seem inappropriate to this apparently simple story of love disappointed and then coming to ultimate fruition. But this little history also has its context, although a much less obtrusive one than that of *Tom Jones*. The social world in which the characters live out their personal lives is not unimportant even in *Persuasion*. An aspect of this that has received surprisingly little attention is Jane Austen's attitude to the place of women in the Regency. Raymond Williams remarks that because of the deficiencies of female education, the 'Brontë sisters knew directly a whole structure of repression in their time.'[12] Such an approach might seem entirely alien to the world of Jane Austen, but the earlier novels hint at a darker view which is intensified in *Persuasion* and used for thematic purposes. Anne herself is an implicit plea for equality between the sexes and this surfaces in her moving debate with Captain Harville: '"All the privilege I claim for my own sex...is that of loving longest, when existence or when hope is gone."' (23). And Anne's role here is mirrored by an unusually strong and explicit stress on the value of femininity. Mrs Smith, although far from Sir Walter's dismissive 'a mere Mrs Smith, an every day Mrs Smith' (17) is hardly perfect, as we see in her shameless manipulation, through Nurse Rooke, of pity for financial gain. But we are surely also meant to admire the solitary woman's 'elasticity of mind, that disposition to be comforted, that power...of finding employment which carried her out of herself.' (17). Again, and surprisingly, the novel sees the emergence, however faintly, of a figure from that world below the landed gentry which Jane Austen is usually content to ignore, in the person of Nurse Rooke. Patterns of implicit contrast abound in *Persuasion* and thoughts of Elizabeth and Mary Elliot rise irresistibly to mind when Mrs Smith praises Nurse Rooke:

> She is a shrewd, intelligent, sensible woman. Hers is a line for seeing human nature; and she has a fund of good sense and observation which, as a companion, make her infinitely superior to thousands of those who having only received 'the best education in the world,' know nothing worth attending to. (17)

But the most striking example of this highlighting of feminine values is Mrs Croft. Sir Walter's man of business, Mr Shepherd, prepares our response to her at an early stage: '"And a very well-spoken, genteel, shrewd lady, she seemed to be...asked more questions about the house, and terms, and taxes, than the admiral himself, and seemed more conversant with business."' (3). His judgement is validated by everything we see of her in the novel. She is, significantly, not beautiful:

> Mrs Croft, though neither tall nor fat, had a squareness, uprightness, and vigour of form, which gave importance to her person. She had bright dark eyes, good teeth, and altogether an agreeable face; though her reddened and weather-beaten complexion, the consequence of her having been almost as much at sea as her husband, made her seem to have lived some years longer in the world than her real eight and thirty. (6)

But this lack of conventional attractiveness does not mean that she is merely a surrogate male, as we can see in her argument with her brother, Wentworth, about women going to sea: '"But I hate to hear you talking so, like a fine gentleman, and as if women were all fine ladies, instead of rational creatures. We none of us expect to be in smooth water all our days."' (8). Rather, she embodies Jane Austen's sense that a woman's life can be something more than a round of dances, child-bearing (the Crofts are childless) and empty accomplishments. Through travelling with her husband in almost constant companionship Mrs Croft seems virtually to participate in his profession, as in a passage where Anne observes them together in Bath:

> She always watched them as long as she could; delighted to fancy she understood what they might be talking of, as they walked along in happy independence, or equally delighted to see the Admiral's hearty shake of the hand when he encountered an old friend, and observe their eagerness of conversation when occasionally forming into a little knot of the navy, Mrs Croft looking as intelligent and keen as any of the officers around her. (18)

In fact, Mrs Croft is in some respects portrayed as her husband's superior, as in her calm response to the Admiral's undiscriminating praise of the Musgrove girls ('"I hardly know one from the other"') which 'made Anne suspect that her keener powers might not consider either of them as quite worthy of her brother.' (10). The often-quoted passage of their driving together is, finally, a definitive embodiment of the role of women so strikingly figured in this novel:

> But by coolly giving the reins a better direction herself, they happily passed the danger; and by once afterwards judiciously putting out her hand, they neither fell into a rut, nor ran foul of a dung-cart; and Anne, with some amusement at their style of driving, which she imagined no bad representation of the general guidance of their affairs, found herself safely deposited by them at the cottage. (10)

One must be careful not to exaggerate: 'structure of repression' would be too strong for this aspect of Jane Austen's work, but it reveals a keen awareness of how social pressures can impinge on her own sex. Although this subject has not received much attention, it would be surprising if such a great writer should not have some sense of how environmental pressures might affect women. What is more crucial for my argument is to see if she has a wider grasp of social forces. I suggested earlier that the characters of *Persuasion* live within a context larger than themselves; I shall try now to trace some of its elements.

A start can be made by asking why the novel opens with an extract from the Baronetage concerning Sir Walter and his family, an unusual beginning which, amongst other things, serves the functional purpose of conveying a great deal of information in a brief space. When we remember the extent to which Sir Walter is placed and limited by his social position, we can see that it has an important thematic function. It introduces an obsession with birth that is pervasive, a preoccupation that makes itself felt within a very wide range of characters, and which invariably takes the form of snobbery rather than an arguably permissible pride in good-breeding as an aspect of civilization. We are not surprised that Anne and Mr Elliot should differ on this question: 'They did not always think alike. His value for rank and connexion she perceived to be greater than hers. It was not merely complaisance, it must be a liking to the cause, which made him enter warmly into her father and sister's solicitudes on a subject which she thought unworthy to excite them.' (16). But it is more significant that similar feelings should be shared by that 'very good woman', (24) Lady Russell: 'She had a cultivated mind, and was, generally speaking, rational and consistent – but she had prejudices on the side of ancestry; she had a value for rank and consequence, which blinded her a little to the faults of those who possessed them.' (2). If such feelings are to be found in a woman of Lady Russell's 'sense and honesty', then we are dealing with a social phenomenon of wide ramifications, and the humanly destructive effects of these feelings are touched in with great delicacy. After Louisa Musgrove's recovery, Anne and Lady Russell visit an Uppercross which Anne feels is 'already quite alive again' in contrast to 'the last state she had seen it in':

> Immediately surrounding Mrs Musgrove were the little Harvilles, whom she was sedulously guarding from the tyranny of the two children from the Cottage, expressly arrived to amuse them. On one side was a table, occupied by some chattering girls, cutting up silk and gold paper; and on the other were tressels and trays, bending under the weight of brawn and cold pies, where riotous boys were holding high revel; the whole completed by a roaring Christmas fire, which seemed determined to be heard, in spite of all the noise of the others. . . . It was a fine family piece. (14)

The scene is almost worthy of Dickens in its combination of human observation and celebratory delight. Across its warmth cuts Lady Russell's chillingly well-bred, '"I hope I shall remember in future... not to call at Uppercross in the Christmas holidays."'(14).

The richness of this pattern is evident in the light it can shed on the character of the novel's heroine. The poignancy of the 'elegant little woman of seven-and-twenty' (17) has a fineness that might be mistaken for lack of spirit. But considering that Anne's life is spent amidst a futile preoccupation with birth, her rejection of it has the liveliness of real independence: '"My idea of good company, Mr. Elliot, is the company of clever, well-informed people, who have a great deal of conversation."' Elliot counters with an argument of convenience: '"Will it not be wiser to accept the society of these good ladies in Laura Place, and enjoy all the advantages of the connexion as far as possible?"' But Anne has the last word: '"I certainly am proud, too proud to enjoy a welcome which depends so entirely upon place."' (16). That these are not idle words; that Anne really does prefer conversation to birth, is validated by her friendship with Mrs Smith to which she holds in the face of her family's strongly expressed disgust.

Discussion of the social context within *Persuasion* demands critical tact. There is no question but that the novel's foreground is occupied by Anne Elliot and the touching growth to fruition of her love for Wentworth, and I shall eventually bring this foreground into relation with the present material. Consideration of this material is justified, however, partly by the relatively little attention given to it, but above all by its own intrinsic importance. The book's concern with birth is linked to another interest which is part of the social context I am trying to clarify. The Musgroves, whose noisiness was so offensive to Lady Russell, occasion an interesting paragraph on social mobility:

> The Musgroves, like their houses, were in a state of alteration, perhaps of improvement. The father and mother were in the old English style, and the young people in the new. Mr and Mrs Musgrove were a very good sort of people; friendly and hospitable, not much educated, and not at all elegant: their children had more modern minds and manners. There was a numerous family; but the only two grown up, excepting Charles, were Henrietta and Louisa, young ladies of nineteen and twenty, who had brought from a school at Exeter all the usual stock of accomplishments, and were now, like thousands of other young ladies, living to be fashionable, happy and merry. Their dress had every advantage, their faces were rather pretty, their spirits extremely good, their manners unembarrassed and pleasant; they were of consequence at home, and favourites abroad. Anne always contemplated them as some of the happiest creatures of her acquaintance; but still, saved as we all are by some comfortable feeling of superiority from wishing for the possibility of exchange, she would not have given up her own more elegant and cultivated mind for all their enjoyments. (5)

As a letter of 1804 suggests, the exactness of this linking of the social and personal stems from observation of the real world: 'I called...on Miss Armstrong and was introduced to her father and mother. Like other young ladies she is considerably genteeler than her parents.'[13] We recognise 'improvement' as one of the key words in Jane Austen's fictional vocabulary, especially if *Mansfield Park* is read with care. The dispassionateness characteristic of the whole passage is sounded in the 'perhaps of improvement' and there is no doubt that the entire family is subjected to critical scrutiny. But they emerge from the ordeal fairly well. The 'old English style' of friendliness and hospitality makes up for the lack of education and elegance, and if the young ladies possess only the 'usual stock of accomplishments' their simple pleasure in themselves and their lot is not contemptible.

But Jane Austen places them by comparison with a more developed human organism, Anne Elliot. Anne is saved from envy of the Miss Musgroves by a 'comfortable feeling of superiority', 'as we all are' if we compare ourselves with others, and yet Anne's feeling is more than just a universal human weakness. She *is* genuinely distinguished and throughout the novel forms a standard by which others are judged. She is that paradox, an ideal norm, whose distinction is rooted not in saintliness or eccentricity, but in the best aspects of common humanity, however rare they may be in reality. But Anne's superiority does not annihilate the Musgroves and this is suggested in a way that reinforces Jane Austen's concern with the human aspect of her novel's social context. The announcement of the second Musgrove engagement evokes this exchange between Anne and Charles Musgrove:

> 'I am extremely glad, indeed,' cried Anne, 'particularly glad that this should happen: and that of two sisters, who both deserve equally well and who have have always been such good friends, the pleasant prospects of one should not be dimming those of the other – that they should be so equal in their prosperity and comfort. I hope your mother and father are quite happy with regard to both.'
>
> 'Oh! yes. My father would be well pleased if the gentlemen were richer, but he has no other fault to find. Money, you know, coming down with money – two daughters at once – it cannot be a very agreeable operation....' 'Such excellent parents as Mr and Mrs Musgrove,' exclaimed Anne, 'should be happy in their children's marriages. They do everything to confer happiness, I am sure. What a blessing to young people to be in such hands! Your father and mother seem so totally free from all those ambitious feelings which have led to so much misconduct and misery, both in young and old!' (22)

It is only human for the father to wish that 'the gentlemen were richer', but the whole process makes a striking contrast with the breakdown of Anne's first contact with Wentworth, and with the marriage arrangements of the book's aristocratic and upper class characters in general. If this is one of the fruits of social mobility it seems no bad thing.

Again, the slightly mindless happiness of the Musgrove girls is quite healthy when compared with the general quality of social life presented in the book. To make too much of a writer's final work is a besetting sin of criticism, especially when finality is the result of accident, but *Persuasion* does represent a shift in Jane Austen's artistry and vision. For example, her discontent with routine socializing is given its most extended treatment in this novel. What I have in mind can be illustrated by a few words from *Sense and Sensibility*, although examples could be taken from all the novels: 'After some time spent in saying little and doing less.' (28). Much has been made of Jane Austen's tolerance of social conventions, but there is plenty of evidence in the letters to show the other side of the story:

> Another stupid party last night; perhaps if larger they might be less intolerable, but there were only just enough to make one card table, with six people to look on, & talk nonsense to each other.[14]

The tedium that could be involved in the endless round of unavoidable visiting is well caught in another letter:

> Our acquaintance increase too fast. He was recognised lately by Admiral Bertie, and a few days since arrived the Admiral and his daughter Catherine to wait upon us. There was nothing to like or dislike in either. To the Berties are to be added the Lances, with whose cards we have been endowed, and whose visit Frank and I returned yesterday. . . . We found only Mrs Lance at Home, and whether she boasts any offspring besides a grand pianoforte did not appear. She was civil and chatty enough, and offered to introduce us to some acquaintance in Southampton, which we gratefully declined.[15]

This does not destroy the delightful Jane Austen for whom to 'sit in idleness over a good fire in a well-proportioned room is a luxurious sensation.'[16] But the previous quotation reveals the pressure of genuine frustration in the controlled savagery of 'nothing to like or dislike in either', being 'endowed' with cards and the wonderful thought of 'a grand pianoforte' as an 'offspring'.

Although touched on in earlier work and letters this revulsion at the empty frivolity of much social life is a major concern of *Persuasion*. The subject is opened as early as the novel's first chapter in a scathing passage on Anne's sister:

> Such were Elizabeth Elliot's sentiments and sensations; such the cares to alloy, the agitations to vary, the sameness and the elegance, the prosperity and the nothingness, of her scene of life – such the feelings to give interest to a long, uneventful residence in one country circle, to fill the vacancies which there were no habits of utility abroad, or talents or accomplishments for home, to occupy. (1)

This is an existence that might well evoke memories of Thackeray's Captain Macmurdo from *Vanity Fair:* 'There can scarcely be a life lower, perhaps, than his.'[17] In a way highly characteristic of Jane

Austen the emptiness of this social life is very much a matter of personal responsibility, although exacerbated by the weight of custom and convention. Elizabeth Elliot's neglect of personal development ensures that she has nothing to contribute to the lives of others, and the stylistic rendering of her nullity is a *tour de force:* 'the sameness and the elegance, the prosperity and the nothingness ... no habits of utility... no talents or accomplishments.' Numerous small examples keep the topic in the forefront of our attention: the Elliots, for example, 'whose evening amusements were solely in the elegant stupidity of private parties' (19); 'after a period of nothing-saying' (20); 'saying the proper nothings' (22). The defining contrast is to be found not merely in Anne Elliot's '"ideal of good company... of clever, well-informed people, who have a great deal of conversation"' (16); it can be found much lower down the social scale, with Nurse Rooke who, when she has '"half an hour's leisure to bestow on me... is sure to have something to relate that is entertaining and profitable, something that makes one know one's species better."' (17). Such a passage, similar in intention to that in which Mr Knightley lavishes his praise on Robert Martin, reveals a more flexible attitude to social hierarchy than Jane Austen is sometimes credited with. And the usefulness of Nurse Rooke's life makes an interesting comparison with a final example:

> Charles Musgrove was civil and agreeable; in sense and temper he was undoubtedly superior to his wife; but not of powers, or conversation, or grace to make the past, as they [he and Anne] were connected together, at all a dangerous contemplation; though, at the same time Anne could believe, with Lady Russell, that a more equal match might have greatly improved him; and that a woman of real understanding might have given more consequence to his character, and more usefulness, rationality, and elegance to his habits and pursuits. As it was, he did nothing with much zeal, but sport; and his time was otherwise trifled away, without benefit from books, or anything else. He had very good spirits, which never seemed much affected by his wife's occasional lowness; bore with her unreasonableness sometimes to Anne's admiration; and, upon the whole, though there was very often a little disagreement... they might pass for a happy couple. (6)

The futility of one aspect of society portrayed in the novel is thus complete. We see it in the barrenness of Elizabeth Elliot's inner life, the meaninglessness of much social activity and, perhaps most crucially, in the limitation of 'passing for' a happy couple which, in another example of the novel's pattern of implicit contrasts, reminds us of such really happy couples as the Crofts.

The fact that the Crofts belong to the novel's naval group suggests that a pattern of contrasts may exist at the unifying level of the book's larger structure as well as in numerous small details. But if it is permissible to order the novel's characters in this way (there seems enough in common between Sir Walter, Elizabeth, Mary, Charles Musgrove and Mr Elliot to justify one grouping), it must not be conceived in abstract terms. The novel's stress falls on the human values of both groups and the human values of the navy group are worth some attention not only because there is clearly a generalizing intention on Jane Austen's part – the Harvilles are another reinforcing example of naval domestic happiness – but also because they form such a consistent contrast to the Elliots and their like. The naval group has its own round of social pleasures, but they are far from routine and mechanical; the crucial difference with the Elliots lies in the inner meaning of apparently similar activities, as in the question of hospitality: 'There was so much attachment to Captain Wentworth in all this, and such a bewitching charm in a degree of hospitality so uncommon, so unlike the usual style of give-and-take invitations, and dinners of formality and display.' (11). It is significant that even Anne is at first staggered on entering the Harvilles' tiny cottage. The spontaneity towards strangers places Elizabeth's decision not to entertain even her own relations properly in Bath:

> It was a struggle between propriety and vanity; but vanity got the better, and then Elizabeth was happy again. These were her internal persuasions. – 'Old fashioned notions – country hospitality – we do not profess to give dinners – few people in Bath do – Lady Alicia never does; did not even ask her own sister's family, though they were here a month: and I dare say it would be very inconvenient to Mrs Musgrove – put her quite out of her way. I am sure she would rather not come – she cannot feel easy with us. I will ask them all for an evening; that will be much better – that will be a novelty and a treat.' (22)

The thematic importance of this is unmistakable, especially when we notice a passage that brings the Musgroves, Harville and Wentworth into direct contact with the Elliots:

> Their preparations, however, were stopped short. Alarming sounds were heard; other visitors approached, and the door was thrown open for Sir Walter and Miss Elliot, whose entrance seemed to give a general chill. Anne felt an instant oppression, and wherever she looked, saw symptoms

of the same. The comfort, the freedom, the gaiety of the room was over, hushed into cold composure, determined silence, or insipid talk, to meet the heartless elegance of her father and sister. How mortifying to feel that it was so! (22)

The complexity of the redefinition of manners going on in *Persuasion* is emphasized by the fact that Lady Russell also finds the naval group antipathetic. We remember that she was instrumental in ending the first stage of Anne and Wentworth's relationship, but her prejudice emerges in much smaller examples of social response; in her reaction, for example, to Admiral Croft's comment on the accident at Lyme:

'Ay, a very bad business indeed. – A new sort of way this, for a young fellow to be making love, by breaking his mistress's head! – is it not, Miss Elliot? – This is breaking a head and giving a plaister truly!'

Admiral Croft's manners were not quite of the tone to suit Lady Russell, but they delighted Anne. His goodness of heart and simplicity of character were irresistible. (13)

In relation to this a small part of the novel's total movement is that at the end there 'was nothing less for Lady Russell to do, than to admit that she had been pretty completely wrong, and to take up a new set of opinions and of hopes' (24) with regard to Wentworth and Mr Elliot. The Admiral's tone is the outward sign of such qualities as a perception of Anne's feelings when she visits her former home, '"Now, this must be very bad for you...to be coming and finding us here"'(13) and a complete absence of vanity '"I have done very little besides sending away some of the large looking-glasses from my dressing-room, which was your father's."' (13) In its turn, this relates to a set of interests and abilities which make the strongest possible contrast with, say Charles Musgrove's trifling away of his time, as Anne finds on a visit to the Harville home:

On quitting the Cobb, they all went indoors with their new friends, and found rooms so small as none but those who invite from the heart could think capable of accommodating so many. Anne had a moment's astonishment on the subject herself; but it was soon lost in the pleasanter feelings which sprang from the sight of all the ingenious contrivances and nice arrangements of Captain Harville, to turn the actual space to the best possible account, to supply the deficiencies of lodging-house furniture, and defend the windows and doors against the winter storms to be expected. The varieties in the fitting up of the rooms, where the common necessaries provided by the owner, in the common indifferent plight,

were contrasted with some few articles of a rare species of wood,
excellently worked up, and with something curious and valuable from all
the distant countries Captain Harville had visited, were more than
amusing to Anne: connected as it all was with his profession, the fruit of its
labours, the effect of its influence on his habits, the picture of repose and
domestic happiness it presented, made it to her a something more, or less,
than gratification. (11)

Quite clearly, then, the naval group embodies attractive human
qualities. Can we go beyond this and suggest that it is something more
than a fortuitously related collection of people, that it might
reasonably be called a social group? However tempting, the
beckoning delights of class must surely be avoided. A schematic
reduction of the novel to a class struggle between a decaying landed
gentry and a facet of the rising bourgeoisie would be to see Jane
Austen, in the words of David Daiches, as 'the only English novelist
of stature who was in a sense a Marxist before Marx.'[18] The question
of class in this period is a difficult one, involving as it does the
problem of when the word, and hence the concept, began to be used
in our modern sense. For the eighteenth century, as Diana
Spearman remarks, social grouping was more a question of 'interests
rather than classes': 'the expression "the middling rank or station"
did not convey the idea of a class bound together by a similar origin
or education, which in relation to the middle class, is a
nineteenth-century invention.'[19] Part of this chapter's wider
purpose is to suggest that Jane Austen occupies a very special place as
a focus of change in relation to society between the eighteenth and
nineteenth-century novel. And this place is partly justified by some
profoundly new emphases in this, her last complete work. If we ask
what can bind together a social group, other than 'a similar origin or
education', then one answer might be the economic activity that
distinguishes it from at least some others; in short, work. It is obvious
that this is not a topic of interest for the eighteenth-century novel.
Fielding's heroes and Richardson's villains have in common the fact
that they need do nothing to earn a living; both have the leisure to
pursue their different activities. Defoe might seem an obvious
exception, but his fascination with the mechanics of things is
concentrated on the odd or peripheral. Moll Flanders may work
hard at being a thief and Robinson Crusoe at staying comfortably
alive on his island, but of work as profession and its deep influence
on the personal life, as with Captain Harville, we hear little if
anything. Jane Austen, however, discovers this subject early in her

fiction and it is of central importance to *Persuasion*.

As early as *Sense and Sensibility* the idea of work is given an element of thematic continuity by being associated with the personal difficulties of Edward Ferrars in his secret engagement to Lucy Steele:

> 'It was a foolish, idle inclination on my side...the consequence of ignorance of the world – and want of employment. Had my mother given me some active profession when I was removed at eighteen from the care of Mr. Pratt, I think – nay, I am sure, it would never have happened.... But instead of having anything to do, instead of having any profession chosen for me, or being allowed to chuse any myself, I returned home to be completely idle.... I had therefore nothing in the world to do, but to fancy myself in love. (49)

This quotation, and the one following, clearly disprove Marilyn Butler's statement that the 'idea that a gentleman ought to be socially useful does not appear at all in *Northanger Abbey* or *Sense and Sensibility*, whereas it is crucial in all of the last three novels.'[20] Although General Tilney is not exempt from the ironic scrutiny characteristic of *Northanger Abbey*, there is no doubt that this passage carries the weight of its author's approval:

> 'Perhaps it may seem odd that with only two younger children I should think any profession necessary for him [Henry]; and there are moments when we could all wish him disengaged from every tie of business. But though I may not exactly make converts of you young ladies, I am sure your father, Miss Morland, would agree with me in thinking it expedient to give every young man some employment. The money is nothing, it is not an object; but employment is the thing. Even Frederick, my eldest son, you see, who will perhaps inherit as considerable a landed property as any private man in the country, has his profession.' (22)

For Wentworth, on the other hand, the money may not be everything but it is certainly an object, and a similar emphasis is to be found in *Pride and Prejudice*, in the positive role assigned to Elizabeth Bennet's uncle *vis à vis* her mother and father:

> Mr Gardiner was a sensible, gentleman-like man, greatly superior to his sister as well by nature as education. The Netherfield ladies would have had difficulty in believing that a man who lived by trade, and within view of his own warehouses, could have been so well bred and agreeable. Mrs Gardiner...was an amiable, intelligent, elegant woman, and a great favourite with all her Longbourn nieces. Between the two eldest and herself especially, there subsisted a very particular regard. (25)

133

Jane Austen goes out of her way to suggest that the personal qualities which eventually win the respect and even affection of Mr Darcy are inseparable from the pursuit of a worthwhile activity in the world, just as Mr Bennet's weaknesses are intimately bound up with his dilettantism. The same point is neatly made in reverse in Elizabeth's attitude to the patroness of Mr Collins: 'She had heard nothing of Lady Catherine that spoke her awful from any extraordinary talents or miraculous virtue, and the mere stateliness of money and rank, she thought she could witness without trepidation.' (29)

The relevance of this line of argument to *Persuasion* is clear, especially when we remember one of Sir Walter's key objections to the naval profession (the other, of course, is the wonderful complaint that '"it cuts up a man's youth and vigour most horribly; a sailor grows older sooner than any other man"'):

> As being the means of bringing persons of obscure birth into undue distinction, and raising men to honours which their fathers and grandfathers never dreamt of.... A man is in greater danger in the navy of being insulted by the rise of one whose father, his father might have disdained to speak to... than in any other line. (3)

And the point is developed as we would expect, and hope, by the egregious Mrs Clay in a passage that is both delightfully amusing and a deeply serious comment on the England of Jane Austen's time:

> 'Sir Walter... is not it the same with any other professions, perhaps most other? Soldiers, in active service, are not at all better off; and even in the quieter professions, there is a toil and a labour of the mind, if not of the body, which seldom leaves a man's looks to the natural effect of time. The lawyer plods, quite care-worn; the physician is up at all hours, and travelling in all weather; and even the clergyman—' she stopped a moment to consider what might do for the clergyman—'and even the clergyman, you know, is obliged to go into infected rooms, and expose his health and looks to all the injury of a poisonous atmosphere. In fact, as I have long been convinced, though every profession is necessary and honourable in its turn, it is only the lot of those who are not obliged to follow any, who can live in a regular way, in the country, choosing their own hours, following their own pursuits, and living on their own property, without the torment of trying for more; it is only *their* lot, I say, to hold the blessings of health and a good appearance to the utmost. (3)

This could hardly be more direct and, if pondered, surely warrants some displacement of the commonly viewed balance of tradition and innovation in Jane Austen. At the very least, it seems impossible to deny a change of earlier views in the careful thematic development of this novel. The way of life praised by Mrs Clay may have been that of Darcy and Knightley (although in a manner she could never dream of) but its representative here is Sir Walter, the strongest possible contrast with Wentworth who, at the beginning of his career, 'had nothing but himself to recommend him, and no hopes of attaining affluence, but in the chances of a most uncertain profession, and no connexions to secure even his farther rise in that profession.' (4). That the opposition between Sir Walter and Wentworth can be seen in social, as well as personal terms, and that *Persuasion* has a vision of society that takes account of some of the objective social changes of Jane Austen's own time is registered with unmistakable force in the book's last chapter:

> Captain Wentworth, with five-and-twenty thousand pounds, and as high in his profession as merit and activity could place him, was no longer nobody. He was now esteemed quite worthy to address the daughter of a foolish, spend-thrift baronet, who had not had principle or sense enough to maintain himself in the situation in which Providence had placed him, and who could give his daughter at present but a small part of the share of ten thousand pounds which must be hers hereafter. (24)

On this point it seems fair to claim that with *Persuasion* the stage is being set for an important preoccupation of Victorian fiction, the treatment of work as vocation and profession, a preoccupation that possibly reaches its apex in a novel by one of Jane Austen's greatest admirers, *Middlemarch*. Michel Zeraffa has pointed to the significant omission of work from the novel:

> Of course, the novel is more concerned with commenting on facts than on revealing them, but it remains true that Western fiction avoids work activity and work value. Work makes its appearance in novels in a rather artificial way, and man as worker dwells within them in some kind of implicit fashion. Work takes time, and time is needed for human relationships, and human emotions.[21]

As Zeraffa suggests, this gap may result as much from technical as ideological reasons. It is difficult to see how the repetitive nature of work could be adapted to the demands of fiction, at least in the traditional novel. (This is perhaps an area where the methods of the *nouvelle roman* can come into their own.) Raymond Williams is surely right in claiming that in Jane Austen the land 'is seen primarily as an index of revenue and position... while the process of working it is hardly seen at all.' Yet this omission is scarcely blameworthy. Williams himself shows that Jane Austen sees with great clarity the money behind, or within, things.

> Her eye for a house, for timber, for the details of improvement, is quick, accurate, monetary. Yet money of other kinds... has no visual equivalent; it has to be converted to these signs of order to be recognized at all.[22]

In doing this, she might be thought to be fulfilling her essential role as a novelist. Jane Austen does not show us a Captain Wentworth in action or a Mr Knightley working at his estate business, but she brings out the relationship between this activity and character. A connection is demonstrated between what they are and what they do for basically economic reasons that is hard to find in earlier novels.

This interest is yet another way of revealing *Persuasion's* climactic position in Jane Austen's career. She was interested from the beginning in the idea of the profession but her earlier heroes, Mr Knightley and Darcy for example, embody the idea of the gentleman in their well-rounded self-cultivation which, amongst other things, includes an active concern for the estate that is their economic base. But although Wentworth has much of the cultivation of these earlier figures, he has a single-minded energy which directs him towards financial success in his chosen field. There is a one-to-one relationship between the individual and work here which of necessity denies the leisure central to the previous ideal and which, in artistic terms, can lead to the almost Dickensian fusion of character and work activity in Captain Harville. Can this shift in Jane Austen's interests be explained? Her stress on conservatism makes Marilyn Butler see Jane Austen as, on this point as in many other ways, a reflector: 'Because in very general terms they reflect "established" ideas, Jane Austen's novels share society's growing seriousness of tone during the period of her writing life.'[23] This leaves out the possibility, crucial to my argument, that by introducing the theme of professionalism into the English novel she is extending the boundaries of consciousness about human and social life. If this is so, a wider historical perspective is required, in which it becomes hard to quarrel with this descriptive comment of Lionel Trilling's: 'A salient fact of French and English society up to a hundred years ago is the paucity of honourable professions which could serve the ambitious as avenues of social advancement.'[24] And his view is complemented by the professional historian's:

> In the first half of the eighteenth century the professions did not have a good image... only soldiers appear to have escaped the general censure.

Few of the professional men in Fielding and Richardson, Parson Adams
and Harrison apart, appear in a good light. Fielding especially castigated
doctors and lawyers; the most vicious criticisms appear in *Amelia* but
Amelia's husband, by contrast, was a soldier.[25]

Moving from description to analysis, we might isolate from a host of
historical forces the ever-increasing shift from an aristocratic to a
middle-class view of life, in its turn inseparably bound up with the
profound general influence of the Industrial Revolution. Auerbach's
exposition of this shift is perhaps the most brilliantly pointed:

> We observed before that in Molière (as everywhere else in the literature
> of the time) not only peasants and other characters from the lowest classes
> but also merchants, lawyers, physicians, and apothecaries appear
> exclusively as comic adjuncts. This is connected with the fact that the
> social ideal of the time required the most general development and
> attitude possible from the *honnête homme*. The trend was away from any
> kind of specialization, even that of the poet or scholar. Anyone who
> wanted to be socially unexceptionable must not allow the economic basis
> of his life to be conspicuous, nor his professional specialty if he had one.
> Failing that, he was considered pedantic, extravagant, and ridiculous.
> Only such abilities could be shown as might also pass as an elegant
> dilettantism and which contributed to easy and pleasant social
> intercourse... professional specialization thus came to be socially and
> aesthetically impossible; only in the category of the grotesque could it
> appear as the subject of literary imitation. In this the tradition of farce
> certainly played a part, but this is still not enough to explain why the
> grotesque conception of the professional man was maintained so generally
> and consistently in the new genre of the elegant social comedy in the
> intermediate style.[26]

The richness of reinforcing examples in English literature from
Shakespeare and Ben Jonson onwards is sufficient to show that this
was not merely a French phenomenon. Indeed, as late as *Persuasion*
itself there is a touch of the older attitude to men of business in the
treatment of Mr Shepherd, Sir Walter's 'civil, cautious lawyer' who
leaves Lady Russell to do his dirty work in persuading his master to
economize and who laughs, 'as he knew he must', at Sir Walter's
'wit'. (3). The recognition of this historical shift is, in fact, something
of a touchstone of nineteenth century novelists. Thackeray's urge
towards the gentlemanly in life as well as art, surfaces partly in his
reliance on soldier-heroes. On the other hand, professionalism is
central in George Eliot, and Dickens's work is studded with
examples, positive and negative, of equal power. One thinks
particularly of such contrasting pairs as Allan Woodcourt (the

doctor who marries Esther Summerson) and Harold Skimpole from *Bleak House,* Daniel Doyce and Henry Gowan from *Little Dorrit.*

Here surely lies the importance of the navy for *Persuasion.* Of course, we recognize its personal significance in that two of Jane Austen's brothers were naval officers, became admirals in fact, but the interest where the great writer is concerned lies in how such biographical accidents are used. The novelist as actor not reflector is seen in Jane Austen's seizing on the general significance of elements of her own life, a significance amply indicated by Lionel Trilling:

> Indeed, in the nineteenth century there was widespread belief that England produced a moral type which made it unique among nations...This moral type...had as its chief qualities probity and candour. That...the moral type shoud be discovered in officers of the Navy is scarcely fortuitous, for the English themselves gave the seafaring profession a special place in their imagination of the moral life....Gentleman though he was, he *worked.* [27]

The last sentence is the key emphasis for my argument. Given the originality of discovering this theme, it is hardly to be expected that Jane Austen could leap directly into the creation of civilian professional types. There is enough in common between Wentworth and a Darcy or a Knightley for Jane Austen to feel on secure ground and still achieve her essential shift of emphasis. Interestingly the importance of these naval characters is recognized by an able early critic, Richard Simpson, who denies any social dimension to most of Jane Austen's work:

> Indeed there is nothing in her novels to prove that she had any conception of society itself, but only of the coterie of three or four families mixing together, with differences of intellect, wealth, or character, but without any grave social inequalities. Of organized society she manifests no idea. [28]

This general view is modified in favour of the naval characters of *Persuasion:* 'Her naval officers are really social portraits.'[29] What is new for Jane Austen is the extension of gentlemanliness into professionalism, not the birth and upbringing of the naval officer himself. In this she differs greatly from Fanny Burney's treatment of Captain Mirvan, in *Evelina,* who has been described as a 'narrow-minded buffoon, with the sense of humour of a fourth-form schoolboy of inferior upbringing.'[30] Fanny Burney, however, defended the character in her diary of 1780 – 'The more I see of sea-captains the less reason have I to be ashamed of Captain

Mirvan.'[31] – in terms which would appear to justify the view that a radical transformation had taken place in the backgrounds from which naval officers were drawn. But although G.M. Trevelyan writes that 'naval officers were now the sons of gentlemen of modest means (Nelson was a poor parson's son)' he goes on to point out that, at their best, they combined sea-going experience with 'the manner and thought of an educated man.'[32] Such sailors, and Captain Wentworth, are epitomized in Macaulay's ideal: 'a man versed in the theory and practice of his calling, and steeled against all the dangers of battle and tempest, yet of cultivated mind and polished manners.'[33]

The appositeness of Jane Austen's imaginative insight into the social order as well as personal life is revealed if we turn for a moment to a specialist historian. She is writing at a time when, in the words of Professor Lewis in his *England's Sea-Officers*, 'the officer is changing his nature, that is between 1794 and 1860.'[34] This change of nature is towards a higher degree of professionalism which, while it implies no derogation from the gentlemanly ideal, is less dependant than in the past on the higher reaches of birth:

> One thing is sure. Somehow or other as the war grew older there
> appeared upon the quarter-decks of His Majesty's ships an appreciable
> group of men whose social qualifications were some way below those
> required in earlier days and far below those desired by the older sort of
> officer.[35]

Sir Walter is right, then, in claiming that a 'man is in greater danger in the navy of being insulted by the rise of one whose father, his father might have disdained to speak to...than in any other line.' (3) And, while demonstrating from a statistical analysis that by far the highest percentage, nearly a quarter, of naval officers came from naval backgrounds, Professor Lewis offers a comment which possibly illuminates Sir Walter's attitude to new creations in the baronetcy:

> Many of these sailor-sons of baronets had fathers who were first creations,
> for the honour was one which the governments of the day bestowed freely
> as a reward for fighting services of not quite first-class order.[36]

By relying on another analysis, Lewis is able to suggest that during the period from 1793 to 1815 fifty per cent of naval officers' parents were from the professions, while only slightly over a quarter were landed gentry, but he also finds it necessary to clarify a possible ambiguity in the figures:

Indeed, such inside personal information as the author happens to possess all goes to show that, had every officer of 'business and commerce' affinities come out boldly with the information, that category would have been the largest of all.[37]

So we can see that in making Wentworth a 'young man, who had nothing but himself to recommend him...and no connexions to secure even his farther rise in that profession' (4), Jane Austen is being both original in fictional terms and representative of an objective social reality. Literary conventions often lag behind changes in the social life which gave them validity; indeed, part of the function of genius is to bring both into a new alignment. For example, B.C. Southam accounts for some of the adverse contemporary response to Jane Austen as resulting from her rejection of widespread novelistic conventions:

The convention of love in sentimental fiction required aristocratic connections for at least one, if not both of the lovers, and this social elevation was to be matched with the peculiar moral elevation of romantic attachment.[38]

By placing *Persuasion* in something of its contemporary context, one sees the grounds for a view different from that of Marilyn Butler: 'she wants to show that the realization of self, an apparently ideal goal, is in fact necessarily destructive and delusory.'[39] More surprisingly one is forced to disagree with Lionel Trilling on a similar point:

The once common view was that, although her characters are rooted in social actuality, Jane Austen does not conceive of society as being in any sense problematical...a large part of the interest in her work is now thought to be exactly in the sensitivity of her response to social change. This she envisages...not directly and in its gross manifestations but in terms of the new consciousness with which...it is associated.... To none of these traits of the new consciousness does Jane Austen give her approval.[40]

Professor Lewis demonstrates a paradox typical of British life in showing that while contemporary naval officers came from a wider spectrum of society than previously, the dominating ethos of the wardroom remained that of the gentleman. Jane Austen seizes this opportunity to create a hero who, while cultivated, is related only to a sister whose manners 'without any approach to coarseness' are 'open, easy, and decided' (6), and a brother about whom Sir Walter is misled ' "by the term *gentleman*. I thought you were speaking of

some man of property" ' (3). In short, he is as much of a new man as
it is reasonable to expect and in giving him both material success and
the lovely Anne, Jane Austen seems clearly to be fashioning her
novel in approval of some at least 'of the traits of the new
consciousness.'

Jane Austen's use of the naval officer is yet another example of the
quite widely held view that *Persuasion* is a novel of new
departures which has a particularly rich relation to the life of its own
time. Those who find claims for this writer's social awareness
doubtful might consider her *Advertizement* for *Northanger Abbey*
where she apologized for 'those parts of the book which thirteen
years have made comparatively obsolete. The public are entreated
to bear in mind that thirteen years have passed since it was finished,
many more since it was begun, and that during that period, places,
manners, books and opinions have undergone considerable
changes.'[41] Nothing could reveal more clearly a mind attuned to
public change as well as private nuance. Scholars have recently been
filling in some gaps in our knowledge of the novel's development by
arguing for the importance of the Jacobin and anti-Jacobin novel at
the turn of the century. A relationship has been suggested between
the general social and political ferment caused by the French
Revolution and the intellectual upheavals generated by those who
took different views of that event. There is no reason to doubt that
this battle of ideas was a factor in the heightening of consciousness
about the nature of society in which the mature Jane Austen
participated, although she is too great a writer to be unambiguously
of only one camp, which is where Marilyn Butler attempts to place
her for the conservative position in *Jane Austen and the War of Ideas*.
Gary Kelly makes interesting claims for the artistry, not merely the
content, of the English Jacobin novel but, with the enthusiasm of the
specialist, he overstates his case in arguing that 'the four major
English Jacobin novelists—Robert Bage, Elizabeth Inchbald,
Thomas Holcroft and William Godwin—took the form and matter
of the English novel from the eighteenth into the nineteenth
century.'[42] Jane Austen has been shown to be aware of at least some
of this work, but my claim for her pre-eminence in effecting this
shift, above all in *Persuasion*, is based on her centrality within the
tradition of the great English novelists. Her direct relationship to the
eighteenth century novel through Richardson and mediated by way
of Fanny Burney leads on, via her own discoveries, to George Eliot
and, through her, to James, above all in the theme of a 'certain

young woman affronting her destiny.'[43]

A reiterated theme of my exposition has been the almost experimental exploration of new possibilities for the novel and Jane Austen's own art in *Persuasion*. Again, Marilyn Butler sees it differently: 'But enveloping this nineteenth-century novel of the inner life is an eighteenth-century novel in search of a centre.... In no other Austen novel is the social group surrounding the heroine so thin as the Elliot's circle at Bath.'[44] My point would be that this thinness is thematic, a sign of attenuation in a social group which is no longer of primary interest to the writer. Also, Anne *is* surrounded by another group, the naval, of real texture and human density, which will eventually form the permanent context for her venture into a new life.

The movement forward into a new world of experience for Anne works against another view of Marilyn Butler's, that *Persuasion* 'is the only one of Jane Austen's novels that is not whole-heartedly partisan, and it is none the better for it.'[45] She thus admits that the book diverges somewhat from her conservative view of the writer, but sees it as eccentric to Jane Austen's main line of development. A contrary view has been developed in the preceding pages, that *Persuasion* picks up and advances diverse thematic threads from the earlier work. The concluding marriages of the other novels place a rewarding stamp of finality on their heroines' progress towards self-knowledge, so that there is a sense in which they may legitimately be seen as what have been called 'closed forms',[46] a fictional rounding-off which contains no hint of further alarms and excursions. This is not to say that these marriages are empty of significance. The balance of human forces embodied in, say, Emma and Mr Knightley promises a dialectical relationship in which liveliness and good sense will be tempered to the benefit of both. Anne's marriage to Wentworth is the infinitely touching reward of an exquisite fidelity, rather than the climax of a growth towards maturity, but it has another dimension in its prophetic relationship to nineteenth-century fiction. The social symbolism of marriage in the Victorian novel is a commonplace—we might take as poles of success and failure the union of Lizzie Hexam and Eugene Wrayburn in *Our Mutual Friend* and Disraeli's shameless manipulation of the same device in *Sybil*—and this is what is anticipated in *Persuasion*. Alastair Duckworth, however, disagrees:

> The 'final marriage' of the novel is not a 'social marriage' in the way that previous marriages are in Jane Austen; Anne's union with Wentworth

fails to guarantee a broader union of themes and attitudes in
Persuasion.... Anne and Wentworth... do not really resolve conflicting
themes by their union; they exemplify rather a deep and private
relationship in a novel where the resolution of public divisions has
become of secondary concern.[47]

My study has assented, with many critics, to the depth of personal
response in *Persuasion,* but to restrict the novel to this sphere alone is
a debilitating limitation which runs counter to the book's complexity
of interests. Malcolm Bradbury strikes a truer note, but is a shade
too enthusiastically one-sided: 'Anne, originally persuaded towards a
caution appropriate to rank and security, comes to question the
values associated with these for those of energetic uncertainty and
promise.'[48] There is, surely, not too much uncertainty about the
marriage's financial stability! Raymond Williams contributes to the
point interestingly—'An openly acquisitive society, which is
concerned also with the transmission of wealth, is trying to judge
itself at once by an inherited code and by the morality of
improvement.'[49]—although one is puzzled by the passivity of 'is
trying to judge itself'. It is surely Jane Austen who is doing the
judging. But that the relationship has an important social as well as
personal dimension seems clear. Wentworth's share in the equation
is obvious; he brings Anne energy, warmth, ability. But Anne's
contribution is less clear. Not only does she belong to the suspect
Elliot group; she appears to have little of her own to offer. What she
really has to offer is, of course, herself and the absolute value of her
gift is focused by the unadorned perfection of its setting. The essence
of her delicate character is conveyed in her reasons for not loving a
second time:

> More than seven years were gone since this little history of sorrowful
> interest had reached its close; and time had softened down much, perhaps
> nearly all of peculiar attachment to him—but she had been too
> dependent on time alone; no aid had been given in change of place...or
> in any novelty or enlargement of society. No one had ever come within
> the Kellynch circle, who could bear a comparison with Frederick
> Wentworth, as he stood in her memory. No second attachment, the only
> thoroughly natural, happy, and sufficient cure, at her time of life, had
> been possible to the nice tone of her mind, the fastidiousness of her taste,
> in the small limits of the society around them. (4).

This passage is a little miracle of observation and insight, a perfect
fusion of realism and idealism, of Augustan common-sense and

143

Romantic truth to the self. There is a complete lack of sentimentality in the circumstantial detail that helps partly to account for Anne's not marrying: the lack of a new or wider social circle and the force of Wentworth as he remains fixed in the transfiguring glow of memory. On the other hand, this does nothing to depreciate the personal value of Anne's constancy. The whole impression is embodied in the tension between the 'nice tone of her mind, the fastidiousness of her taste' and the 'small limits of the society around her.' Marvin Mudrick is surely right to see Anne's personality as more than her own individual creation: 'The proper parochial society that for a quarter of a century Jane Austen had been laughing at and amusing, despising and defending, at all events copiously memorializing, comes to its late flower in the unassuming grace, the finely balanced feelings, the secret strength and charm of character, of Anne Elliot.'[50] But this is also to take the matter a little too lightly. There is a certain slackness in the 'laughing at and amusing, despising and defending' which Mudrick sees as Jane Austen's controlling oppositions. As I have tried to show, the laughter at the Elliots in this novel is rather fierce and there is precious little defending of them to be found anywhere.

The problem facing Jane Austen at this point is similar to that in Fielding's creation of Sophia Western: the necessity of taking the full measure of social evils combined with a commitment to the concept of society as such. Are we right in sensing that this commitment is slackening just a little in *Persuasion*? Auerbach's comments on Molière seem entirely appropriate to the earlier Jane Austen:

> Molière's criticism is entirely moralistic; that is to say, it accepts the
> prevailing structure of society, takes for granted its justification,
> permanence, and general validity, and castigates the excesses occurring
> within its limits as ridiculous.[51]

It would be a delightful irony if we could see some agreement between this last novel and the German playwright Kotzebue whose *Lover's Vows* plays such a demonic role in *Mansfield Park*. In *Virgin of the Sun*, the good Inca high priest remarks: 'Compulsive institutions are no longer necessary to preserve decency'.[52] However far this may seem from the world of Jane Austen, morally compulsive institutions do little to improve Sir Walter, Elizabeth or William Elliot and the novel puts an unusually strong emphasis on Anne's qualities of private judgement, as in her silent ignoring of Lady Russell on the question of Charles Musgrove's proposal where 'in this case, Anne had left nothing for advice to do.' (4). But this questioning, if it exists, still accepts the best that can be created by the older world; as Duckworth says: 'Anne does not reject with the loss of her home a whole moral inheritance.'[53] Anne Elliot's delicacy is a personal quality which is, simultaneously, the fruit of an ideal civilization. Like Fielding, Jane Austen presents in her heroine the vision of what the finest elements of her world might be at their best. And *Persuasion's* openness of form is evident in its hint that these qualities may be tested against dangerous experience, that a price is exacted for the escape from the sterile safety of the Elliot world into a new realm of experience: 'She gloried in being a sailor's wife, but she must pay the tax of quick alarm for belonging to that profession which is, if possible, more distinguished in its domestic virtues than in its national importance.' (24). 1814, the novel's setting in time, was not quite the year which initiated a generation of peace in Europe. Is there any reason to doubt that, beginning *Persuasion* in 1815 as she did, Jane Austen had the thought of Napoleon's return as a specific instance of a tax to come on Anne and Wentworth's mutual happiness?

It seems appropriate to end as I began, with Virginia Woolf and her prophecy of what might have been Jane Austen's future development, a guess which puts the final gloss on the special nature of *Persuasion* as revealed by the preceding argument:

> She would have stood farther away from her characters, and seen them more as a group, less as individuals. Her satire...would have been more stringent and severe.[54]

Further Reading

The number of important books and articles on Jane Austen is now very large. Among the more interesting are:

Jane Austen and her Art by Mary Lascelles (Oxford, 1939).

Jane Austen: Irony as Defence and Discovery by Marvin Mudrick (Oxford, 1952).

Jane Austen's Novels: a Study in Structure by Andrew H. Wright (London, 1953).

'A Critical Theory of Jane Austen's Writings,' by Q. D. Leavis, *Scrutiny* X (1941-42).

Some critical works with a social dimension are:

The Improvement of the Estate: a Study of Jane Austen's Novels by Alistair M. Duckworth (London, 1971).

Jane Austen, Feminism and Fiction by Margaret Kirkham (Brighton, 1982).

Jane Austen in a Social Context edited by David Monagham (London, 1981).

'Regulated Hatred: an Aspect of the Work of Jane Austen,' by D. W. Harding, *Scrutiny* VIII (1940).

'The Economic Determinism of Jane Austen,' by Leonard Woolf, *New Statesman and Nation* XXIV (1942).

6

Vanity Fair

For a critical work which aspires also to suggest a historical reading of the development of the novel, the lapse of time between *Persuasion* and *Vanity Fair* must be acknowledged. To ignore the works written between them is excusable, perhaps, in the interests of keeping the topic within manageable proportions. The English novel is such a vast edifice that only its major features can be noticed in detail; counting individual bricks would swell this book to gargantuan size. But also, as I have argued earlier,[1] selection and omission are of the nature of any intellectual enterprise: our house of fiction may disappear entirely if it is enveloped in a fog of detail.

Some omissions, however, are more serious than others and require more detailed justification. Scott's absence is clearly the largest void here, especially as his creative discoveries relate so closely to the problems under discussion. Lukács makes the point with great clarity:

> Scott's contact with the historical problems of the epoch produces less a
> new historical novel than a further development of the social-critical
> novel of the eighteenth century, with certain elements of the new
> historicism worked in as a means of intensifying and enriching its realistic
> features.[2]

He goes on to place the development in a European context: 'This continuation of the historical novel, in the sense of a consciously historical conception of the present, is the great achievement of his outstanding contemporary, Balzac.'[3] This suggests that the historical colouring of Scott's novels is the prerequisite, however indispensable, to something more profound, his conviction that history is *meaningful* in relation both to its own time and to the present, a distinction which separates good from bad in Scott's variable output. In *Ivanhoe*, say, history is mere icing on the cake of a love and adventure story, a weight of detail created for its own sake. *Waverley's* central concern, on the other hand, is the antagonism and resolution of historical forces through the lives of individuals; if 'history' is substituted for 'society' Irving Howe's definition of the political novel becomes directly applicable, that is, a book 'in which the *idea* of society, as distinct from the mere unquestioned workings of society, has penetrated the consciousness of the characters in all of its profoundly problematic aspects.'[4]

Writers as diverse as George Eliot and Faulkner are, at their best, writing of the present through the past: there is no antiquarianism in *Middlemarch* or *Absolom, Absolom!*, a point which highlights the importance of form in considering the social aspects of literature. The modernism of writers such as Faulkner and T. S. Eliot exists in the artistic pulse of their work rather than the self-conscious trappings of contemporary life, like the pylons which sometimes obtrude into the poetry of the 1930s. The rhythms of the car and of film montage exist in Eliot's work at the level of detailed texture and, conversely, Faulkner is notably feeble when he confronts directly the cocktail party element of modern life, as in *The Wild Palms*. But in his greatest historical reconstructions the artistic treatment is never anything but modernist, often in the most radical ways. Clearly, one aspect of Eliot's greatness was a total sensitivity to the distinctive beat of modern existence, whereas Faulkner was perhaps fortunate to be born in an area where history *was* the present in a peculiarly rich way. Again, we may not go to Shakespeare for the almost documentary feel of the Jacobean world we find in Jonson's *Bartholomew Fair*. But the superficial archaism of *King Lear* is the vehicle for the most deeply felt response to the pressures of conflict between an old and a new order. However remote its historical setting, nothing could be more up-to-date, in its own terms, than Edmund's almost modish anarchism. Similarly, the dating of *Middlemarch* is more than the Victorian convention of setting novels at a period slightly earlier than their writing. George Eliot clearly regarded the first Reform Bill as an event of momentous importance in English history and, more than this, as meaningful for her in the context of her own time. It is entirely appropriate that her characters should move in an atmosphere of reform because reform in its widest sense, of personal change and amendment, is one of the novel's central themes.

Complex problems arise here which are partly clarified by the acceptance of the continuities which Lukács sees between the historical and social novel:

An analysis of the work of the important realists will show that there is not a single, fundamental problem of structure, characterization, etc. in their historical novels which is lacking in their other novels...they flow from a similar aim: the portrayal of a total context of social life, be it present or past, in the narrative form.[5]

The insight is echoed by Andrew Sanders in a passage specifically related to Thackeray (the question of whether or not one is in total agreement with his critical views can be avoided):

The interplay of fictional and factual references within the narrative [of *Henry Esmond*] suggests that we must accept the 'reality' of the whole imagined situation in a complex manner. The imagined world is not an escape from modern reality; it is seen to be as open to criticism as any other world, real or unreal. The eighteenth-century novels are in this way at least of the same 'type' as those set in Thackeray's own age; his criticism does not extend over two different societies, but over an England which is substantially unchanged in political and social fashions.[6]

From the point of view of characterization, the historical and social novel have in common, again in Lukács's words, the 'derivation of the individuality of characters from the historical peculiarity of their age,'[7] another way of formulating his famous concept of typicality. Well taken as these points are, at a certain stage common-sense withdraws from dissolving entirely the obvious differences in genre between the social novel set more or less in its own time and the historical novel proper. And it is this which forbids Scott's assimilation into the present work. There can be no doubt that he helped to make possible the panoramic novel of later European and American fiction, but to give his work an acceptable social reading requires the controlled interaction of at least three variables. The novels' artistry, in the narrowly aesthetic sense; their validity as depictions of specific historical settings; their relation to the period in which they were written – all would demand attention, while consideration of the second would inevitably take this study too far from its chosen path.

Vanity Fair itself teeters on the very edge of involving us in these problems. It is clearly a borderline case between the historical novel and the social panorama, set as it is around the time of Thackeray's birth in 1811. Its occupation of this grey area is seen perhaps most clearly in his decision, recorded in a footnote to the novel's first edition, to make the book's illustrations anachronistic:

It was the author's intention, faithful to history, to depict all the characters of this tale in their proper costumes, as they wore them at the commencement of the century. But when I remember the appearance of people in those days, and that an officer and lady were actually habited like this [drawing] – I have not the heart to disfigure my heroes and heroines by costumes so hideous; and have, on the contrary, engaged a model of rank dressed according to the present fashion.[8]

This suggests some unwillingness on Thackeray's part to take his historical vision with full seriousness and presents one of the novel's most striking dichotomies, that between text and illustration. It also suggests the possibility of avoiding a full-scale theoretical examination of the issues involved in seeing the book as a historical novel proper, although even the most severely practical critic will be unable to avoid the issue entirely.

Such a practical approach might well begin with *Vanity Fair's* element of social criticism as this is clearly a part of its intended aesthetic effect. If we do, the divergence of view is bewildering. For Seymour Betsky, Thackeray is the first novelist who 'sinks bull-dog teeth into every single abuse of rank and privilege.'[9] That alarming prospect contrasts with one of the novelist's great scourges, Grieg: 'Lacking a coherent, integrated social theory, he grew timid and unsure, like a sniper who decamps when the battle grows warm.'[10] Two critics agree, at least, on an almost unconscious radicalism in Thackeray's social criticism. A. E. Dyson stresses the 'intensity' with which Thackeray 'always responded to the human comedy' and which 'pushed him towards a more radical criticism than perhaps he intended.'[11] Barbara Hardy urges a recognition of the fullest possible range of effects in the novels:

> As critic of society, if we take him only at the face value of his explicit attacks, and of his conspicuous jokes, we will find him fervent, witty, sharp, but limited in range and depth. But if we attend to his implicit, as well as his explicit, analysis, we see his full range and depth of attack.[12]

It might be thought, however, that such a catch-all phrase as 'social criticism' is bound to arouse a clash of opinions, whereas a degree of specificity might quieten the uproar. But this is certainly not the case if the subject is money. For Frank O'Connor, Thackeray has, with Balzac, the 'best descriptions of the money mania that swept Europe during the Industrial Revolution';[13] in Talon's view, to Thackeray 'economics were an unknown country.'[14] The most comprehensive positive reassessment in recent years is Barbara Hardy's *The Exposure of Luxury: Radical Themes in Thackeray:* 'Thackeray is the great sociologist of nineteenth-century fiction, the great accumulator of social symbols of class and money. To read him is to read a fictional form of Veblen's *The Theory of the Leisure Class.*'[15] There is, of course, no difficulty in finding many points in the novel which testify to Thackeray's general interest in money. We are told that 'money and fair repute are the chiefest good', that 'people in Vanity Fair fasten on to rich folks quite naturally.' (20). Of great interest, because it occurs in a casual passage of dialogue, is George Osborne's '"Ours is a ready money society."' (20). But the real difficulty is the nature of Thackeray's concern with cash. Does he see it as one cog among others – such as envy and snobbery – which keeps the social machine in motion? Or does it have a status and power unique to itself? Again, how deep does his interest go? Does money operate on the surface of his vision of society as an easily understood motive for human action? Or is it in some sense working below the surface, motivating society in ways of which individuals are not always fully conscious? Answers to these questions might be found by examining a small aspect of the book in close detail. Chapters 36 and 37, 'How to live well on Nothing a Year', promise a concentrated treatment of the role of money in society and so also a crucial imaginative working out of Thackeray's interest in this subject.

How is it possible, then, to live well on nothing a year? Chapter 36 begins with an incisive thumbnail sketch of Jenkins who, although only a 'Commissioner of the Tape and Sealing-Wax Office, with £1200 a year for a salary' is able to live in a style which fills his friends and acquaintances with wonder. And in a way we learn to see as typical of the novel, these chapters are an extended treatment of an aspect of life that Thackeray had hinted at a couple of hundred pages earlier:

> Everybody in Vanity Fair must have remarked how well those live who are comfortably and thoroughly in debt: how they deny themselves nothing; how jolly and easy they are in their minds. Rawdon and his wife had the very best apartments in the inn at Brighton; the landlord, as he brought in the first dish, bowed before them as to his greatest customers; and Rawdon abused the dinners and wine with an audacity which no grandee in the land could surpass. Long custom, a manly appearance, faultless boots and clothes, and a happy fierceness of manner, will often help a man as much as a great balance at the banker's. (22)

The heart of this subject, as it is contained in the first of the two chapters, can be found in a paragraph dealing with Rawdon's exploits at billiards and cards. It is, naturally, impossible literally to live on nothing a year, well or otherwise: 'The truth is...we used the word "nothing" to signify something unknown; meaning, simply, that we don't know how the gentleman in question defrays the expenses of his establishment.' The truth about Rawdon is that 'from being only a brilliant amateur, [he] had grown to be a consummate master of billiards' and his mastery of this game, and cards, consists of nothing less than being a shark who plays clumsily at the beginning of an evening but, once the bets are running against him, invariably comes in to triumph at the end. Thackeray touches in lightly, without overt moralizing, the unpleasant nature of the combined operation run by Rawdon and Becky: 'the young fellows gathered round Mrs Crawley' but 'came from her parties with long faces, having dropped more or less money at her fatal card-tables.' The chapter continues by way of some brilliant observations on the quality of the Crawleys' existence—'Easy and pleasant as their life at Paris was, it was after all only an idle dalliance and amiable trifling; and Rebecca saw that she must push Rawdon's fortune in their own country' – to Becky's successful settling of Rawdon's huge debts for a minimal sum. The last paragraph, though, promises a more detailed treatment of the subject in hand:

> And so, Colonel and Mrs Crawley came to London: and it is in their
> house in Curzon Street, Mayfair, that they really showed the skill which
> must be possessed by those who would live on the resources above named.

Up to this point there is a certain disparity between the largeness of scope suggested by the chapters' heading and the rather 'private' nature of the explanation provided for the particular case. But if so, the passage just quoted suggests that our disappointment will be assuaged, that we will move from the individual case to a wider generality. This is precisely what is indicated by the opening sentence of the following chapter: 'In the first place, and as a matter of the greatest necessity, we are bound to describe how a house may be got for nothing a year.' Thackeray then creates a fascinating little vignette of how Miss Crawley's former Butler, Raggles, bettered himself to the point where he was able to buy, in order to rent out, the house in Curzon Street.

> He was a good man; good and happy. The house brought him in so
> handsome a yearly income, that he was determined to send his children to
> good schools, and accordingly, regardless of expense, Charles was sent to
> boarding at Dr Swish-tail's, Sugarcane Lodge, and Little Matilda to Miss
> Peckover's, Laurentinum House, Clapham.

An old family retainer of the Crawleys, with whom his connection 'had been kept up constantly', Raggles is delighted to let his property to Rawdon who 'knew it and its owner quite well' – and the stage is now set for the final explanation, dazzling in its simplicity; 'Nobody in fact was paid':

> It was wonderful to see the pertinacity with which the washerwoman from Tooting brought the cart every Saturday, and her bills week after week.... The bill for servants' porter at the Fortune of War public-house is a curiosity in the chronicles of beer. Every servant also was owed the greater part of his wages, and thus kept up perforce an interest in the house... and this I am given to understand is not infrequently the way in which people live elegantly on nothing a year.

The personal result of this is that eventually Raggles is 'utterly ruined by the transaction, his children being flung on the streets, and himself driven into the Fleet Prison' which leads Thackeray into a paragraph of generalized moral indignation:

> I wonder how many families are driven into roguery and to ruin by great practitioners in Crawley's way? – how many great noblemen rob their petty tradesmen, condescend to swindle their poor retainers out of wretched little sums, and cheat for a few shillings? When we read that a nobleman has left for the Continent, or that another noble nobleman has an execution in his house – and that one or other owes six or seven millions, the defeat seems glorious even, and we respect the victim in the vastness of his ruin. But who pities a poor barber who can't get his money for powdering the footmen's heads; or a poor carpenter who has ruined himself by fixing up ornaments and pavilions for my ladies' *déjeuner*; or the poor devil of a tailor whom the steward patronizes, and who has pledged all he is worth and more, to get the liveries ready, which my lord has done him the honour to bespeak? When the great house tumbles down, these miserable wretches fall under it unnoticed: as they say in the old legends, before a man goes to the devil himself, he sends plenty of other souls thither.

After this, the subject is abandoned and the chapter continues with Becky's 'pursuit of fashion under difficulties' – her triumphs in male society and her snubs by the ladies – her acquisition of a companion as a weapon in her counter-attack, the partial reconciliation of Rawdon and Sir Pitt, the savage description of Lord Steyne at one of Becky's evening parties, the differing relations of Rawdon and Becky with their son and, finally, the meeting between little Rawdon and the child of George Osborne.

The heart of the problem lies clearly in this moralizing paragraph, which raises tricky problems of response and judgement in relation to the question of narrative stance and, above all, the novel's treatment of time. The narrative runs 'I wonder how many families are driven to roguery and to ruin by great practitioners in Crawley's way?' 'Are' not 'were'; in other words, the moral comment seems intended to bear some relation to the time at which the book is being written. The novel's action moves from 1813 to 1830 and in addition to its period detail it contains, according to J. I. M. Stewart, 'topical asides relevant to the 1840s'[16]. That this is likely is indicated by the novel's opening phrase, 'While the present century was in its teens' (1), which suggests that we shall be looking at the recent past from the standpoint of the present. But the implications of this raise many problems. The Victorian novelists' habit of setting their work at some point earlier than the act of composition is so well established as to have the status of a convention, one which it is difficult for the modern reader to appreciate fully, like the use of boy actors in Elizabethan times. From our standpoint it is hard to grasp in what sense *Little Dorrit*, say, was not a contemporary work for its first readers. On the other hand, unless a writer draws special attention to time we can be fairly safe in assuming that the past setting is essentially a matter of convenience and that the work is, to all intents and purposes, contemporary. No one is bothered, surely, or even aware (unless notes draw attention to it) of the anachronism of the Spanish refugees in *Bleak House*.[17] No double vision is required here; we can feel confident that Dickens's later novels are imaginative statements about the nature of Victorian society as he saw it. This is obviously not the case with *Vanity Fair* where time, and perhaps especially the movement backwards and forwards in time, is of central importance.

The relation of this to social criticism is that it is unmistakably evident that our paragraph deals, at the very least, with the reprehensible social behaviour of individuals: 'When we read that a nobleman has left for the Continent...and...owes six or seven millions, the defeat seems glorious even...But who pities a poor barber....' And the whole weight of the book is to suggest that this is typical of *Vanity Fair*, to an extent that implicates society as a whole: 'When the great house tumbles down, these miserable wretches fall under it unnoticed: as they say in the old legends, before a man goes to the devil himself, he sends plenty of other souls thither.' Clearly, then, the passage is critical of Regency society, but if this were all, the degree of moral indignation seems excessive, especially if we remember that as a man of his time Thackeray could hardly avoid taking a critical stance towards his own period. The evidence suggests that the Hungry Forties in which he was writing made indifference to social evils a difficult matter for the intelligent and sensitive. And this relates to the grammar of the passage: '...how many families *are...*' A connection must be intended between the evils of the past and present. If, then, the paragraph does represent social criticism of the England of 1847, what are we to say about it? Criticism of the worship of money is an old subject in English, to say nothing of European, literature. It exists in the Chaucer of 'The Pardoner's Tale', in the line of bourgeois comedy begun by Ben Jonson, in the eighteenth-century novel. The initiation and development of a literary tradition which relates to ethical behaviour involves a degree of generalization, despite the insistent particularity of poems, plays and novels. This, in its turn, demands the creation of representative types to bear the weight of general commentary. The miser figure comes to mind and suggests that, in the beginning, such generalized figures embody human vices in a markedly unspecialist manner. As the organization of human life that we call society becomes increasingly complex, however, this weight of generalization shifts from broadly allegorical types to figures with a specialized economic function. At a certain point in history, the money-lender and the merchant may have to carry the burden; at a later period, the speculator and the industrialist. (For the twentieth century, the salesman has been a resonant figure.) The moment at which these changes take place is never precise, but they nonetheless represent important shifts of which great writers are aware. One of the most elaborate defences of *Vanity Fair* centres on its 'pattern of juxtaposition'[18] and it is wonderfully characteristic of Thackeray that the two fathers who figure prominently in the novel stand on either side of this historical watershed.

Sedley and Osborne are, of course, markedly different in character, but hard to discriminate in terms of economic function. Osborne is firmly presented as a British merchant of the old school, crude and overbearing, proud of his position – '"The British merchant's son shan't want, sir."'(13) – and yet grovellingly eager to be associated with the aristocracy: whenever 'he met a great man...my-lorded him as only a free-born Briton can do.' (13). This is how the occupier of a '"proud position...in the tallow trade and City of London"' (13) presents an idealized version of his life and family in an effort to impress the mulatto heiress, Miss Swartz:

'You won't find...that splendour and rank to which you are accustomed at the West End, my dear Miss, at our humble mansion in Russell Square. My daughters are plain, disinterested girls, but their hearts are in the right place, and they've conceived an attachment for you which does them honour – I say, which does them honour. I'm a plain, simple, humble British merchant – an honest one, as my respected friends Hulker & Bullock will vouch, who were the correspondents of your late lamented father. You'll find us a united, simple, happy, and I think I may say respected family – a plain table, a plain people, but a warm welcome, my dear Miss Rhoda – Rhoda, let me say, for my heart warms to you, it does really. I'm a frank man, and I like you. A glass of champagne! Hicks, champagne to Miss Swartz.' (21)

Sedley lacks Osborne's moral brutality, but betrays a sufficiently similar insensitivity in his treatment of his son, Jos, and in his enjoyment of Becky's tortures in eating curry followed by a chili (although neither, of course, are especially misplaced targets for his barbs): 'Mr Sedley burst out laughing (he was a coarse man, from the Stock Exchange, where they love all sorts of practical jokes).' (3). On his first appearance in *Vanity Fair*, Sedley enters 'rattling his seals like a true British merchant' (3), but the fact is that we are dealing with 'John Sedley, Esquire, of Russell Square, and the Stock Exchange.' (4). What difference, if any, does it make to the book that he is a stock-broker? At this point, we must consider one of the novel's most persistent dichotomies, what might be called its Regency-Victorian duality, the tension between its setting and the period when it was written. The word 'stock-broker' was coined in 1706 and the activity was encouraged by the 'financial revolution... the product of the unprecedented needs for borrowing money which arose after 1688, when William committed England to major wars against France.'[19] A more extreme form of this situation existed as a result of the Napoleonic Wars and so Thackeray's decision to make Sedley a stock-broker is part of his careful recreation of the Regency atmosphere. Perhaps the best example of this in strictly economic terms is the description of old Sir Pitt's speculative activities:

He speculated in every possible way; he worked mines, bought canal-shares; horsed coaches; took government contracts, and was the busiest man and magistrate of his county. As he would not pay honest agents at his granite quarry, he had the satisfaction of finding that four overseers ran away, and took fortunes with them to America. For want of proper precautions, his coal-mines filled with water: the government

flung his contract of damaged beef upon his hands; and for his
coach-horses, every mail proprietor in the kingdom knew that he lost
more horses than any man in the country, from underfeeding and buying
cheap. (9)

Historians have shown that the notion of a total split between the
aristocracy and entrepreneurial activity in the eighteenth and
nineteenth centuries is quite false.[20] Again from the Regency
perspective, the similarities between Osborne and Sedley are not
perhaps surprising. The Stock Exchange as such only emerged as
late as 1773, out of the coffee-house world in which earlier
eighteenth-century financial transactions took place. And although
both men have achieved the separation between home and place of
business characteristic of modern enterprise, they retain elements of
an earlier world which have quite credibly lasted into their own
time. After his economic collapse, John Sedley attempts rehabili-
tation as a merchant, in wine and coal, while Osborne's invitation to
his son through Dobbin for a reconciliation is expressed in terms
which reject the new dichotomy between home and business:
"'Come along, and dine in Russell Square today: both of you. The
old shop, the old hour.'" (24). The underlying sentimentality of the
brutal old cynic is wonderfully caught in this appeal through earlier
forms of living. Again, his anger at the presence of Amelia in his
house is interpreted by Miss Wirt, the governess, as a sign that "'the
funds are falling'" (13), precisely the form in which Sedley's downfall
is recorded: 'in the month of March, Anno Domini 1815, Napoleon
landed at Cannes, and Louis XVIII fled, and all Europe was in
alarm, and the funds fell, and old John Sedley was ruined.' (18).

In other words, Thackeray seems to draw no particular distinction
between his merchant and stock-broker, either personally or in
terms of economic activity:

All his speculations had of late gone wrong with the luckless old
gentleman [Sedley]. Ventures had failed; merchants had broken; funds
had risen when he calculated they would fall. What need to particularize?
If success is rare and slow, everybody knows how quick and easy ruin is.
Old Sedley had kept his own sad counsel. Everything seemed to go on as
usual in the quiet, opulent house; the good-natured mistress pursuing,
quite unsuspiciously, her bustling idleness, and daily easy avocations; the
daughter absorbed still in one selfish, tender thought, quite regardless of
all the world besides, when that final crash came, under which the worthy
family fell. (18)

From the Regency perspective, there is nothing particularly wrong with this. Industrial and financial capitalism were, of course, well established by the turn of the century, but general recognition of such changes is partly a process of absorption over a fairly lengthy period. And so, if *Vanity Fair* is mainly a reconstruction of early nineteenth-century society, Thackeray's fusion of merchant and stock-broker is quite valid. But by 1848 their creation as distinctive literary types was a real possibility. By then, the socially aware novelist could see that the merchant was beginning to decline as a representative of rising social and economic groups; the industrialist and speculator were the men of the moment and, even more, of the future. Such historical complexities demand careful treatment. 1848 is the year of *Dombey and Son* as well as *Vanity Fair* and although Dickens is often credited with a powerful imaginative presentation of Victorian society, his protagonist is also a merchant. Dickens might seem even more at fault as a social observer if we accept Kathleen Tillotson's view that *Dombey* is the first of Dickens's novels 'in which a pervasive uneasiness about contemporary society takes the place of an intermittent concern with specific social wrongs' and that his use of the railways underlines the 'contemporary intention of the novel and its offered social commentary.'[21] Professor Ray's comparison between Dickens and Thackeray on this point is very much to the former's disadvantage: 'To compare him [Osborne] with a similar personage, Mr Dombey . . . is to see how greatly Thackeray profited by his position as an insider in portraying upper-middle-class character.'[22] Although this refers specifically to Osborne, his view (if accepted) would obviously apply also to old Sedley. There is undoubtedly great psychological penetration in Thackeray's portrait of Osborne (much less in Sedley) but the treatment of his representative role lacks originality. Osborne's palpable crudities, his brutal outspokenness and roughness of manner are part of an eighteenth-century, or even earlier literary tradition, and might be related to the 'thingness' of his world, his economic dealings in stuff of different kinds, his sense of money and power as almost tangible counters to be grasped in the selfish manoeuvring of his own game. A similar externality is observable, much later, in the Melmotte of Trollope's *The Way We Live Now*. Both possess an element of debased heartiness, a physical grossness, quite absent from Mr Dombey's chilly reserve, the almost frozen immobility which looks forward to the masterly presentation of spiritual paralysis in the great financial manipulator of Dickens's *Little Dorrit*, Mr Merdle. Merdle's physical intangibility (his digestive processes are significantly impaired) relates to the fact that his vast financial empire rests on nothing more solid than paper. The modernity of the conception is evident and, compared with its symbolic and psychological richness, Mr Osborne can only appear as a somewhat flat creation from an earlier world. In short, from the perspective of 1848, Thackeray assimilates his merchant/stock-broker figures and displays little grasp of the economic realities of the period in which he is writing.

These points may clarify the problems of 'How to live Well on Nothing a Year' with its troublesome 'how many families are driven to roguery and to ruin by great practitioners in Crawley's way?' (37). This satire is of little representative significance with regard to the conditions of mid-Victorian life. Attacks on the aristocracy for ruining tradesmen by running up bills which they have no intention of paying is a traditional form of social criticism, found in Restoration Comedy, Swift and the novels of Fielding. Such criticism belongs to a pre-industrial society in which the behaviour of the aristocracy is all-important. By Thackeray's time it is shadow boxing because it fails to mirror any important social reality. No doubt aristocrats were still ruining tradesmen in 1848, but the historical centre of the credit system had shifted to the manipulations of high finance whose defectors could ruin thousands because of the links binding individuals to institutions in a complex modern society. Thackeray's failure to grasp this aspect of his world suggests that his turning to the past for his subject matter, which intensifies as his career proceeds, relates to a deep unease in the face of the complex problems of his contemporary society. This unease is also evident in a persistent ambiguity in Thackeray's use of the concept of society itself. Too often, society in the interesting imaginative and intellectual sense dwindles into 'high society', the tiny world of '"the best"' (51) which sometimes seems to exert as strong a fascination over the narrator as he continuously asserts that it does over us, his readers. This social élite is presented at one point by way of a list of guests reminiscent of those attending Gatsby's parties, although its Victorian knock-about lacks Fitzgerald's wit:

'Yesterday, Colonel and Mrs Crawley entertained a select party at dinner at their house in Mayfair. Their Excellencies the Prince and Princess of Peterwaradin, H.E. Papoosh Pasha, the Turkish Ambassador (attended by Kibob Bey, dragoman of the mission), the Marquis of Steyne, Earl of Southdown, Sir Pitt and Lady Jane Crawley, Mr Wagg, etc. After dinner Mrs Crawley had an assembly, which was attended by the Duchess

(Dowager) of Stilton, Duc de la Gruyère, Marchioness of Cheshire, Marchese Alessandro Strachinor, Comte de Brie, Baron Schapzuger, Chevalier Tosti, Countess of Slingstone, and Lady F. Macadam, Major-General and Lady G. Macbeth, and (2) Miss Macbeths; Viscount Paddington, Sir Horace Fogey, Hon. Sands Bedwin, Bobbahy Bahawder,' and an etc., which the reader may fill at his pleasure through a dozen close lines of small type. (51)

These figures make an instructive contrast with Bar, Bishop, and the rest, of *Little Dorrit*. Dickens's treatment leaves no doubt as to his attitude towards these satirical personifications. They are accurately placed by his continuously ironic narrative tone. But there is fascination as well as disgust in *Vanity Fair*, the sense that Thackeray himself (and not just his juggling narrator) half desires to be part of this world. This is an area of critical disagreement, although even Barbara Hardy, who sees Thackeray as fiercely radical in his social criticism, is forced to an admission on the point:

> Thackeray writes against the great world as one who knows its excesses and ennuis from the inside, but also, from time to time, as one who likes to distinguish *la belle societé* from the smaller world, where the company is not so good and the claret, food and service decidedly inferior. [23]

The nub of the problem is, of course, the extent of that 'from time to time.' Professor Ray questions even Thackeray's inside knowledge of high society, at least as far as *Vanity Fair* is concerned: 'Conceivably he succeeded so incomparably well in conveying the charms of high life in this novel because he was not yet familiar with it at first hand.'[24] Ray suggests, too, a Gatsbian complexity in Thackeray's portrayal of this world: 'In *Vanity Fair* Thackeray...contrives both to display the glamour of fashionable life within its own frame and to suggest the doubts which occur to the thoughtful onlooker once fashionable life is viewed in a larger context.'[25] But he also provides evidence for what I would see ultimately as Thackeray's compromised position on this issue. For Ray, Thackeray's ambiguity about high life is an important ingredient of the novel's success with the public:

> The resulting picture of high society was precisely what the intelligent Victorian reader desired. He still had, in Gladstone's phrase, 'a sneaking kindness for a lord'; but he had lost his assurance in the essential rightness of the aristocratic system. Thackeray satisfied both his taste and his conscience. [26]

Again, one senses something of Thackeray's own glee in the pleasure taken in the social fruits of his achievement by G. M., a possible original of old Miss Crawley: 'Indeed the success of *Vanity Fair* enchanted her, not least because it took Thackeray into the best society. "I tell G. M. of the Lords I meet," he wrote to his mother; "it delights the old lady hugely."'[27] The decorative flourishes of the opening of Chapter 7, 'Crawley of Queen's Crawley' are relevant here, and analogous to the treatment of the Steyne family in the Gaunt House chapter. Thackeray's attitude to this material may be ambiguous, but we hardly need him to criticise it for us; its imperfections are all too evident, especially when they remain unsupported by the fictionalized analysis so characteristic of Dicken's great social novels.

This is an aspect of the book in which Thackeray indulges his digressive tendencies to the full, as with the 'few words' he insists 'ought to be said regarding' Lady Southdown, a series of pages which ends with the following:

> Oh, my dear brethren and fellow-sojourners in Vanity Fair, which among you does not know and suffer under such benevolent despots? It is in vain you say to them, 'Dear Madam, I took Podgers' specific at your orders last year, and believe in it. Why, why am I to recant and accept Rodgers' articles now?' There is no help for it; the faithful proselytizer, if she cannot convince by argument, bursts into tears, and the recusant finds himself, at the end of the contest, taking down the bolus, and saying 'Well, well, Rodgers' be it.' (33)

I shall deal later with the use of 'Vanity Fair' epitomized by this passage, but is not the answer to the narrative's question: 'Perhaps, yes, maybe?' Lady Southdown is too particularized, and uninterest-ing, a case to evoke the assent commanded by George Eliot's novelistic generalizations, although Professor Ray is willing to accept the relevance of the passage where Lady Southdown forces Becky to swallow her filthy medicine: 'In *Vanity Fair* this sort of unforced comic detail is always at Thackeray's command...yet...what he relates is always directly pertinent to his story.'[28] This seems a fairly desperate claim for organic unity or, put another way, for a typicality which would lift such characters above the level of personal trivia. Even Professor Fleishman's admiration for *Vanity Fair* is tempered by his admission that, finally, 'the historical and the universal...remain distinct from each other.'[29] The dichotomy results from these figures inhabiting a world which is richly enough detailed in its surface, but which lacks a context which is either historical or social in a meaningful sense. The equivalent characters in Dickens – the Tite Barnacles. the Eugene Wrayburns and Mortimer Lightwoods – are understandable both in their personal lives and, crucially, in the social context of which they are imaginatively a part. It is in his handling of the novel's social context above all that we feel Thackeray's uneasiness, a lack of grip which causes the book to slide into confusion and lapse into *longueurs*. These weaknesses are attributable to what J. I. M. Stewart sees as one of the novel's strengths, the fact that 'the predominant feel of the book is one of brilliantly resourceful improvisation.'[30] Such praise demands reflection, particularly in relation to the indissolubility of form and content which is central to my argument. If a novel is being improvised, however brilliantly, what is being improvised in the end is a view of human life and not merely form in some limited sense. And the question arises, whether improvisation is nourishing enough to sustain a large-scale work of art. What, to be precise, is the quality of the vision of human society with which we are presented in *Vanity Fair*? This is, surely, an admissible question to raise about the book. It may not possess a hero and the stress may fall continually on the mildness of the tune being piped: 'we are only discoursing at present about a stock-broker's family in Russell Square, who are taking walks, or luncheon, or dinner, or talking and making love as people do in common life.' (6) But the novel's ambition is panoramic, even hugely so, and it seeks to create, in the very act of unfolding its story to us, a sense of lives being lived in relation to social forces. On occasion, we see these private lives juxtaposed with the largest historical events:

> Our surprised story now finds itself for a moment among very famous events and personages, and hanging on to the skirts of history. When the eagles of Napoleon Bonaparte, the Corsican upstart, were flying from Provence, where they perched after a brief sojourn in Elba, and from steeple to steeple until they reached the towers of Notre Dame, I wonder whether the Imperial birds had any eye for a little corner of the parish of Bloomsbury, London, which you might have thought so quiet, that even the whirring and flapping of those mighty wings would pass unobserved there?...Yes; Napoleon is flinging his last stake, and poor little Emmy Sedley's happiness forms, somehow, part of it. (18)

Two qualities seem necessary to the successful achievement of this kind of novelistic interest: breadth of scope, the ability to deploy a great range and variety of detail; and coherence, the power to fuse disparate elements into a unified perspective. Thackeray's relative success and failure here may be gauged by the examination of a

single important strand in the novel, his use of the phrase 'Vanity
Fair' itself, which is singled out by Geoffrey Tillotson as one of
Thackeray's dominant images.[31]

I propose to ignore the phrase's cumulative meaning in its descent
from Bunyan and concentrate on it as a conceptual term. This has its
dangers, especially in demanding a higher degree of abstract
coherence than should be asked of a work of art: who would care to
endorse the precise wording of Grieg's charge that Thackeray
'lacked...a stable and undeviating mind?'[32] On the other hand,
works of art are products of the imagination; that is, structures which
combine emotion *and* intelligence. Thinking and feeling are just as
important to the reader's response as they are to the writer's act of
creation. And this is especially true in considering the novelist's
vision of society. The writer who undertakes a fictional view of
society must be presumed to aspire to some degree of coherence, if
only for the duration of any specific work, the coherence we mean
when we talk, following Coleridge, of the 'world' of a Shakespeare
play, that creation of 'a local habitation and a name' which possesses
its own patterns of the possible forms of human behaviour and its
own consistent atmosphere. It is, of course, of the essence of
Shakespeare's genius that he should be able to create worlds of such
bewildering diversity, from the somewhat chilly sunshine of *As You
Like It* through the moral anarchy of *Troilus and Cressida* to the
complex acceptance of *The Tempest*. But in each case we are drawn
into an experience which, at least while we read or watch, impresses
us as an image of the real world, an image which has, in the words of
Middlemarch, 'that distinctness which is no longer reflection but
feeling – an idea wrought back to the directness of sense, like the
solidity of objects.'[33] Even a novelist as great as Dickens fails to
achieve the creation of this series of self-contained and radically
dissimilar worlds. Rather, his mature work might be seen as
variations on a continuous theme, the exposure of his relationship
with Victorian society. But individually his greatest novels possess
this quality in microcosm. *Little Dorrit* is not an attempt to deal with
an *aspect* of Victorian civilization, but the creation of a fictional
object that can stand, however obliquely, for a moment in Dickens's
response to that civilization as a whole. And although his vision is
embodied in appropriately novelistic terms, in symbolism and
imagery for example, this represents a richly intelligent as well as
emotional reaction to the facts of Victorian life as Dickens saw them.
It is clear that Dickens has a conception of his society, and the lives

belonging to it, which forms an active soil for the growth of symbols such as the prisons of *Little Dorrit* and the dust-heaps of *Our Mutual Friend*. The following pages will try to discover if such a conceptual unity is at work in *Vanity Fair*.

The first mention of the phrase comes as early as the opening, 'Before the Curtain': 'Yes, this is VANITY FAIR: not a moral place certainly; nor a merry one, though very noisy,' a place of which 'the general impression is one more melancholy than mirthful,' from which one returns home in a 'sober, contemplative, not uncharitable frame of mind.' Vanity Fair, is, then, a 'very vain, wicked, foolish place, full of all sorts of humbugs and falsenesses and pretentions' (8) and when we couple that with 'this Vanity Fair of ours' (21) it seems fairly clear that what we are dealing with is an image of the world, of human life in the widest sense. But as we would expect from any serious nineteenth-century novel, Thackeray is not simply spreading before us a slice of raw human experience, of life unmediated by vision. This is a fictional image of reality, not the reality of Virginia Woolf's 'air of probability embalming the whole so impeccably that if all his [the realistic novelist's] figures were to come to life they would find themselves dressed down to the last button of the coats in the fashion of the hour.'[34] As such, it possesses its own system of internal laws which are the concrete expression of Thackeray's reading of existence. One of these is the suggestion that it is part of the nature of this world to exert a deterministic influence over its inhabitants, as in a passage concerning Sir Pitt's second marriage to the daughter of an ironmonger who should have married a young man of her own class:

> O Vanity Fair – Vanity Fair! This might have been, but for you, a cheery lass: Peter Butt and Rose a happy man and wife, in a snug farm, with a hearty family; and an honest portion of pleasure, cares, hopes, and struggles: but a title and a coach and four are toys more precious than happiness in Vanity Fair: and if Harry the Eighth or Bluebeard were alive now, and wanted a tenth wife, do you suppose he could not get the prettiest girl that shall be presented this season. (9)

'But for you' suggests strongly that the values of Vanity Fair are so powerful that they constitute a system against which the individual is relatively helpless. In keeping with this strand of determinism there are several passages which generate a feeling of the inevitable decay of love and happiness; for example, on the fact that in Vanity Fair 'there are no better satires than letters':

> Take a bundle of your dear friend's of ten years back – your dear friend

whom you hate now. Look at a file of your sister's! how you clung to each
other till you quarrelled about the twenty pound legacy! Get down
the round-hand scrawls of your son who has half broken your heart with
selfish undutifulness since; or a parcel of your own, breathing endless
ardour and love eternal, which were sent back by your mistress when she
married the Nabob – your mistress for whom you now care no more than
for Queen Elizabeth. Vows, love, promises, confidences, gratitude, how
queerly they read after a while. (19)

Precisely the same is true of portraits: 'Some few score of years
afterwards, when all the parties represented are grown old, what
bitter satire there is in those flaunting childish family portraits, with
their farce of sentiment and smiling lies, and innocence so
self-conscious and self-satisfied' (24). There is little doubt that the
handling of time is one of *Vanity Fair*'s triumphs, especially in its
stress on the movement from youth to age with its attendant decay of
beauty and energy (the corresponding cycle, towards new life, is felt
much less strongly). Another of the 'laws' of the Thackerayan
universe is discernible here, that the passage of time brings, in its
very nature, sorrow, regret and a withering of spontaneous impulse.

And so we have our impression that Vanity Fair is an image of the
world coloured by the dark tones of Thackeray's individual vision, a
world in which greed creates hatred among brothers (11), in which
cheating is almost an accepted part of gambling (17), and in which
mothers and daughters regularly collaborate in the degrading
manoeuvres of the marriage market (15). All of this might suggest a
work which is sombre to the point of depression, but this would be
false to our experience of reading moment-by-moment. Thackeray
himself said that his 'object... is to indicate, *in cheerful terms*, that we
are for the most part abhominably foolish and selfish people'[35] and he
succeeds in creating a form which often works against the negative
aspects of the content, above all in the verbal brilliance of his style
and the witty manipulation of narrative, qualities central enough to
Thackeray's vision to be worth extended examination:

What a dignity it gives an old lady, that balance at the banker's! How
tenderly we look at her faults if she is a relative (and may every reader
have a score of such), what a kind good-natured old creature we find her!
How the junior partner of Hobbs and Dobbs leads her smiling to the
carriage with the lozenge upon it, and the fat wheezy coachman! How,
when she comes to pay us a visit, we generally find an opportunity to let
our friends know her station in the world! We say (and with perfect truth)
I wish I had Miss MacWhirter's signature to a cheque for five thousand

pounds. She wouldn't miss it, says your wife. She is my aunt, say you, in an
easy careless way, when your friend asks if Miss MacWhirter is any
relative. Your wife is perpetually sending her little testimonies of
affection, your little girls work endless worsted baskets, cushions, and
footstools for her. What a good fire there is in her room when she comes
to pay you a visit, although your wife laces her stays without one! The
house during her stay assumes a festive, neat, warm, jovial, snug
appearance not visible at other seasons. You yourself, dear sir, forget to go
to sleep after dinner, and find yourself all of a sudden (although you
invariably lose) very fond of a rubber. What good dinners you have –
game every day, Malmsey–Madeira, and no end of fish from London.
Even the servants in the kitchen share in the general prosperity; and,
somehow, during the stay of Miss MacWhirter's fat coachman, the beer is
grown much stronger, and the consumption of tea and sugar in the
nursery (where her maid takes her meals) is not regarded in the least. Is it
so, or is it not so? I appeal to the middle classes. Ah, gracious powers! I
wish you would send me an old aunt – a maiden aunt – an aunt with a
lozenge on her carriage, and a front of light coffee-coloured hair – how
my children should work workbags for her, and my Julia and I would
make her comfortable! Sweet – sweet vision! Foolish – foolish dream! (9)

These lines constitute a striking example of some of the best aspects
of *Vanity Fair*; especially noteworthy is the digressive nature
of the unit taken as a whole. The conclusion of the previous
paragraph runs: 'Miss Crawley was, in consequence, an object of
great respect when she came to Queen's Crawley, for she had a
balance at her banker's which would have made her beloved
anywhere.' It is delightful to see how Thackeray takes up the hint of
his own little nugget of factual information to launch into an
encomium on the 'dignity' that a 'balance at the banker's' gives to an
'old lady'. Recent discussion of Victorian narrative conventions has
shown that, far from being an artistic weakness, a device such as
direct address may have a complex function in drawing readers into
a sense of communal experience.[36] Thackeray fuses a comic
awareness of this possibility with the time-honoured technique of
satirical involvement in his parenthetical 'and may every reader have
a score of such'. With amazing spareness, he builds the sense of a tiny
segment of comic life: we move swiftly from the 'junior partner of
Hobbs and Dobbs' to a 'she' who rapidly becomes 'Miss
MacWhirter' and then to the cause of all this agitation, the old lady's
'signature to a cheque for five thousand pounds.' Thackeray avoids
interruption in the narrative's easy flow by omitting quotation marks
from the airy statements of husband and wife. A flurry of detail

follows, pointed by the 'You yourself, dear sir', climaxed by the clinching generalization: 'Is it so, or is it not so? I appeal to the middle classes.' And the passage ends with a marvellously ridiculous series of 'personal' fragments: 'an old aunt...with...a front of light coffee-coloured hair...how...my Julia and I would make her comfortable! Sweet – sweet vision! Foolish – foolish dream!' The irony here is manifold, of course; directed at the narrator himself, at us the readers, in other words at Vanity Fair. Verbally the satire is aimed at the Fair's very means of communication, its language. The ruthless pursuit of personal gain is parodied in the commonplaces of Victorian sentimentality ('sweet vision...foolish dream'); the rubbishy language of the novelettes Thackeray knew so well from his days as a parodist is also the sign of the hypocrisy and corruption of the novel's created world. Actual social observation and artistic embodiment are brought together in a satisfying whole.

On many pages of this exhilarating novel, then, we see a unifying element at work – 'Vanity Fair' as an image of the real world – binding together the digressions which are of the essence of Thackeray's 'brilliant improvisation'. But when we consider the full range of the ways in which the phrase is used, we may have doubts about Thackeray's ability to endow it with conceptual coherence, especially if we notice two major deviations from the use I have been trying to bring out. In a passage on Mr Sedley's ruin we find: 'And so it is that the French Emperor comes in to perform a part in this domestic comedy of Vanity Fair which we are now playing, and which would never have been enacted without the intervention of this august mute personage.' (18) It would be foolish to make too much of a brief passage, but it seems unfortunate that Thackeray should draw a distinction between Vanity Fair and the world of public events. One aspect of Thackeray's purpose, of course, is to emphasise that this is a novel without a hero: a work that deals with the real lives of real people. But part of the book's force lies in the ways in which it attempts to demonstrate a connection between private life and the great impersonal forces of history. John Sedley is, after all, ruined by large-scale economic trends and, in what is perhaps the novel's most memorably dramatic moment, George Osborne's death, the 'bullet through his heart' (32) has been fired in one of the momentous battles of history, not a private duel. We sense here a certain lack of self-awareness in Thackeray despite all his brilliance and wit. There are moments in *Vanity Fair* which embody George Eliot's insight that there is no life 'that is not greatly determined by what lies outside it.'[37] But they are not developed with the consistency to convince one that Thackeray has fully grasped it as an imaginative fact.

A similarly damaging disjunction is suggested by the language of the following:

> But, without preaching, the truth may surely be borne in mind, that the bustle, and triumph, and laughter, and gaiety which Vanity Fair exhibits in public, do not always pursue the performer into private life...O brother wearers of motley! Are there not moments when one grows sick of grinning and tumbling, and the jingling of cap and bells. This, dear friends and companions, is my amiable object – to walk with you through the Fair, to examine the shops and the shows there; and that we should all come home after the flare, and the noise, and the gaiety, and be perfectly miserable in private. (19)

The essence of the question here is one of metaphor. The richness of Dickens's metaphorical system in, say, *Little Dorrit* is that it applies over the novel's whole range. No matter which character we are dealing with, no matter if the subject be public or private, the prison metaphor has a total appropriateness. As a series of physical locations, as an embodiment of the inner state of individuals, as an image of society and, ultimately, of human life itself (the 'bars of the prison of this lower world') the metaphor is equal to all the demands that are made on it. In contrast, although Thackeray's metaphor has its own kind of vividness, an impression that stems partly from its traditional resonance, it works against that feeling of the Fair as an image of the whole of human life that I began with.

The imaginative suggestion of this passage is that Vanity Fair is a something out there, a something into which we go but out of which we return into the privacy of private life ('we should all come home...and be perfectly miserable in private'). And this contradicts a passage just dealt with where private life is the essential Vanity Fair. The distinction is clear at a moment when Amelia seeks refuge in prayer from the early disappointments of her marriage, the kind of passage where we feel Thackeray is hardly at his strongest: '...sought for consolation, where as yet, it must be owned, our little girl had but seldom looked for it.' This prompts a question: 'Have we a right to repeat or to overhear her prayers? These, brother, are secrets, and out of the domain of Vanity Fair, in which our story lies.' (26) The failure of nerve here is damaging. Of course, we feel relief that 'our little girl's' banalities are not inflicted on us, but the serious point is that such an area should be avoided altogether if it cannot be brought successfully within the range of the novel's framework. Thackeray fails here as both satirist and novelist, in an area of common ground between the two, in his inability to deal adequately with material that he himself has introduced. The creator of a fictional world must convince us that his world is total and complete. It does not matter that reason tells us that this image is, in fact, simply an extract from the multifariousness of experience. If our 'willing suspension of disbelief' is evoked, then a world will seem to be called into being before us. If Vanity Fair *is* an image of the world, then Amelia's prayers must form a part of it, along with all the other elements that Thackeray chooses to introduce into his novel. If there is a world of private life apart from the Fair, then the novel has no unifying element but a catch-all phrase that Thackeray can manipulate from moment to moment as the more limited exigencies of the work demand. In short, we are back with 'improvisation', although now perhaps of a less brilliant kind. Or, to put it another way, we are back with Thackerayan ambiguity. We might well remember that 'our little girl' was, on only the previous page, sitting 'indulging in her usual mood of selfish brooding.' (26)

One way, then, in which Vanity Fair loses conceptual coherence is in this move from being an image of human life in general to the suggestion that there are areas of experience which it fails to cover. But the phrase also moves in another direction, as is suggested in a passage on Sir Pitt:

> Vanity Fair – Vanity Fair! Here was a man, who could not spell, and
> did not care to read – who had the habits and the cunning of a boor,
> whose aim in life was pettifogging: who never had a taste, or emotion, or
> enjoyment, but what was sordid and foul; and yet he had rank, and
> honours, and power, somehow: and was a dignitary of the land, and a
> pillar of the state. He was high sheriff, and rode in a golden coach. Great
> ministers and statesmen courted him; and in Vanity Fair he had a higher
> place than the most brilliant genius or spotless virtue. (9)

This highlights a crucial dichotomy between realistic and non-realistic elements in *Vanity Fair*. In his own day Thackeray was famous for his apparent fidelity to the truths of normal human experience, an aspect of his work that appeared with all the greater clarity in comparison with the sometimes exaggerated tone of the writer he seemed to challenge, Dickens. (Perhaps the best known example of this is Charlotte Bronte's praise of Thackeray in the preface to *Jane Eyre* where she refers to him as the 'first social regenerator of the day.') English fiction is fortunate in possessing two contemporaries in Dickens and George Eliot who were capable of taking the symbolic and realistic modes to an extreme point of development but, to borrow Dr Leavis's threat about Joyce and Lawrence, to admire one is not to reject the other. What is striking is the relative consistency with which these novelists cleave to their vision of art and reality. We may feel that George Eliot strays a little unhappily from the path of her true genius in, say, the Raffles episodes of *Middlemarch*, but this is not a divergence that can weaken the book at its centre. And even in the most psychologically realistic of his novels, *Great Expectations*, Dickens does not depart from his essentially symbolic viewpoint. In the passage under discussion, however, Thackeray is positing a specifically social figure in a specific social context. In other words, we are in the realm of Bar and Bishop from *Little Dorrit* or the patriarchal Casby of *Our Mutual Friend*, figures who make no pretence at human complexity but who owe their sense of life to their emblematic relationship with a fictional world that is not a reflection of reality but a vision governed by laws that are essentially non-realistic. This is clarified by Roland Barthes when he writes of how nineteenth century novels construct an 'autarkic world which elaborates its own dimensions and limits, and organizes within these its own Time, its own Space, its population, its own set of objects and its myths.'[38] These worlds may be organized on either realistic or non-realistic lines, but it is essential to their artistic success that they should possess a central adherence to the mode in which their creators have chosen to work. When, to give another example, Thackeray writes the following of 'sweet, blooming, orange flowers' we feel more in the world of Lady Tippins than the realistic manoeuvring of Becky Sharp:

> The other day I saw Miss Trotter (that was), arrayed in them, trip into the travelling carriage at St George's, Hanover Square, and Lord Methuselah hobbled in after. With what an engaging modesty she pulled down the blinds of the chariot – the dear innocent! There were half the carriages of Vanity Fair at the wedding. (12)

And the sense of disjunction is heightened by the words that come immediately after the passage: 'This was not the sort of love that finished Amelia's education; and in the course of a year turned a good young girl into a good young woman – to be a good wife presently, when the happy time should come' An element of sheer unbelievability is involved here, an unbelievability forced on us by

Thackeray's own juxtaposition. What is to prevent Amelia from becoming another Miss Trotter if Vanity Fair is as powerful as we have been led to believe and if Amelia is a part of it, as in a sense she appears to be? The contrast between the total evil of Blandois and the total goodness of Little Dorrit is acceptable because they inhabit a poetic world in which symbolic opposition is the norm. Again, Dorothea and Rosamund (in *Middlemarch*) may ultimately be poles apart in terms of moral sensibility, but they co-exist in our imagination because they belong to a world where none is free from fault and none incapable of goodness. Miss Trotter and Amelia belong to different universes of discourse, to aspects of Vanity Fair that cannot, finally, be subsumed in a coherent vision. The vacuous generalizing of 'when the happy time should come' is utterly at odds with the moral atmosphere of large parts of the story.

One sign of an absence of full control over this side of the novel is Thackeray's tendency to trivialize it. A seriously revealing passage, and one crucial to my argument, occurs when Amelia is preparing for her son to live with his grandfather:

> So poor Amelia had been getting ready in silent misery for her son's departure, and had passed many and many a long solitary hour in making preparations for the end. George stood by his mother, watching her arrangements without the least concern. Tears had fallen into his boxes; passages had been scored in his favourite books; old toys, relics, treasures had been hoarded away from him, and packed with strange neatness and care – and of all these things the boy took no note. The child goes away smiling as the mother breaks her heart. By heavens it is pitiful, the bootless love of women for children in Vanity Fair. (50)

With this passage we leave behind all of the various forms that Vanity Fair has taken up to now: we are clearly not in the realms of social satire, domestic privacy or, even, Vanity Fair as an image of human life. This aspect of the relation of mothers to children is as timeless and universal as anything could well be, and the attempted localization of it within Vanity Fair serves to demonstrate that the phrase lacks unifying power for Thackeray himself. It has all the air of a happy idea, brilliantly improvised on occasion, but with none of the sustaining force of a fictional concept imaginatively worked out.

My suggestion is, then, that a social reading of a novel which invites such an approach can be a valid tool for aesthetic judgement. There is no question that *Vanity Fair* is in many ways a remarkable book, never more so than in the coruscation of Thackeray's wit, as in this passage concerning Becky's life in Paris in the aftermath of victory: 'But, as we have said, she was growing tired of this idle social life; opera-boxes and restaurateur-dinners palled upon her: nosegays could not be laid by as a provision for future years: and she could not live upon nicknacks, laced handkerchiefs, and kid gloves. She felt the frivolity of pleasure, and longed for more substantial benefits.' (36) Or there is the larger play of invention contained in, say, the amusing thirty-fourth chapter, 'James Crawley's Pipe is Put Out', where in James's attempt at an ingratiating visit to Miss Crawley we see the disastrous result of his father's advice: 'put him on the old woman, hey; and tell him to thrash Pitt if he says anything' (34); an attempt which ends in failure precisely because the inexperienced James '*had* in fact...done what he menaced to do. He had fought his cousin Pitt with the gloves.' (34) Such moments have the aptness suggested by improvisation at its best. But I have argued that the novel attempts an extended image of society which purports to reveal the corruptions engendered by materialism, power and snobbery. The danger of improvisation is that it will simply go on and on, not knowing when to stop, a weakness fatally linked to the digressive nature of Thackeray's imagination. This *can* work brilliantly, as one happy idea leads to another, but it is also the cause of the novel's collapse into a series of unresolved dichotomies: its Regency and Victorian elements, for example; the tension between Amelia and Becky as suspect heroine and lively villainess; Thackeray's revealing phrase 'Satire and Sentiment' (17) or, as we might feel tempted to substitute, Cynicism and Sentimentality. The Satire has wit, force, edge, but leaves out too much and in its eagerness to see only the darker side of human life eventually becomes wearisome. And Sentiment's power to move is too often weakened by a cloying emotionalism. Neither singly nor together are they strong enough to constitute an artistic vision that can sustain *Vanity Fair* thematically and stylistically. This weakness, despite the novel's many brilliancies, brings to a focus Thackeray's inability to unify his book at the personal or social level. The inconsistencies within his use of Vanity Fair are so pervasive as to weaken and distort the novel as an image of society.

Further Reading

For this and subsequent chapters bibliographical assistance will be found in:

Victorian Fiction: A Second Guide to Research by George H. Ford (New York, 1978).

A general work with a social dimension is:

The English Novel from Dickens to Lawrence by Raymond Williams (London, 1970).

The classic study of the historical novel from a Marxist standpoint is:

The Historical Novel by Georg Lukács (Penguin, 1976) translated by Hannah and Stanley Mitchell.

Two other interesting studies are:

The English Historical Novel: Walter Scott to Virginia Woolf by Avrom Fleishmann (London, 1971).

The Novelist as Historian by James C. Simons (The Hague, Paris, 1973).

For Scott himself see:

Scottish Literature and the Scottish People 1680-1830 by David Craig (London, 1961).

Scott and Society by Graham McMaster (Cambridge, 1982).

Scott and Scotland by Edwin Muir (London, 1936).

The Hero of the Waverley Novels by Alexander Welsh (Yale, 1963).

Some of the more important work on Thackeray is:

The Exposure of Luxury: Radical Themes in Thackeray by Barbara Hardy (London, 1972).

Thackeray: Prodigal Genius by John Carey (London, 1977).

Thackeray and the Form of Fiction by John Loofbourow (Princeton, 1964).

Thackeray the Novelist by Geoffrey Tillotson (London, 1954).

7

Dickens:
The Early Novels

A distinctively modern bias is revealed by the fact that 'scientific' is
so frequently coupled with the word 'discovery'. Scientific discovery
is the paradigm of intellectual enquiry for the twentieth century. But
it is worth remembering that what deserve to be called discoveries
occur in the world of literature also. Distinguished, and even great,
writers often work within conventions which they are content only
to modify, but others create shifts in the previously accepted patterns
of form and content that have to be called discoveries of expression
and subject-matter. Shakespeare, Wordsworth and T. S. Eliot
caused seismic disturbances of this order. Scholars may patiently
demonstrate that all three did not spring naked from the mind of
God: they trail their clouds of influence from, to be brief, Marlowe,
the pre-Romantics and Laforgue. But the fact remains that even
when read within these contexts they still seem irresistibly new.
Their lives and output embody Coleridge's distinction between
fancy and the imagination. Looked at closely, the work reveals traces
of the iron filings of already existing materials, but the magnet of
genius has arranged them in previously unknown patterns. In the
fourth number of *The Pickwick Papers,* the twenty-four-year-old
Dickens made a discovery of this order:

'My father, sir, wos a coachman. A widower he wos, and fat enough for
anything – uncommon fat, to be sure. His missus dies, and leaves him four
hundred pound. Down he goes to the Commons, to see the lawyer and
draw the blunt – wery smart – top boots on – nosegay in his button-hole
– broad-brimmed tile – green shawl – quite the gen'lm'n. Goes through
the archway, thinking how he should inwest the money – up comes the
touter, touches his hat – "Licence, sir, Licence?" – "What's that?" says my
father. – "Marriage licence," says the touter. – "Dash my veskit," says my
father, "I never thought o' that." – "I think you want one, sir," says the

touter. My father pulls up, and thinks a bit – "No," says he, "damme, I'm too old, b'sides I'm a many sizes too large," says he. – "Not a bit on it, sir," says the touter. – "Think not?" says my father. – "I'm sure not," says he; "we married a genl'm'n twice your size, last Monday." – "Did you, though," says my father. – "To be sure, we did," says the touter, "you're a babby to him – this way, sir – this way!" – and sure enough my father walks arter him, like a tame monkey behind a horgan, into a little back office, vere a feller sat among dirty papers and tin boxes, making believe he was busy. "Pray take a seat, vile I makes out the affidavit, sir," says the lawyer. "Thankee, sir," says my father, and down he sat, and stared with all his eyes, and his mouth vide open, at the names on the boxes. "What's your name, sir," says the lawyer. – "Tony Weller," says my father. – "Parish?" says the lawyer. – "Belle Savage," says my father; for he stopped there wen he drove up, and he know'd nothing about parishes, *he* didn't. – "And what's the lady's name?" says the lawyer. My father was struck all of a heap. "Blessed if I know," says he. – "Not know!" says the lawyer. – "No more nor you do," says my father, "can't I put that in arterwards?" – "Impossible!" says the lawyer. – "Wery well," says my father, after he'd thought a moment, "put down Mrs Clarke." – "What Clarke?" says the lawyer, dipping his pen in the ink. – "Susan Clarke, Markis o' Granby, Dorking," says my father; "she'll have me, if I ask, I des-say – I never said nothing to her, but she'll have me, I know." The licence was made out, and she *did* have him, and what's more she's got him now; and *I* never had any of the four hundred pound, worse luck. Beg your pardon, sir," said Sam, when he had concluded, 'but when I gets on this here grievance, I runs on like a new barrow vith the wheel greased.'(10)

Whatever literary antecedents for Sam Weller are dragged into the light of day, the pristine freshness of his first appearance in the novel remains undimmed. Suddenly, all the ingredients of Dickens's comic art erupt into the book: the liveliness of Sam's idiomatic speech ('"draw the blunt"'), the richness of detail ('"we married a genl'm'n twice your size, last Monday"'), the element of comic fantasy that remains rooted in a recognizable world and, above all, the dramatic vividness with which the whole episode is brought imaginatively alive. The vision of Mr Weller 'like a tame monkey behind a horgan' is perhaps the wildest flight and yet it is firmly linked to the life of which Sam is so rich a part.

That life is the idiosyncratic diversity of the streets of London and, in creating Sam Weller, Dickens discovered a subject matter that was to be central to his art for the rest of his career: the forms of life made possible, or inevitable, by the great modern city. In *The English Novel*, Raymond Williams argues against a simplistic dismissal of the Industrial Revolution as the destroyer of any possibility of a culture amongst the broad mass of the people. Professor Williams distinguishes between a folk culture that *was* destroyed and a popular culture that came into existence in the nineteenth century, a culture intimately bound up with the development of the metropolis:

> The central case we have to make is that Dickens could write a new kind of novel – fiction uniquely capable of realizing a new kind of reality – just because he shared with the new urban popular culture certain decisive experiences and responses. . . . He takes and transforms certain traditional methods . . . in his own way, into a dramatic method which is uniquely capable of expressing the experience of living in cities. [1]

Dickens's exuberantly comic version of these historical processes is everywhere present in *The Pickwick Papers,* but is intensified into its richest focus in Sam and Mr Weller, and the relationship between them. It is, of course, an almost unbelievable fusion of genius in the youthful Dickens which combines a purely artistic grasp of social forces with the celebration of a pre-industrial, pre-Victorian, even pre-lapsarian world. All the novel's best critics, from Chesterton to W. H. Auden, comment on its mythical freshness, that sense of an England inhabited by gods. Mr Weller functions as a genial minor deity of this sunlit universe, dispensing boozy wisdom and, ultimately and gloriously, kicks in the behind to Mr Stiggins, but his sheer solidity of person and character suggest the confidence of a being totally at one with his social world. Mr Weller can imagine no more splendid vocation than his own, but there is no question of Sam's following in his footsteps, or coachwheels. Sam, in fact, presents the clearest possible example of upward social mobility:

> 'I worn't always a boots, sir,' said Mr Weller, with a shake of the head. 'I wos a wagginer's boy, once.'
>   'When was that?' inquired Mr Pickwick.
>   'When I wos first pitched neck and crop into the world, to play at leap-frog with its troubles,' replied Sam. 'I wos a carrier's boy at startin': then a vagginer's, then a helper, then a boots. Now I'm a gen'l'm'n's servant. I shall be a gen'l'm'n myself one of these days, perhaps, with a pipe in my mouth, and a summer-house in the back garden. Who knows? *I* shouldn't be surprised, for one.'(16)

And Mr Weller has assisted this process by means of his son's '"eddication"' over which he took '"a good deal o' pains"' by letting him '"run in the streets when he was wery young, and shift for his-self. It's the only way to make a boy sharp, sir.'"(20).

Whatever the distance between Sam and his creator, they have some things in common. During the blacking-factory episode, the twelve-year-old Dickens ran in the streets and shifted for himself, and this early acquaintance with the raw life of his times was developed, as all who knew him testify, into a 'knowledge of London' which, like Sam's, was 'extensive and peculiar.' (20). There is no mystery, then, as to where Dickens developed his interest in, and knowledge of, the life of the streets – the mystery lies in the genius that grasped the wider social meaning of this interest and rendered it into inexhaustibly varied artistic forms. It was this interest, for example, which enabled Dickens to accomplish an anatomy of Lawyers' Clerks, themselves a sub-group of a whole of increasing importance in a London devoted to the law, commerce, finance and bureaucracy:

> Scattered about, in various holes and corners of the Temple, are certain dark and dirty chambers, in and out of which, all the morning in Vacation, and half the evening too in Term time, there may be seen constantly hurrying with bundles of papers under their arms, and protruding from their pockets, an almost uninterrupted succession of Lawyers' Clerks. There are several grades of Lawyers' Clerks. There is the Articled Clerk, who has paid a premium, and is an attorney in perspective, who runs a tailor's bill, receives invitations to parties, knows a family in Gower Street, and another in Tavistock Square: who goes out of town every Long Vacation to see his father, who keeps live horses innumerable; and who is, in short, the very aristocrat of clerks. There is the salaried clerk – out of door, or in door, as the case may be – who devotes the major part of his thirty shillings a week to his personal pleasure and adornment, repairs half-price to the Adelphi Theatre at least three times a week, dissipates majestically at the cider cellars afterwards, and is a dirty caricature of the fashion which expired six months ago. There is the middle-aged copying clerk, with a large family, who is always shabby, and often drunk. And there are the office lads in their first surtouts, who feel a befitting contempt for boys at day-schools: club as they go home at night, for saveloys and porter: and think there's nothing like 'life.' There are varieties of the genus, too numerous to recapitulate, but however numerous they may be, they are all to be seen, at certain regulated business hours, hurrying to and from the places we have just mentioned. (31).

In one of the many different senses of the word, this is surely an aspect of the city's culture and in exposing it for our delight and instruction, as well as that of his contemporaries, Dickens is stripping away some of the layers of anonymity supposedly so characteristic of metropolitan life. The dulled vision of the conventional observer is suddenly defamiliarized as these scurrying figures are rendered known and knowable. Dickens brings a similar vibrancy to the streets themselves; as in the description of Lant Street that begins Chapter 32:

> In this happy retreat are colonised a few clear-starchers, a sprinkling of journeymen bookbinders, one or two prison agents for the Insolvent Court, several small housekeepers who are employed in the Docks, a handful of mantua-makers, and a seasoning of jobbing tailors. The majority of the inhabitants either direct their energies to the letting of furnished apartments, or devote themselves to the healthful and invigorating pursuit of mangling. The chief features in the still life of the street are green shutters, lodging-bills, brass door-plates, and bell-handles; the principal specimens of animated nature, the pot-boy, the muffin youth, and the baked-potato man. The population is migratory, usually disappearing on the verge of quarter-day, and generally by night. His Majesty's revenues are seldom collected in this happy valley; the rents are dubious; and the water communication is very frequently cut off. (32).

This 'translation' of the apparently blank surface of city life is continued down to such tiny details of vulgar behaviour as that 'very graceful piece of pantomime . . . which was familiarly denominated "taking a grinder"' (31) and the '"over the left", [which] when performed by any number of ladies and gentlemen who are accustomed to act in unison, has a very graceful and airy effect; its expression is one of light and playful sarcasm.' (42). An extended example of Dickens's total grasp of the details of lower class life occurs in Chapter 46, the description of the day out to the Spaniards Tea Rooms by Mrs Bardell and her friends. The unmistakably ideological intention in all this is evident in the grimly triumphant note of the Preface to the Cheap Edition of *The Pickwick Papers* in 1847, on the question of serial publication: 'My friends told me it was a low, cheap form of publication, by which I should ruin all my rising hopes; and how right my friends turned out to be, everyone now knows.'

Part of the force of Dickens's genius stems from the unity of his life and work. One senses a disabling confusion of aims in Thackeray, for example, which crystallizes in his desire to be socially acceptable as well as a professional writer and which may partially account for his move into the artistic safety of historical reconstruction and pastiche after living dangerously with *Vanity Fair*. But Dickens's professionalism, his glorying in an economic dependence on the widest possible public, is all of a piece with his determination to give large sections of that public a place in literature previously denied them. Even now, one of the excitements of reading *The Pickwick Papers* is the spectacle of a great creative mind fumbling with its material and gradually coming to self-understanding as the work progresses. The oft-told tale of Dickens's writing of his first novel makes it quite clear, in fact, that he discovered how to write it as he went along. He did, of course, have plenty of material to help him with the task, including his by then immense experience of life as working boy, lawyer's clerk, journalist and brilliantly successful parliamentary reporter; his own early experiments in writing, such as *Sketches by Boz;* and his omnivorous reading in the eighteenth-century novel. But the discovery of an appropriate form for his vision of the social world was essentially self-generating. And this process of self-discovery can be seen as a paradigm of the argument of this book. Dickens moves rapidly towards mastery, from an initial uncertainty about his form and content, like a violently speeded-up version of the development of the English novel from its eighteenth-century beginnings. Added to this is the fact that his lifetime encompassed important changes in society, from his beginnings in a Regency world through the various phases of Victorianism. He thus provides a test case of a novelist who discovers artistic forms that embody a complex series of images of society.

What is the nature of the form that Dickens creates in the process of writing *The Pickwick Papers?* Critics display a fondness for one of two ploys in discussing the work. Some talk of ways in which it anticipates aspects of Dickens's later writing. Others, such as W. H. Auden in his perceptive essay, 'Dingley Dell and the Fleet,' advance theories about the novel's coherent thematic meaning; Auden's view in a nutshell, is that the novel's real theme is 'The Fall of Man.'[2] Neither approach is wholly satisfactory. The first plays down the novel's own intrinsic nature; the second imposes a unity that is false to one's experience of reading the book page by page. In short, both reveal an inability fully to get to grips with a work that is not susceptible to a reading in the general terms established by the classic modern theories of the novel, all of which are marked by some adherence to the idea of organic form; that is, an absence of elements in excess of those required for the work's inner aims. But literary history presents many correctives to the easy dismissal, as aesthetic failures, of poems and plays which lack this quality. *The Canterbury Tales*, *The Faerie Queene* and Marlowe's *Dr Faustus* are not organically unified, but this hardly suggests their relegation to the dustbin. It is necessary to make a distinction here between *Vanity Fair* and Dickens's early work. Thackeray's novel and *The Pickwick Papers* may both rely on improvisation, but my earlier discussion of *Vanity Fair* attempts to show that it fails ultimately because its inner logic is driving towards an organic unity which the novelist's improvisational skill cannot accomplish. *Pickwick* and *Nicholas Nickleby* remain frankly episodic and so can be evaluated by different criteria.

A work of literature may, then, be successful and still lack organic unity, but it must presumably have some principle of organization. A series of fragments, however vivid, cannot give substance to a novel, a play or a long poem. Perhaps episodic unity would be the best description of the structure of the works under consideration, although such a label gives rise to some difficult questions. Whether, for example, episodic has a unity different from organic unity; whether in episodic unity all the episodes have to possess the same kind of relationship to some overall aim; whether an episodic work has to have a theme, as opposed to a subject. If we accept the definition of theme as 'a thesis or doctrine which an imaginative work is designed to incorporate and make persuasive to the reader,'[3] then it is immediately apparent that *Pickwick* lacks one. But it does have a subject or, rather, a series of related subjects. One constant pattern is the discomfiture of the upper by the lower classes: street arabs cheeking elderly gents, cabbies arguing about fares, Eatanswill voters jostling their betters. In the broadest sense, though, the book's subject could be said to be the celebration of goodness, a generality rendered substantial by Dickens's increasingly cunning arrangement of his episodes as the novel develops. Following up this point may go some way towards answering the questions posed a moment ago, at least as far as one novel is concerned.

Sam and Mr Weller, for example, are not simply a major comic centre; they come to have a functional relationship to Mr Pickwick, as a corrective to his innocence. They are not brutally cynical, of course, but Sam especially introduces a note of hard-headed realism which balances Mr Pickwick's simplicity. This is a traditional aspect of the literary servant-master relationship, but one that Dickens revives with his own characteristic power, as in Sam's suspicions of Mr Pickwick's amorous activities: '"Rum feller, the hemperor," said

Mr Weller, as he walked slowly up the street. "Think o' his making up to that ere Mrs Bardell – vith a little boy, too! Always the vay vith these here old 'uns hows'ever, as is such steady goers to look at. I didn't think he'd ha' done it, though – I didn't think he'd ha' done it!" Moralising in this strain, Mr Samuel Weller bent his steps towards the booking-office.' (18). Nothing could express more clearly an essential shift in sensibility than this delightful passage. Through his comic moralising, Sam is invested with a human equality in relation to Mr Pickwick. However deferential he may be to his master, Sam's inner life is his own and within it he is free to comment on the motives and behaviour of his 'betters'. With the significant exception of Nurse Rooke, it is impossible to imagine a similar licence being granted by Jane Austen. The social and the literary are united here in a way that makes it difficult to give precedence to either. Again, despite Mr Weller's dislike of widders and marriage, both father and son show a healthy interest in the opposite sex; one remembers the 'several very unfatherly winks' (56) that Mr Weller bestows on Mary, Sam's intended. And Sam is one of the principal channels through which the novel's strong element of macabre comedy is presented. At the level of characterization, then, Dickens creates an unforced consistency in the roles of the Wellers and Mr Pickwick which gives their encounters a meaning, without destroying the exuberance of the novel's flow of episodes. At the wider, structural level, Mr Pickwick's supposed proposal to Mrs Bardell occurs as early as the fifth monthly part, in Chapter 12, and this leads eventually to the Fleet Prison by way of the trial of Bardell against Pickwick, one of the timeless fantasies of all literature. However fantastic, though, the trial is rooted in the corrupt nature of real human institutions and raises, in its comic way, profound questions about the status of language, questions that were to preoccupy Dickens for the rest of his career.[4]

And so *Pickwick's* major subject, the celebration of human goodness, is deepened, darkened, given complexity, in a way that does no injury to its comedy or its essentially episodic nature. This flexibility is maintained by the novel's consistent delight in the sheer variety of human life, in 'contemplating human nature in all the numerous phases it exhibits' (12) as Mr Pickwick does from the vantage point of his rooms in Goswell Street. Extending this variety forms a possible justification for the interpolated tales, an outmoded device which Dickens attempts to rehabilitate in *The Pickwick Papers*. Two of the tellers use a strikingly similar phrase in introducing their stories. The dismal man's is '"curious as a leaf from the romance of real life"' (5) while the old man who 'relates a Story about a queer Client' speaks of '"the romance of life, sir, the romance of life."' (21). Many years later, in the preface to its first edition, Dickens asserts that in *Bleak House* I have purposely dwelt upon the romantic side of familiar things' and although by then he is surely using the word more self-consciously (staking a claim for the symbolic transfiguration of reality) that great novel also displays a seemingly inexhaustible range of social types. But tone and artistry have altered and this is more than a narrowly aesthetic development on Dickens's part.

Bleak House, despite its comedy, is a different work from *Pickwick* or *Nickleby* for a host of reasons: because in it Dickens is a maturer, more experienced artist; because he is an older and, in some ways, different man; and because the social world depicted, in a highly stylized manner, by *Bleak House* is radically unlike that of the earlier works. This last point is clearly central to my argument, but it offers a trap that needs to be avoided in any social reading of Dickens's achievement. A facile contrast between the magnificent fun of the early novels and the seriousness of the later has been part of the critical landscape surrounding Dickens for a long time, although efforts have been made to redress the balance in recent years. It would surely be too easy, and predictable, to rehearse the admittedly magnificent power of the later novels as a series of images of society, brilliantly realized variations on the theme of his confrontation of the inner forces, as well as the surface appearance, of his social reality. But one point should be made: Dickens's unquenchably fertile discoveries in the practice of his art. The discovery, for example, of the fictional institution – Chancery, the Circumlocution Office, the Marshalsea – as the focus of social insights in a purely artistic form is one of the greatest advances made by the nineteenth-century novel, one painfully ignored by later writers. Kafka seems almost alone, in *The Castle* and *The Trial,* in having realized the potential of this discovery for the modern novel. For Dickens, the fictional institution operates as an organizing principle in two distinct, but related, ways. It provides a unifying centre artistically, a hub around which the multifarious detail of these vast structures can move in a disciplined, although not regimented, manner. And, simultaneously, it becomes the means by which Dickens can read, as well as record, the appearances of things in terms of their underlying structure. In the end we may not subscribe to the historical accuracy of every last detail of his reading of Victorian life through *Bleak House* but, like Fitzjames Stephen, take a happier view of social developments in the nineteenth century.[5] What cannot be denied, however, is that the objective social reality of 1853 was more complex than that of the 1830's, and that in the form of his later novels Dickens discovered images of society which are a perfect artistic embodiment of a highly organized social world.

But this should not mislead us into thinking that the social interest of the earlier work lies in its merely sketching ideas that will come to fruition later. If Dickens discovered the lives of humble people as an aesthetic subject in *Sketches by Boz*, and brought it to a high level of development in *Pickwick*, it was clearly this aspect of his own genius that he seized on most firmly for his third novel, *Nicholas Nickleby*. The understanding of lower class life shown in the Spaniards Tea Rooms episode of *Pickwick* is here refined and extended in the depiction of the Kenwigs family. We first meet them in all their glory in Chapter 14, 'the anniversary of that happy day on which the Church of England as by law established, had bestowed Mrs Kenwigs upon Mr Kenwigs.' (14). It would take a Chesterton to recreate the comic delight of this section in his own language without recourse to extensive quotation. More mundanely, one can speculate on some of the literary and social developments that made the creation of such scenes possible. The sanction given to the treatment of humble life by the Romantic movement is an obvious factor. And this, in its turn, is part of that democratization of literature which occurred through the gradual shift from an aristocratic domination of social life and values. But several things are new here. The Kenwigs are the urban poor, not Wordsworth's rustics. Since they belong to a class well above the dispossessed – indeed, they already have the distinction of occupying 'the whole of the first floor, comprising a suite of two rooms' (14) and have ambitions towards further improvement – Dickens knows their life from the inside: what they eat, their clothes, furniture, their aspirations. Above all, Dickens's tone and attitude towards the Kenwigs is a key indicator of a change in sensibility. We cannot imagine this little family coming within, say, Jane Austen's artistic horizon, but although funny they are never the object of Dickens's, or our, contempt or ridicule. Although Dickens embeds their absurdities of language and behaviour in a context of comically distancing narrative ('a suite of two rooms'), this places and evaluates without denigration. Again, as with *Pickwick*, there is an ideological intention at work, signalled by the title of the Kenwigs chapter, 'Having the Misfortune to treat of none but Common People, is necessarily of a Mean and Vulgar Character.' (14).

This treatment of Common People, begun so triumphantly with the Wellers, is not merely refined in the Kenwigs; it is made part of a total context which reveals the still youthful Dickens's grasp of the connections between apparently different aspects of the new urban world which forms such an important part of the setting of *Nicholas Nickleby*. Like an ocean, London is swept by 'the giant currents of life that flow ceaselessly on from different quarters.' (4). And when, as early as Chapter 4, Dickens's imagination turns to Newgate and its public executions the scene is 'rendered frightful with excess of human life.' This human saturation of the city is turned to good account by Miss La Creevy for her miniature portraits: '"That's the great convenience of living in a thoroughfare like the Strand. When I want a nose or an eye for any particular sitter, I have only to look out of window and wait till I get one."' (5). Dickens himself has an unerring eye for characteristic and representative activities that arise from this pressure of population. The transience of city life is revealed on Nicholas's return from Yorkshire when he finds it necessary to rent a room: 'For the letting of this portion of the house from week to week, on reasonable terms, the parlour lodger was empowered to treat, he being deputed by the landlord to dispose of the rooms as they became vacant.' (16). Becoming a weekly tenant and 'having hired a few common articles of furniture from a neighbouring broker, and paid the first week's hire in advance, out of a small fund raised by the conversion of some spare clothes into ready money, he sat himself down to ruminate upon his prospects.' (16). In this world nothing need be permanent: clothes are translated into money, a room paid for weekly becomes a home, even furniture does not need to be owned. And institutions exist to enable all these activities to take place. But it is not merely the immaterial that can be hired:

> As there was a board outside, which acquainted the public that
> servants-of-all-work were perpetually in waiting to be hired from ten till
> four, Nicholas knew at once that some half-dozen strong young women,
> each with pattens and an umbrella, who were sitting upon a form in one
> corner, were in attendance for that purpose, especially as the poor things
> looked anxious and weary. (16).

The employment agency is a perfect little image of the institutions necessary to accommodate the pressures of urban living. The masses of people involved in Victorian domestic service clearly precluded any more direct method of employment. And, again, Dickens removes the anonymity of this segment of city life through comic vignettes of potential employers: 'Family of Mr Gallanbile, MP. Fifteen guineas, tea and sugar, and servants allowed to see male cousins, if godly.' (16).

Finally, Dickens humanizes this environment with characters who have adapted to its constraints with a remarkable, if humanly limiting, facility. The mysteriousness of Newman Noggs's activities as he goes about the discovery of the secret of Madeline Bray's fortune is embodied in his paradoxical appearance: 'Newman fell a little behind his master, and his face was curiously twisted as by a spasm, but whether of paralysis, or grief, or inward laughter, nobody but himself could possibly explain. The expression of a man's face is commonly a help to his thoughts, or glossary on his speech; but the countenance of Newman Noggs, in his ordinary moods, was a problem which no stretch of ingenuity could solve.' (3). Tim Linkinwater is always in danger of being sucked into the vortex of sentimentality which is the medium in which the Cheerybles move, but the human impoverishment of his existence as their clerk is plain enough in his description of his own life:

> 'It's forty-four year . . . next May, since I first kept the books of Cheeryble Brothers. I've opened the safe every morning all that time (Sundays excepted) as the clock struck nine, and gone over the house every night at half-past ten (except on Foreign Post nights, and then twenty minutes before twelve) to see the doors fastened and the fires out. I've never slept out of the back attic one single night. There's the same mignonette box in the middle of the window, and the same four flower-pots, two on each side, that I brought with me when I first came. There an't – I've said it again and again, and I'll maintain it – there an't such a square as this in the world. I *know* there an't,' said Tim, with sudden energy, and looking sternly about him. 'Not one. For business or pleasure, in summer time or winter – I don't care which – there's nothing like it. There's not such a spring in England as the pump under the archway. There's not such a view in England as the view out of my window; I've seen it every morning before I shaved, and I ought to know something about it. I have slept in that room,' added Tim, sinking his voice a little, 'for four-and-forty year; and if it wasn't inconvenient, and didn't interfere with business, I should request leave to die there.' (35)

And Miss La Creevy is a brilliant example of Dickens's ability to take the pulse of the new way of life represented by the metropolis:

Here was one of the advantages of having lived alone so long. The little bustling, active, cheerful creature, existed entirely within herself, talked to herself, made a confidant of herself, was as sarcastic as she could be, on people who offended her, by herself... nobody's reputation suffered; and if she enjoyed a little bit of revenge, no living soul was one atom the worse. One of the many to whom, from straitened circumstances, a consequent inability to form the associations they would wish, and disinclination to mix with the society they could obtain, London is as complete a solitude as the plains of Syria, the humble artist had pursued her lonely, but contented way for many years; and, until the peculiar misfortunes of the Nickleby family attracted her attention, had made no friends, though brimfull of the friendliest feelings to all mankind. There are many warm hearts in the same solitary guise as poor Miss La Creevy's. (20)

Solitariness, eccentricity and celibacy are the hallmarks of all three characters, individualized fragments of a mass of humanity visible only as the crowds that throng the city's streets. For them London has taken the place of the family and friends which we have seen as important human units in earlier fiction and, in doing so, has limited their possibilities of normal human development. Marriage, children, community play no part, at least in their younger lives. Community *can* exist in this world, the Kenwigs demonstrate that, but Dickens's revelation of the lives existing below the surface of urban anonymity shows as much, if not more, loneliness as communion.

Brilliant as these insights are—profound, even, on occasion—they are more than isolated perceptions. Although *Nicholas Nickleby* is frankly episodic in structure, as its excursions into Yorkshire and the Crummles world show, Dickens's sense of London is beginning to develop a pattern which suggests connections between different parts of its social reality. This has nothing of the rigour and completeness of, say, *Bleak House*, but the roots of the later vision are clearly taking a strong hold in Dickens's imagination even at this early stage. On his first, chance meeting with Mr Charles Cheeryble, Nicholas's remark that he is a '"stranger in this wilderness of London"' is immediately taken up: '"Wilderness! Yes it is, it is. Good. It *is* a wilderness.....It was a wilderness to me once."' (35) The idea of London as a wilderness relates to Dickens's general theme of revelation, of reading the anonymity of city life in such a way as to reveal its underlying forms of individual and group existence. If London is a wilderness then it needs its explorer, a role which deeply excites him. Such explorations emphasise a paradox which will be of central importance to his development as artist and visionary critic of Victorian society.

The chaos of London is modified in one highly significant way, as we are told in the words of Tim Linkinwater: '"Why, I don't believe now...that there's such a place in all the world for coincidences as London is!"' (43) This claim is prompted by the accidental meeting of Nicholas and Frank Cheeryble, an encounter which forms part of a little series of repeated events in the novel. This is how Nicholas stumbles on his overhearing of Sir Mulberry and Lord Verisopht discussing his sister, Kate:

> He walked on a few steps, but looking wistfully down the long vista of gas-lamps before him, and thinking how long it would take to reach the end of it – and being besides in that kind of mood in which a man is most disposed to yield to his first impulse – and being, besides, strongly attracted to the hotel, in part by curiosity, and in part, by some odd mixture of feelings which he would have been troubled to define – Nicholas turned back again, and walked into the coffee-room. (32)

There is an obvious uncertainty in the handling of this moment, a hint almost of supernatural prompting, which suggests that Dickens lacks confidence in making the coincidence acceptable; he seems happier, at this stage, with such broad strokes as Smike's relationship to Ralph Nickleby. Nonetheless, scenes such as this, and Nicholas's first sight of Madeline, are chance encounters of great importance to Dickens's vision of London life, an importance reinforced by the novel's images of entanglement. In trying to dissuade Madeline from marrying Arthur Gride, for example, Nicholas reveals his knowledge of the money-making scheme of which she is the victim: '"I know what web is wound about you."' (53) Ralph Nickleby expresses his ambition of destroying his nephew in a similar way: '"Let me but do this, and it shall be the first link in such a chain, which I will wind about him, as never man forged yet."' (56) And in a pattern that is deeply familiar from Dickens's work as a whole, Smike 'turns out to be' Ralph's son. That Dickens never despised such a device is demonstrated by its importance for *Bleak House* in Esther's relationship to Lady Dedlock. Of course, by that stage it is used as the vehicle for a profound examination of sexuality and materialism, just as Chancery's encircling web is an image of entrapment in a society founded on money. Part of the earlier novel's fascination lies in its more tentative working out of these subtleties at the level of both artistry and social vision; it may even be possible to trace the genesis of this central insight in *Nicholas Nickleby*.

It seems reasonable to divide the novel's episodic structure into three main centres of interest: Dotheboys Hall, Crummles and the theatre, London and the life of the streets. The first is an example of a major aspect of Dickens's social criticism in the early work, the often-noted concentration on a self-enclosed abuse which outrages his compassion and sense of justice, above all where children are concerned. The Crummles scenes are equally self-enclosed in their joyous fun, Dickens's affectionate, but not uncritical, tribute to a world he never ceased to love. But ripples do travel out from the theatrical episodes into the novel as a whole. They are, obviously, steeped in melodrama, and on various levels. The melodramatic nature of the material in which the Crummles company appear before the public is wonderfully created, as in the description, in Chapter 24, of the 'play' Nicholas 'writes' for Miss Snevellicci's Great Bespeak. But the actors not merely appear in melodrama; they are themselves melodramatic. Melodrama is the medium in which they live and have their being, most memorably perhaps in the 'scene' where Mr Crummles takes leave of Nicholas on his return to London:

> In fact, Mr Crummles, who could never lose any opportunity for professional display, had turned out for the express purpose of taking a public farewell of Nicholas; and to render it the more imposing, he was now, to that young gentleman's most profound annoyance, inflicting upon him a rapid succession of stage embraces, which, as everybody knows, are performed by the embracer's laying his or her chin on the shoulder of the object of affection, and looking over it. This Mr Crummles did in the highest style of melodrama, pouring forth at the same time all the most dismal forms of farewell he could think of, out of the stock pieces. Nor was this all, for the elder Master Crummles was going through a similar ceremony with Smike; while Master Percy Crummles, with a very little second-hand camlet cloak, worn theatrically over his left shoulder, stood by, in the attitude of an attendant officer, waiting to convey the two victims to the scaffold. (30)

But although the theatrical episodes form a self-enclosed unit, the melodramatic mode in which they are cast is present everywhere in the novel, as Dickens himself clearly recognises; in the heading to Chapter 28, for example: 'Miss Nickleby, rendered desperate by the Persecution of Sir Mulberry Hawk, and the complicated Difficulties and Distresses which surround her, appeals, as a last resource, to her Uncle for Protection.' In other words, the melodrama which is made fun of in the Crummles scenes is itself an essential part of the novel as a whole. There would be ample scope for discussion at this point of the book's self-reflexiveness if that were the direction of my argument: *Nicholas Nickleby* is about melodrama not just in terms of its subject, but as an aspect of its texture at every level. However, this study centres on how fiction gestures towards the outside world and not just to itself. No matter how ludicrous its excesses, Dickens's willing participation in the popular culture of his own time means that this is the area within which his imagination is at home.

Dickens is probably the last great literary artist in the English tradition for whom melodrama is a completely serious business, as well as the cause of wild comedy; in European terms his preoccupation passes to Dostoevski, partly by way of Dickens's direct influence. There is thus an opportunity at this stage to round off one of my study's minor themes, the role of melodrama in English literature. We have seen elements of melodramatic excess in the externalised gesturing that passes for emotion, whether of joy or grief, in Defoe and Smollett; even the incomparably greater genius of Fielding is not entirely free from such mechanical substitutes for feeling. Richardson must be credited – and it is a tribute to his remarkable originality – as one of the first explorers of the melodramatic mode of consciousness, combining as he does an elemental sense of good and evil with various aspects of literary realism. The force of Richardson's example is at least part of the explanation of how the melodramatic mode becomes widely diffused throughout European literature. But the second section of my first chapter is devoted to showing that the return of melodrama from Europe to, firstly, the English stage is more than a matter of literary influences in the narrow sense. My point is that melodrama enjoys such wide popularity as a form of entertainment and then as a literary device of general currency because it answers to certain psychic needs which are, in their turn, related to the nature of nineteenth-century society. This fact, as I believe it to be, is revealed by Dickens: his brilliant intelligence perceives it as an aspect of his social and personal world, partly as a result of his own experience, and his artistry embodies it in forms that give it the status of imaginative truth as well as social insight.

Dickens's discovery – no other word is appropriate – centres on the recognition that the forms of existence characteristic of his period (the complex interdependencies of Victorian capitalism and the street life of the great metropolis are two of the most obvious) lend themselves to melodramatic treatment because they carry the seeds of melodrama within them. The revelation of this unexpected, or unknown, human dimension might well have the force of melodramatic contrivance in its bringing to light of previously unsuspected connections between groups or individuals. Similarly, the city is the perfect setting for the melodramatic contrast of extremes of wealth and poverty, and the jostling of strangers who will, in fact, 'turn out to be' related, often in mysterious and surprising ways. As Dickens's career progresses his ability to embody these insights in richly varied artistic forms is remarkable, but his attempts in *Nicholas Nickleby*, however loosely episodic the novel may be, suggests that its form deserves to be taken seriously.

Again, if Dickens stumbled into the creation of *The Pickwick Papers*, his faltering steps are still those of a genius and the rapidity with which he took control of the whole venture is mirrored by the firm episodic unity the novel increasingly displays. But the shape Dickens discovers for his early books is more than a matter of falling back on his beloved eighteenth-century novelists to write his way out of a difficult corner. Fielding without the sex, and a toning down of Smollett's brutalities, are not enough to account for the power of *Pickwick* and *Nickleby*. In other words, 'Victorian versions of eighteenth-century fiction' is a hopelessly inadequate formula to describe these works. A brief reminder of the detailed historical context of Dickens's earlier life illustrates how decisively pre-Victorian, in fact, his formative years were. Dickens was as old as 17 when the Stephensons' 'Rocket' won its epoch-making competiton in 1829, 19 when he reported on the passage of the Reform Bill, and 25 when Victoria became Queen in 1837. *The Pickwick Papers* was published in 1836-7, *Oliver Twist* in 1837-8, and *Nicholas Nickleby* in 1838-9. Thus Dickens had the inestimable benefit of knowing, and knowing intimately, as his life and letters testify, a less bureaucratically organized social world than that of the later nineteenth century. In purely economic terms, we may think of the mid-Victorian period as a chaos of slump and boom caused by the free play of market forces, justified by theories of *laissez-faire*. But a deeper underlying pattern, and one which Dickens undoubtedly perceived, was the development of structures and institutions to control the problems caused by large-scale industrialization, increases in the size of cities, and so on: a pattern which reaches its benign apotheosis in the British Welfare State and its cruelly lunatic outcome in Stalinist Russia. Dickens's early life was poised at the very moment when this pattern was beginning to take shape. Straws in the wind are Peel's formation of the London police force in 1829, the foundation of the British Association for the Advancement of Science in 1831, the factory inspectorate of 1833, and the reform of Municipal Corporations in 1835, abolishing the old Charter privileges.

Seen in this light, the form of Dickens's early novels, and his development as a writer, take on a new significance. The crude version of this process is the one which keeps to the narrowest aesthetic focus. That is, that the shape of Dickens's early work is virtually an act of plagiarism of eighteenth-century fiction, although it is admitted that new wine is poured into old bottles. Then, with *Dombey and Son*, begins the development of an artistic conscience and the discovery of ways to build his material into coherent patterns. Within the social context I have just sketched, however, the form of even the earliest work can be seen to be appropriate from the start. There is no point in denying that these books were influenced by Dickens's reading of eighteenth-century fiction. But just as he seized on the popular uses of melodrama for his own purposes by seeing how they could be manipulated to embody the realities of urban living, so there is no reason to suppose that he failed to see how episodic unity could mirror the social organisation of the first thirty years of the nineteenth century. The aesthetically disciplined social panorama of *Bleak House* was necessitated by the demands of social life in the 1850s. The assumption that Dickens's inability to write in this way at the beginning of his career was a weakness stands, therefore, in need of re-examination. The juncture of the Regency and Victorian periods at which the early novels were created suggests that more tightly structured works would have been false to the conditions of living which were at least partly responsible for their birth.

Further Reading

The most detailed listing of Dickens criticism up to 1967 is to be found in *The New Cambridge Bibliography of English Literature*, Volume 3 edited by George Watson (Cambridge, 1969).

Much critical attention has been given to Dickens's treatment of society. One attempt to cover it comprehensively is:

Dickens, Money and Society by Grahame Smith (Berkeley, 1968).

Other work in this area is:

Love and Property in the Novels of Dickens by Ross H. Dabney (Berkeley, 1967).

The Victorians and Social Protest by John Butt and I. F. Clark (Newton Abbot, 1973).

'Dickens' Vision of Society,' by John Holloway in *The Novelist as Innovator* edited by Walter Allen (London, 1966).

'Social Criticism in Dickens: Some Problems of Method and Approach', by Raymond Williams, *Critical Quarterly* (1965).

Among the more notable general studies are:

The Violent Effigy: A Study of Dickens's Imagination by John Carey (London, 1973).

The Dickens Theatre by Robert Garis (Oxford, 1965).

Dickens the Novelist by F. R. and Q. D. Leavis (London, 1970).

Dickens: From Pickwick to Dombey by Steven Marcus (London, 1965).

Dickens: the World of his Novels by J. Hillis Miller (Cambridge, Mass, 1958).

The City of Dickens by Alexander Welsh (Oxford, 1971).

The World of Charles Dickens by Angus Wilson (London, 1970).

8

Daniel Deronda

Daniel Deronda opens dramatically with a question: 'Was she beautiful or not beautiful?' The drama and the questioning are equally important. The novel's themes are open-ended, speculative, uncertain, and this sense of exploration is rendered by an artistic form which relies on image, symbol and action to an extent unusual in George Eliot.

The point is enforced by a moment of apparently incidental local colour of a kind hardly to be found in her earlier panoramic novels. (The fact that it would not be entirely out of place in *Silas Marner* is significant.) In the midst of the gambling casino 'were gathered two serried crowds of human beings, all save one having their faces and attention bent on the tables':

> The one exception was a melancholy little boy, with his knees and calves simply in their natural clothing of epidermis, but for the rest of his person in a fancy dress. He alone had his face turned towards the doorway, and fixing on it the blank gaze of a bedizened child stationed as a masquerading advertisement on the platform of an itinerant show, stood close behind a lady deeply engaged at the roulette-table. (1)

An earlier George Eliot is present here also, in the rather heavy humour of the child's legs in 'their natural clothing of epidermis.' But the moment remains remarkable on several counts, perhaps above all for its mystery. The sad boy in his fancy outfit may be emblematic of the sordid show of gambling, the ironic contrast between 'bedizened' innocence and its surroundings is obvious enough. At a more complex level, we register the earliest possible introduction of the book's imagery of public entertainment as an image of corruptions in the private world. And we might even trace a connection between this neglected child and a boyish Deronda who is slighted at a depth below the affection and comfort of his surface life when he is asked by his adoptive father whether he would like to be '"a great singer."' (16) But these considerations are secondary to the sheer inexplicable oddity of a fragment of experience. That 'blank gaze' towards the 'doorway' raises unanswerable questions about the fate of this speck of human life, an awareness similar to that aroused by those pathetic cyphers, Gwendolen's sisters, the 'four superfluous girls, each, poor thing – like those other many thousand sisters of us all – having her peculiar world which was of no importance to any one else.' (21). A literary antecedent for this vignette might be found in the great passage of *The Prelude* when Wordsworth sees a beautiful infant like 'A sort of alien scattered from the clouds.':

> Upon a board
> Decked with refreshments had this child been placed
> *His* little stage in the vast theatre,
> And there he sate, surrounded with a throng
> Of chance spectators, chiefly dissolute men
> And shameless women, treated and caressed.
> (Bk. VII, 356-61, Text of 1850).

We know how deeply Wordsworth influenced George Eliot – 'I never before met with so many of my own feelings, expressed just as I could like them'[1] – but the point's interest does not depend on her specific dependence on Wordsworth. It is, rather, part of the general process (seen also in the Dickens of *Bleak House*) whereby Romantic ideas and images are fed into the mainstream of Victorian fiction. Its appearance in this form so early in *Daniel Deronda* signals an important development in George Eliot's themes and techniques in this, her last novel, and justifies a perceptive comment of Edward Dowden: 'In *Daniel Deronda*, for the first time, the poetical side of George Eliot's genius obtains adequate expression, through the medium which is proper to her – that of prose – and in complete association with the non-poetical elements of her nature.'[2]

Like *Persuasion*, *Daniel Deronda* is an ending pregnant with possibilities of new life in both ideas and form, and so of particular value to a study which seeks to catch the novel at some of its crucial points of shift and transition. *Middlemarch* is a finished masterpiece, the high-water in English fiction of the social-psychological novel, just as *Little Dorrit* might be taken as the fullest expression of the social-symbolic novel. In the terms of my argument these are achievements towards which the novel has been moving from its first tentative discovery of its grounding within social and personal life (the two are ultimately indissoluble). This process might be defined as the discovery of genres which are then taken to a point of fulfilment from which the novel does not decline, but from which it moves towards new expressions of the form's possibilities. This continual sense of discovery is a marked feature of Dickens's genius; in his essay 'Wilkie Collins and Dickens' T. S. Eliot draws attention to Dickens's unwillingness to remain safely within his earlier achievements.[3] A similar tribute is due to George Eliot for facing the challenge of pushing her art in new directions in *Daniel Deronda* after the success of *Middlemarch*.

I take it for granted that in living dangerously in the later novel George Eliot takes risks which do not always succeed. The book undoubtedly contains *longueurs*: for example, the tiresomely extended passages of discursive analysis which attempt to explain Deronda's character. And the proffered wisdom of her generalizations – an important aspect of *Middlemarch*'s total artistry – descends on occasion to banality:

> He really did not long to find anybody in particular; and when, as his habit was, he looked at the name over a shop-door, he was well content that it was not Ezra Cohen. I confess, he particularly desired that Ezra Cohen should not keep a shop. Wishes are held to be ominous; according to which belief the order of the world is so arranged that if you have an impious objection to a squint, your offspring is the more likely to be born with one; also, that if you happened to desire a squint, you would not get it. This desponding view of probability the hopeful entirely reject, taking their wishes as good and sufficient security for all kinds of fulfilment. (33)

But these blemishes are more than compensated by a richness of insight and artistry of a new kind. What follows is motivated by the conviction that the book is not two novels (*Gwendolen Harleth* and *Daniel Deronda*), the one great, the other worthless; that the novel's English scenes are not simply a reworking of the *Middlemarch* area of experience with Gwendolen as another version of Rosamund Vincy; that, above all, the Jewish scenes, and the richest part of the English strand, represent George Eliot's attempt to explore new material in a new way. In taking this view, one at least has the satisfaction (trusting tales rather than tellers notwithstanding) of agreeing with the author herself: 'This is better than the laudation of readers who cut the book into scraps and talk of nothing but Gwendolen. I meant everything in the book to be related to everything else there.'[4]

Daniel Deronda is a novel unusually rich in crises, in moments of dramatic power and intense feeling; one of these, following Gwendolen's decision to marry Grandcourt, forms a powerful subsidiary climax on the way to her receipt of Mrs Glasher's letter and its accompanying diamonds. Gwendolen and Grandcourt are approaching Ryelands and the consummation of their marriage:

> Gwendolen had been at her liveliest during the journey, chatting incessantly, ignoring any change in their mutual position since yesterday; and Grandcourt had been rather ecstatically quiescent, while she turned his gentle seizure of her hand into a grasp of his hand by both of hers, with an increased vivacity as of a kitten that will not sit quiet to be petted. She was really getting somewhere febrile in her excitement; and now in this drive through the park her usual susceptibility to changes of light and scenery helped to make her heart palpitate newly. Was it at the novelty simply, or the almost incredible fulfilment about to be given to her girlish dreams of being 'somebody' – walking through her own furlong of corridors and under her own ceilings of an out-of-sight loftiness, where her own painted Spring was shedding painted flowers, and her own foreshortened Zephyrs were blowing their trumpets over her; while her own servants, lackeys in clothing but men in bulk and shape, were as naught in her presence, and revered the propriety of her insolence to them: – being in short the heroine of an admired play without the pains of art? (31)

This connects with the rest of the novel in ways so complex as almost to defy ordered discussion. Its underlying sexual menace is infinitely disturbing. The Gwendolen who faces the frightful confidence of an 'ecstatically quiescent' Grandcourt is the girl who objects 'with a sort of physical repulsion, to being directly made love to' (7) and whose perception of approaching tenderness makes her 'curl up and harden like a sea-anemone at the touch of a finger.' (7). We know enough of Grandcourt by this time to be sure that these fears and delicacies are about to be swept aside; he will not be content 'not to transgress again' as he was in his kiss on Gwendolen's neck that produced the 'marked agitation' which made her 'rather afraid of herself.' (29) It is pathetically appropriate that Gwendolen should be at her 'liveliest': she will not be lively for the rest of the novel. Her desperate attempt to control Grandcourt's desires by taking his hand in 'both of hers' makes one think of her wish 'to mount the chariot and drive the plunging horses herself, with a spouse by her side who would fold his arms and give her his countenance without looking ridiculous.' (13) Her area of domination is now at once more intimate and more precarious, and the physical grossness of the overturning of her desire to dominate through horse-riding is unmistakable. (In passing, we might notice that Gwendolen is one of the earliest manifestations of the European new woman in Victorian fiction; her combination of sexual timidity and obsession with the masculine world reminds one irresistibly of Hedda Gabler.) The 'usual susceptibility to changes of light and scenery' connects with her fear of solitude and space as part of the narrowly social essence of her personality: her 'fulfilment' is neither emotional nor sexual and to be 'somebody' is not to occur through the hard-won discovery of a self, but as a figure passing through 'her own furlong of corridors.' The unnatural emptiness of Gwendolen's ambition is suggested by the 'painted' spring and flowers, and its inhumanity by her desire to be surrounded by servants whose abasement is accentuated by their physical palpability. With a moral stupidity that echoes Emma Bovary's wish to be both dead and in Paris, Gwendolen's ultimate desire is to be 'the heroine of an admired play without the pains of art.'

Passages revealing such new depths of understanding occur frequently in *Daniel Deronda* and display a richness of language demanded by George Eliot's willingness to probe areas not easily susceptible to rational analysis. *Middlemarch* is a daylight world of Apollonian clarity where the moral blankness that can wreck the lives of others is finally explicable. Such explanations are often immensely complex and the novelist must start from the given element of destructive egotism in Casaubon and Rosamund. But this granted, we are made to feel a total understanding of the book's major characters. The web of motives, however ravelled, is disentangled with a completeness that leaves nothing more to be known. The point might be expressed in moral terms. *Middlemarch* is permeated with the differences between right and wrong, *Daniel Deronda* with the conflict between good and evil. This suggests an explanation of why the Raggles episode from the earlier novel is so unsatisfactory. The convenient hold-all of melodrama is frequently invoked here, but the objection has more to do with context than absolute literary value. With Raffles, George Eliot is working in a mode that seems inappropriate to the formal and thematic boundaries of the novel. Would he seem so out of place in the exploratory world of *Deronda?* Jean Sudrann clarifies one's sense of what is new in the book, and its necessity: 'Twentieth century psychologists have given twentieth century novelists their own vocabulary by which to describe the descent into the self. George Eliot uses the idiom available to her, the idiom of melodrama.'[5] This sense of exploration registers in, say, Gwendolen's response to

197

'changes of light and scenery,' a psychological phenomenon at the very threshold of consciousness. There are numerous attempts to deal with these new levels of experience in the book, as in the confusion of reasons that lead Gwendolen to keep the necklace returned to her by Deronda: 'It was something vague and yet mastering.... There is a great deal of unmapped country within us which would have to be taken into account in an explanation of our gusts and storms.' (24). It emerges also in the reference to the 'dark seed-growths of consciousness' (26) and in a significant emphasis in the epigraphs to some of the novel's chapters; that to Chapter 11, for example, with its daunting claim that the 'beginning of an acquaintance whether with persons or things is to get a definite outline for our ignorance', or that to the first: 'No retrospect will take us to the true beginning; and whether our prologue be in heaven or on earth, it is but a fraction of that all-presupposing fact with which our story sets out.' These insights connect with interesting features of the novel's larger structure, its dramatic plunge *in medias res* and the time shifts necessary to accommodate its movement back on itself. These surely imply George Eliot's recognition that a straightforwardly linear development is inadequate to her aims. The complex mysteries of the individual psyche are complemented by a social world of moral emptiness in which means and ends are consistently confused. Image and symbol can penetrate intuitively into private darkness; similarly, the complex layers of a disordered social world can only be peeled back in a 'disorderly' narrative fashion.

But detailed attention is demanded by that searing metaphor which embodies the quality of Gwendolen's desires and ambitions, the wish to be the heroine of a play without the pains of art. The last phrase provides the clue to a starting-point, in the face of the manifold possibilities opened up by the imagery of acting and the stage. Gwendolen is first made aware of the pains of art in the consummate scene of her encounter with Klesmer when she asks his advice on the possibility of a stage career. The scene is presented with all George Eliot's control of the myriad elements that go to make up any complex human encounter. In her best *Middlemarch* manner, we discover how Klesmer is led to be slightly more fierce with Gwendolen than he would wish to be because 'his temperament was still in a state of excitation from the events of yesterday' (23); that is, his contemptuous rejection by the Arrowpoints as a suitor for their daughter. One of the major complications is also, naturally enough, the character and role in the novel of Klesmer himself. He is clearly a creation in the same mould as Will Ladislaw whom Raymond Williams, contrary to the general view, finds a successful attempt on the novelist's part to think 'into mobility not as dislocating but as liberating.'[6] For many, Klesmer may seem the more successful, partly because he has a smaller part to play, but also because on this occasion George Eliot's irony ensures that the admirable does not become the idealized: we smile at Klesmer as well as respect him, a fusion deftly conveyed by his appearance at the archery contest:

> His tall thin figure clad in a way which, not being strictly English, was all the worse for its apparent emphasis of intention. Draped in a loose garment with a Florentine *berretta* on his head, he would have been fit to stand by the side of Leonardo da Vinci; but how when he presented himself in trousers which were not what English feeling demanded about the knees? – and when the fire which showed itself in his glances... was turned into comedy by a hat which ruled that mankind should have well-cropt hair. (10)

In the language of suburbia, Klesmer undoubtedly looks 'arty' and it is clearly part of the author's purpose that we should feel the absurdity of this. On the other hand, the musician's evidently rich hair contrasts strongly with that baldness of Grandcourt's which it is such a shock to encounter for the first time; and his fiery glances are set against Mr Arrowpoint, 'whose nullity of face and perfect tailoring might pass everywhere without ridicule.' (10). Our smile at Klesmer is, then, one of pleasure, that at the English, one of contempt.

As the passage quoted indicates, Klesmer's real differences from the English upper-classes are more than sartorial. He is a man of great talent, perhaps even of genius, but the emphasis falls constantly on how his gifts are controlled and shaped by work. And absence of work, of a sense of vocation, is inseparable from Gwendolen and Grandcourt's inner emptiness.[7] The expression of this vacuity helps to clarify what is new in *Daniel Deronda*. Gwendolen's failure to go to Mirah for singing lessons arises from that 'want of perceived leisure which belongs to lives where there is no work to mark off intervals' (48) and work is central to Deronda's whole development, as we see towards the end of his meeting with his father's friend, Kalonyos:

> 'What is your vocation?'
> This question was put with a quick abruptness which embarrassed

Deronda, who did not feel it quite honest to allege his law-reading as a vocation. He answered—

'I cannot say that I have any.'

'Get one, get one. The Jew must be diligent. You will call yourself a Jew?...'

'I shall call myself a Jew . . . I hold that my first duty is to my own people, and if there is anything to be done towards restoring or perfecting their common life, I shall make that my vocation.'

It happened to Deronda at that moment, as it has often happened to others, that the need for speech made an epoch in resolve. His respect for the questioner would not let him decline to answer, and by the necessity to answer he found out the truth for himself. (60)

In Gwendoline's case, and to some extent Deronda's, this lack is explicable in terms of the daylight world of social forms with which we are familiar from *Middlemarch*, part of the writer's wisdom about social and psychological experience. When we discover Grandcourt, however, in his habit of 'sitting meditatively on a sofa and abstaining from literature' we are at a level deeper than or beyond psychological explanation, although there is still a perceptible link between Grandcourt's character and his total social context. But George Eliot is now entering psychic depths, levels at which her earlier lucidity is no longer appropriate or even possible. Insight into Grandcourt's inner life is obscured by the idle movement of fragments of personality, a subterranean area accessible only to flashes of intuition:

In this way hours may pass surprisingly soon, without the arduous invisible chase of philosophy; not from love of thought, but from hatred of effort—from a state of the inward world, something like premature age, where the need for action lapses into a mere image of what has been, is, and may or might be; where impulse is born and dies in a phantasmal world, pausing in rejection even of a shadowy fulfilment. (28).

Such issues, which arise from even a brief discussion of Klesmer, suggest that he is an important symbolic focus for a whole range of references to art, of which the most important are acting and singing. And he performs this function with magnificent power in his scene with Gwendolen, justifying the narrator's comment, 'Woman was dear to him, but music was dearer' (5) and his own claim, '"My rank as an artist is of my own winning, and I would not exchange it for any other."' (22). His first attempts to convince Gwendolen of her inaptitude for the stage founder on the rock of her invincible egotism: 'The belief that to present herself in public on the stage must produce an effect such as she had been used to feel certain of in private life, was like a bit of her flesh – it was not to be peeled off readily, but must come with blood and pain.' (23). The simile has a poetic intensity, mimicking a repulsive ripping of skin and flesh; her blindness forces him to speak more plainly, in a way that gives detailed force to the symbolic role I have just mentioned: '"You must know what you have to strive for, and then you must submit your mind and body to unbroken discipline. Your mind, I say. For you must not be thinking of celebrity:– put that candle out of your eyes, and look only at excellence."' (23). And in a masterly passage, the novelist makes Klesmer reveal the paradox in Gwendolen's sexual timidity, coupled with her love of personal display:

> 'But – there are certainly other ideas, other dispositions with which a young lady may take up an art that will bring her before the public. She may rely on the unquestioned power of her beauty as a passport. She may desire to exhibit herself to an admiration which dispenses with skill. This goes a certain way on the stage: not in music; but on the stage, beauty is taken when there is nothing more commanding to be had. Not without some drilling, however: as I have said before, technicalities have in any case to be mastered. But these excepted, we have here nothing to do with art. The woman who takes up this career is not an artist: she is usually one who thinks of entering on a luxurious life by a short and easy road – perhaps by marriage – that is her most brilliant chance, and the rarest. Still, her career will not be luxurious to begin with: she can hardly earn her own poor bread independently at once, and the indignities she will be liable to are such that I will not speak of.' (23).

This is yet another example of the novel's rich web of inter-connections in its suggestion of the lower reaches of the stage as a form of prostitution, or at the most the road to a brilliant marriage, a link with the blatant physical display which George Eliot castigates as part of the contemporary marriage market. The Archery Meeting at Brackenshaw Park, for example, has an essentially theatrical air: 'Who can deny that bows and arrows are among the prettiest weapons in the world for feminine forms to play with? They prompt attitudes full of grace and power.' (10). Gwendolen's unconscious fusion of conventionality and sexual inhibition is revealed by her unawareness of the sport's deeper implications: the tarnished echo of Cupid haunts this Victorian equivalent of a beauty contest. And so the '"indignities" that she might be visited with had no very definite form for her, but the mere association of anything called "indignity" with herself, roused a resentful alarm.' (23). However, she is unable to perceive degradation in her attempt to capture Grandcourt's attention by the 'perfect movement of her fine form.' (10).

Such ironies permeate the entire novel. Gwendolen's request for Klesmer's advice stems from a typical self-delusion, his response to her fear of the portrait during the charades scene of Chapter 6: 'He divined that the betrayal into a passion of fear had been mortifying to her, and wished her to understand that he took it for good acting. Gwendolen cherished the idea that now he was struck with her talent as well as her beauty, and her uneasiness about his opinion was half turned to complacency.' (6). This passage leads on to one of the book's most powerful strands of imagery. Early in the novel there is the danger of a clash between Mrs Arrowpoint and Gwendolen, the 'too quick young lady, who had over-acted her *naiveté.'* (5). After her financial disaster, Gwendolen's hopes of salvation 'sometimes turned on the question whether she should become an actress like Rachel, since she was more beautiful than that thin Jewess.' (6). The 'since' is revealing, of course; Gwendolen is sure that her superiority in one area will suffice for another which demands talent and application. In those fascinating verbal encounters between Gwendolen and Grandcourt in which his slowness of speech is stressed we find: 'Always there was the same pause before he took up his cue.' (11). And Deronda's separation from this world of charades and fashionable play-acting is concentrated in his reponse to an odd question of Mirah's, prompted by fear, in the course of his rescue of her: '"Do you belong to the theatre?" "No; I have nothing to do with the theatre," said Deronda, in a decided tone.' (17). Grandcourt's position within it, on the other hand, emerges from the language he himself uses, as well as that used about him by the narrator; this is made clear by his reply to Sir Hugo's little joke about kneeling in prayer on the Abbey's stones: '"A confounded nuisance," drawled Grandcourt. "I hate fellows wanting to howl litanies – acting the greatest bores that have ever existed."'(35). The possibility of howling sincerely doesn't of course occur to him. Pathetically, under the pressure of suffering and Deronda's influence, Gwendolen attempts to widen her horizons by serious reading, but 'it was astonishing how little time she found for these vast mental excursions. Constantly she had to be on the scene as Mrs Grandcourt, and to feel herself watched in that part by the exacting eyes of a husband.' (44). And this social pretence is generalized a few pages later at a moment when Mirah's mind is 'chiefly occupied in contemplating Gwendolen': 'It was like a new kind of stage-experience to her to be close to genuine grand ladies with genuine brilliants and complexions, and they impressed her vaguely as coming out of some unknown drama, in which their parts perhaps got more tragic as they went on.' (45). Finally, there is a rich example of this preoccupation at one of the novel's climactic moments, Deronda's interview with his mother:

> The varied transitions of tone with which this speech was delivered were as perfect as the most accomplished actress could have made them. The speech was in fact a piece of what may be called sincere acting: this woman's nature was one in which all feeling – and all the more when it was tragic as well as real – immediately became matter of conscious representation: experience immediately passed into drama, and she acted her own emotions. In a minor degree this is nothing uncommon, but in the Princess the acting had a rare perfection of physiognomy, voice, and gesture. It would not be true to say that she felt less because of this double consciousness: she felt – that is, her mind went through – all the more, but with a difference: each nucleus of pain or pleasure had a deep atmosphere of the excitement or spiritual intoxication which at once exalts and deadens. But Deronda made no reflection of this kind. All his thoughts hung on the purport of what his mother was saying; her tones and her wonderful face entered into his agitation without being noted. (51)

Daniel Deronda is, then, a novel which fuses George Eliot's mastery of the social-psychological with an exploration of psychic depths in relation to a larger social context than that of *Middlemarch*. From a complex enough vision of a provincial world we move here to the ramifications of high society from a European standpoint, for there is a negative as well as a positive pole of internationalism in the novel. The second, the Jewish theme, will be dealt with later, but the texture of life where 'abroad' is seen in terms of taking the waters and gambling, rather than an extension of personal culture, is initiated as early as the first chapter. With a remarkable similarity to the opening of Dickens's *Little Dorrit*, we begin with gamblers who 'showed very distinct varieties of European type: Livonian and Spanish, Graeco-Italian and miscellaneous German, English aristocratic and English plebeian. Here certainly was a striking admission of human equality.' (1). And at key moments, Gwendolen's limitations are exposed by her unawareness of the great historical events of the day:

> Could there be a slenderer, more insignificant thread in human history than this consciousness of a girl, busy with her small inferences of the way in which she could make her life pleasant?—in a time, too, when ideas

were with fresh vigour making armies of themselves, and the universal
kinship was declaring itself fiercely: when women on the other side of the
world would not mourn for husbands and sons who died bravely in a
common cause, and men stinted of bread on our side of the world heard
of that willing loss and were patient: a time when the soul of man was
waking to pulses which had for centuries been beating in him unheard,
until their full sum made a new life of terror or of joy. (11)

It is doubtful if Gwendolen ever heard of the American Civil War.
And just as those who take part in the Archery Contest are oblivious
of the larger beauties of nature, so English high society as a whole is
'busy with a small social drama as little penetrated by a feeling of
wider relations as if it had been a puppet-show.' (14).

An important, and related, theme makes *Daniel Deronda* a
latter-day condition-of-England novel, although far removed from
the direct pressure of material deprivation which characterized the
genre in the 1840s. George Eliot raises questions about the nature of
England and Englishness to which her answers are not encouraging.
This generalizing impulse is embodied most fully in Deronda's
character and the plot concerning him; it is brought into focus by a
question of Sir Hugo's: '"So you don't want to be an Englishman to
the backbone after all?"'(16). Although Daniel still believes at this
stage that he 'was somehow to take his place in English society' (17),
his own doubts about this fate are beginning to surface and the
narrator has already provided ample evidence to justify them. This
ominous thread runs throughout the book: the 'correct Englishman...
seeming to be in a state of internal drill, suggests a suppressed
vivacity, and may be suspected of letting go with some violence
when he is released from parade' (11); the 'new English' who 'should
look at themselves dispassionately in the glass, since their natural
selection of a mate prettier than themselves is not certain to bar the
effect of their own ugliness.' (11); and the 'English gentleman' who
'may make a good appearance in high social positions...at a small
expense of vital energy.' (15). This controlled savagery is epitomized
in the implied contrast between Grandcourt and Deronda.
Grandcourt's manners, which in the end are the surface expression
of his intellectual and spiritual nullity, 'might be expected to present
the extreme type of the national taste' (35); while Sir Hugo's tenants,
if Daniel had been his heir, would have 'regretted that his face was
not as unmistakably English as Sir Hugo's.' (36).

Taken as a whole, George Eliot's novels display one of the
characteristic movements of feeling in nineteenth and twentieth-

century life. In *The Mill on the Floss* we are made to experience the possibilities for life inherent in the rootedness of an organic existence where 'life seemed like a familiar smooth-handled tool that the fingers clutch with loving ease.'[8] That this is more than simple nostalgia is revealed by the complex moral purpose to which the novel's sense of the past is put. Despite being carried away with Stephen, in both senses, Maggie discovers the meaning of her own past as a moral defence against Stephen's almost Lawrentian imperative of acting in accordance with a purely personal emotional truth. That victory achieved, however, there is no way forward for either Maggie or George Eliot. Maggie's limitations of social position and place are widened in *Middlemarch* to a larger stage for conflicts of every kind. An aspect of the earlier book is carried over in the Garths, but their essentially rural, craftsmanlike certainties no longer hold the centre of attention. Although the novel is imbued with a feeling of tragic irony, its ending affords a qualified optimism in Dorothea and Will's movement to the metropolis. But that centre is itself under attack in *Daniel Deronda*. Klesmer's function in the novel is again instructive here. He enjoys independence and fame, but as a socially dubious provider of culture as entertainment for high society. Appreciation of his true worth is restricted to a handful of individuals; there is no widespread recognition of the relationship between his social role and his inner life.

How does this darkly questioning view of the possibilities of English life connect with the psychic depths whose exploration is such a striking feature of the novel's originality? We have seen that Gwendolen's sexual nature is deeply troubled, a complexity that gives her a dimension of interest beyond the socially oriented Rosamund Vincy. This psychic disturbance relates to a network of personal problems: her fear of solitude, of large open spaces, of being alone in the night. These neuroses, if that is not too strong, give her a richness of character perfectly compatible with a totally con- ventional outlook on life. She sees marriage as inevitable because it 'was social promotion; she could not look forward to a single life.' (4). Marriage for Gwendolen represents the power of leadership, for she *is* ambitious and 'such passions dwell in feminine breasts also':

> In Gwendolen's, however, they dwelt among strictly feminine furniture, and had no disturbing reference to the advancement of learning or the balance of the constitution; her knowledge being such as with no sort of standing-room or length of lever could have been expected to move the world. She meant to do what was pleasant to herself in a striking manner;

or rather, whatever she could do so as to strike others with admiration and get in that reflected way a more ardent sense of living, seemed pleasant to her fancy. (4)

The fact that she 'had about as accurate a conception of marriage...as she had of magnetic currents and the law of storms' (27) does not make her view of it any the less representative of her social world. Mr Gascoigne is one of George Eliot's most accurate portraits of the combination of worldliness and benevolent good sense; with Sir Hugo (we notice that they become friends) he represents the best the English gentlemen can achieve in this social world, but Gwendolen's marriage lacks any private dimension for him:

> This match with Grandcourt presented itself to him as a sort of public affair; perhaps there were ways in which it might even strengthen the Establishment. To the Rector, whose father (nobody would have suspected it, and nobody was told) had risen to be a provincial corn-dealer, aristocratic heirship resembled regal heirship in excepting its possessor from the ordinary standard of moral judgements; Grandcourt, the almost certain baronet, the probably peer, was to be ranged with public personages, and was a match to be accepted on broad general grounds national and ecclesiastical. (13)

Mr Gascoigne takes love, or affection, for granted, but this is strictly secondary to social advancement in his eyes. Part of Miss Arrowpoint's distinction lies in seeing through this game: 'There were as usual many guests in the house, and among them one in whom Miss Arrowpoint foresaw a new pretender to her hand: a political man of good family who confidently expected a peerage, and felt on public grounds that he required a larger fortune to support the title properly.' (22). Miss Arrowpoint has the will, so signally lacking in Gwendolen, to mould her own fate by virtually proposing to Klesmer through what amounts to a definition of real marriage: '"I am afraid of nothing but that we should miss the passing of our lives together."' (22).

Attacks on the marriage market aspect of English high life are one of the staples of social criticism in Victorian fiction, but George Eliot makes her version of it profound by linking it to Gwendolen's sexual deprivation. We understand that her frigidity relates to a coldness at the very heart of her personality. Her childhood selfishness is amply documented; a more fascinating example of her egotism occurs, however, at the moment when she is ready to return home because of the failure of the family fortune:

And even in this beginning of troubles, while for lack of anything else to do she sat gazing at her image in the growing light, her face gathered a complacency gradual as the cheerfulness of the morning. Her beautiful lips curled into a more and more decided smile, till at last she took off her hat, leaned forward and kissed the cold glass which had looked so warm. How could she believe in sorrow? If it attacked her, she felt the force to crush it, to defy it, or run away from it, as she had done already. Anything seemed more possible than that she could go on bearing miseries, great or small. (2)

Gwendolen can kiss herself and kiss, or be kissed by, her mother; a man's kiss is another matter. We might notice, in passing, a possibly hereditary element in all this: poor Mrs Davilow 'disliked what is called knowledge of the world; and indeed she wished that she herself had not had any of it thrust upon her.' (29). And Gwendolen's deepest fears – of the night, of open spaces and changes of light – clearly relate to psychic phenomena akin to those generated by sexual excitement. Gwendolen's sense of self can only be maintained within a rigidly conventional social mould: her egotism is so far-reaching that it cannot bear self-surrender. Put another way, she cannot submerge herself in anything beyond a narrow round of social pleasures; music, nature, ideas and causes, sexual union, all are beyond her range. By a painful irony, she learns to accept physical contact from Deronda, a man committed to another woman: 'That grasp was an entirely new experience to Gwendolen: she had never before had from any man a sign of tenderness which her own being had needed, and she interpreted its powerful effect on her into a promise of inexhaustible patience and constancy.' (56). But the wider social irony is that Gwendolen's very private sexual failure represents an extreme form of the barrenness of her society's view of life, while Grandcourt's behaviour is an extreme form of the sexual activity it is prepared to condone. Sex takes a terrible revenge on Gwendolen, in the form of Grandcourt's moral brutality, for acquiescence in her world's public and mechanical view of marriage. Gwendolen sees marriage as a means (to power, money and position) rather than as an end and at this point George Eliot fuses the social and the personal in complete inter-relation.

Here, as in many other places, a link exists with the novel's Jewish scenes. It is hard to be selective on this because, as Dickens hoped for his interpolated tale of Miss Wade in *Little Dorrit*, 'the blood of the book' flows through all its aspects. This is reinforced at a minute level by a whole series of correspondences, analogies, ironic contrasts: Gwendolen's step-father stole her mother's jewellery as Lapidoth steals Daniel's ring; Mirah's and Daniel's mothers are both Jewish, but relate to the stage and singing in totally different ways; like Gwendolen, Daniel's mother sought freedom and power in marriage; Mirah's admiration for Klesmer is an ironic reversal of his interview with Gwendolen; the novel's complex use of letters – these are only a few of the most important examples. A major sexual contrast operates in the novel also: 'when the bridal veil was around Mirah it hid no doubtful tremors – only a thrill of awe at the acceptance of a great gift which required great uses.' (70). Her relationship with Deronda promises to involve them in large public issues, as well as the intimacies of personal life; the tremor-laden nature of Gwendolen's response to Grandcourt, indeed to all men except Deronda, justifies acceptance of the hint that Daniel and Mirah will know happiness in the fullest sense.

The Jewish aspect of *Daniel Deronda* prompts questions of artistry and meaning, the answers to which highlight George Eliot's aesthetic daring. The mode in which she is working here justifies a long quotation, Daniel and Mordecai's meeting by the river:

When the wherry was approaching Blackfriars Bridge where Deronda meant to land, it was half-past four, and the grey day was dying gloriously, its western clouds all broken into narrowing purple strata before a wide-spreading saffron clearness, which in the sky had a monumental calm, but on the river, with its changing objects, was reflected as a luminous movement, the alternate flash of ripples or currents, the sudden glow of the brown sail, the passage of laden barges from blackness into colour, making an active response to that brooding glory.

Feeling well heated by this time, Deronda gave up the oar and drew over him again his Inverness cape. As he lifted up his head while fastening the topmost button, his eyes caught a well-remembered face looking towards him over the parapet of the bridge – brought out by the western light into startling distinctness and brilliancy – an illuminated type of bodily emaciation and spiritual eagerness. It was the face of Mordecai, who also, in his watch towards the west, had caught sight of the advancing boat, and had kept it fast within his gaze, at first simply because it was advancing, then with a recovery of impression that made him quiver as with a presentiment, till at last the nearing figure lifted up its face towards him – the face of his visions – and then immediately, with white uplifted hand, beckoned again and again.

For Deronda, anxious that Mordecai should recognise and await him, had lost no time before signalling, and the answer came straightway.

Mordecai lifted his cap and waved it – feeling in that moment that his inward prophecy was fulfilled. Obstacles, incongruities, all melted into the sense of completion with which his soul was flooded by this outward satisfaction of his longing. His exultation was not widely different from that of the experimenter, bending over the first stirrings of change that correspond to what in the fervour of concentrated prevision his thought has foreshadowed. The prefigured friend had come from the golden background, and had signalled to him: this actually was: the rest was to be. (40)

This passage suggests a fruitful conjunction of the greatest novelists of the Victorian period. Just as Dickens attempts a more psychologically rounded portrait in the Pip of *Great Expectations* than his earlier characterization seemed to make likely, so George Eliot might be seen as working in Dickens's mode of symbol, image and, even, melodramatic coincidence. But the suggestion that this mode is incongruous with the English sections of *Daniel Deronda* must be resisted. When Gwendolen is introduced to Grandcourt, 'Lord Brackenshaw moved aside a little for the prefigured stranger to come forward.' (11). And nothing could be more mysterious than the terrifying picture at Offendence which prefigures the face of the drowning Grandcourt. The Jewish scenes embody only an intensification of a style that is everywhere present in *Daniel Deronda*. Admittedly, these scenes lack the satirical savagery, and so the humour, characteristic of George Eliot's devastating portrayal of high society. Mirah and Mordecai, although not Daniel, are exempt from the irony which flickers around even Klesmer. There is a shadowiness here which may seem to compare unfavourably with the crystalline clarity of the great set-pieces of English life. And Mordecai is allowed a degree of verbal laxity which sometimes makes one long for the laconic utterances of Grandcourt. But this vagueness of outline and dialogue is perhaps necessary, or at least unavoidable, in that it represents a certain lack of clarity in George Eliot herself about he novel's direction.

What then, in the widest sense, are the Jewish scenes for and about? The novel's analysis and definition of England and Englishness embodies, in my view, something like a total rejection by George Eliot of her society, certainly at the imaginative level. Her criticism is set within a context of references to a wider world of effort and activity, a pattern that makes Deronda's character more comprehensible than is sometimes suggested:

> But how and whence was the needed event to come? – the influence that
> would justify partiality, and making him what he longed to be yet was
> unable to make himself – an organic part of social life, instead of roaming
> in it like a yearning disembodied spirit, stirred with a vague social
> passion, but without fixed local habitation to render fellowship real? (32)

The George Eliot who has moved, literally and artistically, from
country village to provincial town to the metropolis can no longer
find the answer to such yearnings within any coherent and workable
picture of English society. And this dissatisfaction is pregnant with
thematic and formal consequences. George Eliot is not abandoning
her search for rootedness, of course, it is too profoundly a part of the
very texture of her thought and being. But Deronda's attachment,
emotional and intellectual, to the cause of a small racial homeland is
at the same time a relationship with a people that has international
implications. The prefigured home for Daniel is ultimately the state
of Israel, but for his lifetime it will have to be within an idea rather
than, say, in a mill on the banks of the Floss. In keeping with this
largeness of scope in ideas and intention, George Eliot has attempted
a new artistic language to answer to her enhanced sense of the
mysterious complexity of human, social and national life.

The conclusion of this entire argument is that with *Daniel Deronda*
we see the very beginnings of the movement away from the great
European achievement of the social novel. Individual life portrayed
within a rich social context had provided nineteenth-century
novelists with an unrivalled field for artistic exploration. Indeed, the
lack of this interaction was a crucial factor for James in both his
move to Europe and his sense of the differences between
nineteenth-century American fiction and its European counterpart.
In Victorian terms, the social novel as a form had been brought to
perhaps unsurpassable peaks of greatness in *Middlemarch* and the
later novels of Dickens. Dickens himself appears to be changing
direction in the uncompleted *Edwin Drood*. Compared with *Our
Mutual Friend* its scale is reduced and it also develops his symbolic
mode to a point of extremity which creates a suggestive attenuation
of effect, similar to *Deronda's* Jewish scenes, and radically unlike the
dense social particularity of his earlier work. Again, although in a
direction different from George Eliot, the novel moves outside
English society to a wider international perspective. And its possible
avoidance of psychological coherence in favour of an interest in
drugged states of consciousness resembles *Deronda's* fascination with

the 'unmapped country within us.' (24). The social novel will continue to be written – by Gissing, Wells, Bennett and others – but one interest of *Daniel Deronda* is that as early as 1876, George Eliot had both the insight to recognise that the form had perhaps reached its fulness of life in English terms, and the courage to attempt to carry the novel a stage further.

Further Reading

Some important general works on George Eliot are:

The Novels of George Eliot by Barbara Hardy (London, 1959).

The Art of George Eliot by W. J. Harvey (London, 1961).

The Great Tradition by F. R. Leavis (London, 1948).

Critical views of *Daniel Deronda* itself may be found in:

George Eliot and Judaism by William Baker (Salzburg, 1975).

The Truthtellers by Laurence Lerner (London, 1967).

'*Daniel Deronda* and the Landscape of Exile,' by Jean Sudrann, *Journal of English Literary History* (1970).

An unusual, and amusing, form of literary criticism is:

'*Daniel Deronda:* A Conversation' by Henry James which is reprinted in Leavis's *The Great Tradition.*

9

Conclusions

The attempt to read works of literature from a social perspective has suffered badly from the reductiveness of both vulgar Marxism and sociological nit-picking. After such assaults novels, plays and poems often seem barely recognizable: the Procrustean bed of class-consciousness and the tabulation of transient forms of social behaviour lead only to the destruction of works of art. Too frequently, though, this has damned the whole enterprise for those who prefer the cloistered study of literature. This book has tried to show that a social reading is perfectly compatible with a respect for artistry; indeed, given the genesis of the novel that I have suggested, such a reading is unavoidable for eighteenth-century and nineteenth-century fiction: depiction of society is part of the aesthetics of the classic English novel. Implicit in my argument is the hope of ridding the position I advance of the stigma of the hobby-horse, the obsession of the wild-eyed enthusiast who seeks to convert others to the faith that all literary works must always be read from such a perspective. The argument centres on novels, and on novels from within a certain historical period, in the belief that this is its most persuasive strategy. But equally in *The Country and the City*, Raymond Williams has shown that seventeenth-century country house poems can be read skillfully and convincingly by placing them in their historical context. Again, the plays of Shaw and Brecht are not alone in having a social dimension; it is hardly possible to understand *Waiting for Godot* without some reference to the traumas of twentieth-century life. And in his *Ford Madox Ford: Prose and Politics*, Robert Green has shown that a writer who is sometimes seen as the archpriest of formalism in the modernist novel was a 'historical figure, a man who lived through history and was himself a part of that same history.'[1] In short, consideration of a literary work's social aspect should be part of the critic's normal range of techniques, to be applied with discretion and tact in what seem the most appropriate cases.

It is obviously impossible to embark on a full-scale justification of the position at this stage. Poetry and drama must be left to their own advocates. But a word is possible on the twentieth-century novel. At the end of the last chapter I suggested that *Daniel Deronda* represented a move away from the European phenomenon of the panoramic social novel. But the concentration on the personal and psychological, the psychic inwardness, of modernist fiction is far from signalling the complete disappearance of society as an aesthetic concern. Within the modernist perspective, *Sons and Lovers* may strike us as old-fashioned in the relative richness of its depiction of working-class life, and Lawrence certainly felt the need to move forward into his own version of the modernist preoccupation with making it new, in *The Rainbow* and *Women in Love*. But for all its psychic intensity *Women in Love* frequently places its human dilemmas within a social context. An instructive comparison is possible between Chapters 23 and 17, 'Excurse' and 'The Industrial Magnate.' Ursula's total confrontation with death in the former is without parallel in earlier fiction, in the minuteness with which Lawrence explores states of feeling at the very boundary of consciousness – a similarity with *Daniel Deronda* is worth noting here, as well as admiration for the earlier writer, but the grand march of intellect[2] enables him to dive deeper and stay below the surface longer. To invoke the social at this point is as irrelevant as, I have argued, it is in the case of lyric poetry.[3] 'The Industrial Magnate', on the other hand, encompasses a wide spectrum of English society, albeit in an impressionistic style which works by implication rather than through the weight of detail we associate with the realist tradition. In other words, from the perspective of later developments in the novel, it is possible to see that the gradual shift towards the interior landscape in late James, Conrad, Lawrence and Joyce did not involve any cutting of the umbilical cord between character and society. The attempt has been made, however, above all in the French New Novel.[4] A brief consideration of this development will provide the opportunity for a further discussion of the writers central to this book.

The theory and practice of the New Novel posits a view of fiction which involves the necessity of autobiography, or at least the use of the first person singular; which sees the novel as a document rather than as a work of the imagination; and for which character, in the traditional sense, is an irrelevance. This is how the points are made by Nathalie Sarraute in *The Age of Suspicion*: 'According to all appearances, not only has the novelist practically ceased to believe in his characters, but the reader, too, is unable to believe in them.' And she writes of the central figure of a great many contemporary novels as a 'being devoid of outline, indefinable, intangible and invisible, an anonymous "I", who is at once all and nothing, and who as often as not is but the reflection of the author himself.'[5] Again, Alberto Moravia claims that we should look for the 'essay-novel,' written in the first person, a form which he believes corresponds to contemporary notions of reality. What these notions of reality are is indicated, from very different positions, by Lionel Trilling and Fredric Jameson. In noticing the decay of narration in contemporary fiction, Trilling writes that a 'chief part of the inauthenticity of narration would seem to be its assumption that life is susceptible of comprehension and thus of management.'[6] For those writers who are doubtful of the extent to which external reality can be known, it is clearly the self which provides the one more or less secure haven of understanding. This stress on the self is obviously related to a distrust of the novelist's traditional function of story-telling, a phenomenon suggestively accounted for by Jameson:

> In the modern world...in Western Europe and the United States...
> economic prosperity is such that nothing is really irrevocable in this sense
> [of the nineteenth-century novel]: hence the philosphy of freedom, hence
> the modern literature of consciousness...hence also the decay of plot, for
> where nothing is irrevocable...there is no story to tell either, there is only
> a series of experiences of equal weight whose order is indiscriminately
> reversible.[7]

The essence of this position is summarized by Alain Robbe-Grillet, the principal theorist of the New Novel, when he says that avant-garde changes in fictional form reflect a change in 'our relationship with the universe...the dismissal of the old myth of depth.'[8]

It should be immediately obvious that such a dismissal constitutes a direct challenge to the literature of the past. If we attempt to sum up our reactions to the great novels of the nineteenth century, for example, we might easily do so by an appeal to the density of created life, the richness of texture that we find in them. This richness exists not simply because of the detailed recording of external reality which is often held to be their major characteristic. In fact, the use of the word 'realist' to describe the work of Stendhal, Balzac, and others, might well seem troubling. Lukács's failure to give extended treatment to either Dickens or Dostoevski in his famous *Studies in*

European Realism may have strategic implications in relation to his whole argument, or be simply a matter of convenience and the exigencies of space; but it may well connect with his uncompromising view of the nature of literary realism itself: 'realism is not one style among others, it is the basis of literature.. The inevitability of realism is most obvious...where descriptive detail is concerned.'[9] At this point the extremes of dogmatism and neutral definition meet. For Lukács, realism is the foundation of all literature, while in 'On Realism in Art,' Roman Jakobson points out that one use of the term is to comprehend 'the sum total of the features characteristic of one specific artistic current of the nineteenth century.'[10] This second view would appear to be shared by Harry Levin: 'Realism is a literary mode which corresponds, more directly than most of the others, to a stage of history and a state of society.'[11] It is not clear that any of these moves is particularly useful. To suggest that all literature – 'if it is good' must be the implied caveat – is realistic clearly begs more questions than it answers for those who do not share Lukacs's position, while to use the word as a historically descriptive term, like Romanticism, is hardly more illuminating for dealing with specific cases. It seems that some more value-laden definition is called for, but many such formulations raise their own difficulties, as in this comment by Ioan Williams: 'we have come to associate mid-Victorian literature with a naive confidence that Reality consisted in the material and social world.'[12] This is clearly not the case for the Emily Brontë who wrote *Wuthering Heights.* One of the sources of that work's greatness is its firm rootedness in a world of tea-making, roaring fires and influence of the weather on human life, features of the book, convincing in themselves, which help to secure our willing suspension of disbelief in the extraordinary. But can there be any doubt that this central area of concern is utterly opposed to the 'material and social world?' Again, in what sense do the novels of Dickens reveal a 'naive confidence' in mundane reality? The objects which inhabit the Dickens world are charged with an animism one of whose major effects is to imply a doubt as to the fixedness of apparently substantial things.

These over-simplifications are associated with attempts to show that the nineteenth-century novel is a 'closed form' compared to the openendedness of modern fiction,[13] but such views are an exaggeration of the extent to which Victorian novels end neatly with everyone remembered, including the dog. Even J. P. Stern's *On Realism* lends some weight to such one-sided opinions: 'The riches of the represented world; its weightiness and resistance to ideals; its consequential logic and circumstantiality – these I take to be among the attributes one would expect to find in realistic literature.' And the position is carried a stage further by his claim that: 'In realism the relation that obtains between a work of literature and the world outside is positive, expressive of a fundamental assent, whereas in idealism it is negative, expressive of a problematic attitude towards the world.'[14] But can it really be maintained that the endings of, say, *Anna Karenina*, *Middlemarch* and *Great Expectations* (in its original version) are unproblematic? There is a provisionality in Levin's relations with Kitty similar to the conclusion of *Women in Love;* Dorothea's marriage to Will Ladislaw is one of the 'determining acts of her life' that is 'not ideally beautiful';[15] and Pip is left with a future unmapped-out, even by implication. This fusion of negative ideas about the nineteenth-century novel is reinforced by the vulgar Marxism which sees bourgeois realism as accepting bourgeois society together with its values, a generalized liberal humanism which works against the portrayal of 'genuine' anguish. The indispensible word here must be 'genuine'. Without it, the claim that Balzac, Stendhal and the Dickens of, say, *Our Mutual Friend* lack anguish is too nakedly insubstantial. Even Ian Watt is unable to escape some of the confusions generated by the concept of realism, as is shown by the uncertainty of his discussion of Fielding in *The Rise of the Novel*, perhaps the most unsatisfactory aspect of that brilliant and pioneering work.

Watt is so firmly wedded to a realist view of the novel, with Richardson at its head, that he makes a series of bland assumptions about Fielding very much at odds with the closely textured argument of the rest of his book:

> As far as most modern readers are concerned it is not Fielding's moral but his literary point of view which is open to objection. For his conception of his role is that of a guide who, not content with taking us 'behind the scenes of this great theatre of nature,' feels that he must explain everything which is to be found there; and such authorial intrusion, of course, tends to diminish the authenticity of his narrative.... The effect of these references is certainly to break the spell of the imaginary world represented in the novel.... Fielding's interventions obviously interfere with any sense of narrative illusion, and...the prefatory chapters, or Fielding's diverting asides...undoubtedly derogate from the reality of the narrative.[16]

With others, Wayne Booth in his *The Rhetoric of Fiction* has helped us to grasp the limitations of such views.[17] Perhaps most crucially, Watt's position here rests on a highly suspect notion of the nature of our imaginative involvement with works of art. Indeed, this is not far removed from the absurdities of Ford Madox Ford: 'The object of the novelist is keep the reader entirely oblivious of the fact that the author exists – even of the fact that he is reading a book.'[18] Dr Johnson dealt decisively with this kind of thing in relation to the dramatic unities a long time ago; our involvement with a play is not dependent on a naive belief that the actors are those whom they represent. Similarly, the process of reading is surely a complex fusion of subjective engagement and objective judgement. In any case, Clarissa's ability to dash off letters in any situation is just as likely to 'derogate from the reality of the narrative,' supposing this to be the main point at issue; our relationship with the narrator of *Tom Jones* is every bit as valid, artistically and imaginatively, as our breathless pursuit of Clarissa's latest dilemma. Watt's whole argument on the development of the novel rests on the correlation between its realist elements and the historical factors which facilitated this growth, and in his eagerness to give the argument a binding force he ventures the truly amazing statement that in 'his effort to infuse the new genre with something of the Shakespearian virtues Fielding departed too far from formal realism to initiate a viable tradition,'[19] a moment at which the names of Jane Austen, Thackeray and George Eliot come instantly to mind.

More positively, Watt helps to clarify the general problems associated with realism through an admirably succinct statement of a crucial aspect of the term: 'the novel's realism does not reside in the kind of life it presents, but in the way it presents it.'[20] This is helpful, not least because it highlights one of the polarities into which a form as various even as the novel can be resolved: Richardson and Fielding, George Eliot and Dickens, Tolstoy and Dostoevski. The reservations needed to substantiate these oppositions are complex, but there is a genuine dichotomy between works which express 'fidelity to the surface exterior of life' and novels which are poetic and symbolist – 'romances', in Hawthorne's persuasive definition:

> When a writer calls his work a Romance, it need hardly be observed that he wishes to claim a certain latitude, both as to its fashion and material, which he would not have felt himself entitled to assume had he professed to be writing a Novel. The latter form of composition is presumed to aim at a very minute fidelity, not merely to the possible, but to the probable

217

and ordinary course of man's experience. The former . . . has fairly a right to present . . . truth under circumstances, to a great extent, of the writer's own choosing or creation. If he thinks fit, also, he may so manage his atmospherical medium as to bring out or mellow the lights and deepen and enrich the shadows of the picture.[21]

In the last analysis, such categorisation is one of dominant tendency only. Any great novel contains elements of realism and of what I shall call idealism. In fact, their coexistence, in varying proportions, helps to define the classic status of the nineteenth-century novel. A brief explanation of this richness of texture may help to show why the classic novel is aesthetically susceptible to a social reading.

A good starting-point is Lionel Trilling's essay 'Manners, Morals and the Novel,' in which he describes succinctly how the novel arose at a period of change in European history, the movement from the hierarchical structure of mediaeval society to the more fluid social organization of Renaissance and post-Renaissance Europe.[22] These are large counters to deploy, even in a speculative discussion, so it is helpful to turn briefly to some specialist views to justify the essential modernity of the novel form and the impossibility of its arising at an earlier period. Walter Ullmann, for example, comments on the rigid nature of many aspects of mediaeval life: 'The abstract standpoint . . . was an attempt to subject reality to conceptual thinking, to subject – in the public field – the individual's nature to the norm of an a-natural code, to shape and orient natural reality by means of speculative and abstract concepts.'[23] The large exception to these confident generalizations, in the English tradition, is the Chaucer of *The Canterbury Tales,* the Prologue to which possesses the idiosyncratic richness and love of diversity associated with the English novel. But Chaucer's own 'apology' for the sometimes rank humanity of the tales, as well as the ending of *Troilus and Criseyde,* reveal a state of mind that has at least some connections with the formalism of late mediaeval thought commented on by Huizinga: 'The complexity of things is ignored by it in a truly astounding manner. It proceeds to generalisation unhesitatingly on the strength of a single instance. . . . To explain a situation or event, a single motive suffices, and, for choice, the most general motive, the most direct, or the grossest.'[24] If this is compared with the tissue of motives so characteristic of the novel, there may be some grounds for asserting a real continuity between an epoch and its works of art. Nothing could be more remote from the named, heterogeneous individuality of the novel than the anonymity recorded by Ullmann:

'It is assuredly not without coincidence that we know so very little of the personal traits of most of the men who directed the path of mediaeval society. Hardly any personal correspondence has survived; no personal anecdotes are there; none of the stories which grow around great men exists; there are few biographical data; above all, there is hardly any worthwhile contemporary biography or pictorial representation.'[25]

Arising in the way Trilling suggests, then, the novel is involved from the moment of its birth in questions of social mobility, which means questions of station and snobbery; and since this social change is connected with the birth of capitalism, the novel also has money as one of its basic subjects, an interest which involves an engagement with the fantasies engendered by money. All of this leads to Trilling's definition of the novel: 'The novel, then, is a perpetual quest for reality, the field of its research being always the social world.'[26] This is true as far as it goes, but it hardly goes far enough. In discussing what we can take to be the first novel, *Don Quixote*, Trilling suggests that it deals with the typically novelistic clash between what may loosely be called 'reality', and 'fantasy'. It is this hint I wish to take up, one which Trilling leaves undeveloped because he is concerned to present a view of the novel that stresses its realist aspect.

This duality in the novel may tempt one towards a simplistic social reading, especially if subject-matter is stressed at the expense of artistry. In such an account the realist aspects of fiction may be read from a social perspective, but fantasy belongs to a personal realm which would be violated by social considerations. Such a dichotomy would, of course, dissolve the foundations of the view of the novel presented in this book. My claim is that the classic English novels involve an opposition between mundane reality and something other than this. It is the nature of this other element which requires analysis because it can be of more than one kind, negative or positive. To take the negative first, we find conflicts between reality and fantasy, by which I mean the delusions of class, snobbery, money, materialism. In this opposition, reality is of intense value as an aspiration to be achieved. Positively, there is an opposition between reality and the ideal, the striving for some life beyond the mundane, the response to a conception of human life which can infuse reality with an otherwise absent power and beauty. This negative and positive conflict with reality can exist within a single novel, of course, a situation that suggests the image of overlapping circles of reality and the ideal as a way of sketching the form of such a book. If we imagine the novel's protagonist at the centre of these possibilities, living a day-by-day existence which may be either dull or exciting, and surrounded by the temptations of fantasy and a vision of the ideal, then the source of the classic novel's richness of texture in what Robbe-Grillet dismisses as the 'myth' of depth becomes clear. It is also clear that fantasy and the ideal involve the whole reach of a society's culture, both the weakness of its greeds and illusions, and the strength of its spiritual, moral and intellectual life.

The conflict between reality and fantasy is crucial to the comic tradition of the English novel, both in relation to questions of social class and to the universal theme of self-discovery. The fantasies concerning the life of the gentleman in the Pip of *Great Expectations* give rise to pain as well as laughter, responses evoked equally in Jane Austen's exploration of how Emma moves towards an understanding of herself and of the human beings she manipulates to such near-disastrous effect. But the depth and poignancy of the struggles of such characters stem, in part, from their glimpse of the ideal, just as a sense of painful comedy is created by their delusions. Despite living in the metropolis, Pip's daily existence seems almost as circumscribed as Emma's, an occasional evening of pseudo-dissipation with the Finches of the Grove being one of his few excitements. And if Emma is more successful is accommodating her best self to a life in society, to a large extent through her marriage to Mr Knightley, this has as much to do with differences between historical periods as differences between the writers. However, both are capable of moments of experience which transcend the mundane. Emma's patronising insult to the helpless Miss Bates provokes an intense self-scrutiny, as well as Knightley's reproof. And when Pip faces what he belives to be his moment of certain extinction on the marshes at the hands of Orlick, his sense of being in spirit with Joe, Biddy and Herbert, but not Estella, is the apparently instinctive climax of a painful process of moral revaluation.

I hope it is clear by now that such moments of intense – in Pip's case even visionary – experience do not belong to some special world of purely private responses hermetically sealed off from the social. Such moments do exist, of course. I suggested earlier that crises of a totally a-social kind are to be found in *Wuthering Heights*.[27] And this related to my argument that although social elements are always to be found in works of literature, there is a scale of profitability on which it may simply not be critically illumating always to pursue a social reading.[28] But there are large areas of literature where such a reading is of intense aesthetic value, above all in a group of coherently related eighteenth and nineteenth-century English novels. These fictions are social in the large sense I have attempted to clarify; that is, they create their own internal social worlds which are at the same time images of society in that they stand in a complex series of relations to reality. But the private aspiration of Emma or Pip towards an ideal also has its connection with a community of shared moral and religious beliefs which, although it may find expression in individual lives, has its grounding in a socially created framework of what is morally creditable.

The bonds of such a framework loosen between the time of Jane Austen and Dickens, of course, and even more in the twentieth century, but it remains difficult to see how any human life can be quite without a social dimension. The very attempt to demonstrate this, in the French New Novel, is itself susceptible to a social explanation, as Lucien Goldmann has suggested, although his own attempt is perhaps unnecessarily doctrinaire.[29] In short, however alienated and spiritually lonely modern life may be – and it is possible that this modernist inheritance may have hardened by now into an orthodoxy – it remains possible to explain such features of human life at least partly in social terms. The fact is that society is stubbornly reluctant to go away, whether as concept or as actuality. It may even exert its influence as an absence, the loss of an ideal possibility of social living. However conceived, positively or negatively, eighteenth and nineteenth-century society gives the classic novel its 'field of research . . . the social world,' a field of enquiry that I have tried to show is inexhaustibly interesting in, and for, the English novel from Defoe to George Eliot.

Further Reading

The approach followed in this book is intellectually indebted to the work of Lionel Trilling, the classic representative of an undogmatic treatment of the problems of relating literature and society.

For the French New Novel see (in additional to Sturrock, note 5):

The Nouveau Roman: A Study in the Practice of Writing by Stephen Heath (London, 1972).

A useful, short introduction to literary realism is:

Realism by Damian Grant (London, 1970).

More advanced work will be found in:

Man in Society in Nineteenth-Century Realism:Determinism and Literature by Maurice Larkin (London, 1977).

On Realism by J. P. Stern (London, 1973).

The Monster in the Mirror: Studies in Nineteenth-Century Realism edited by D. A. Williams (Oxford, 1978).

The following is a list of works which have a bearing on the issues discussed in this chapter:

Introduction to the Sociology of Music by Theodor W. Adorno (New York, 1976) translated by E. B. Ashton.

Illuminations: Essays and Reflections by Walter Benjamin (London, 1970) translated by Harry John.

The Social Construction of Reality by P. L. Berger and T. Luckmann (Penguin, 1971).

The Social Context of Modern English Literature by Malcolm Bradbury (Oxford, 1972).

Afterthoughts on Material Civilization and Capitalism by Fernand Braudel (London, 1977) translated by P. M. Ranum.

The Illusion: An Essay on Politics, Theatre and the Novel by David Caute (New York, 1972).

Literature and Sincerity by Henri Peyre (Yale, 1969).

Loss of Self in Modern Literature and Art by Wylie Sypher (New York. 1962).

Notes

Preface

1 *The Story of the Novel* (London, 1979), xiii.

Chapter 1

1 F. R. Leavis, 'Sociology and Literature', *The Common Pursuit* (Penguin, 1962), p. 200.

2 Roy Harvey Pearce, 'Historicism Once More', *The Kenyon Review* Vol. XX, No. 4 (1958), p. 563.

3 Ian Watt, *The Rise of the Novel* (Penguin, 1963), p. 9.

4 A. R. Humphreys, *The Augustan World* (London, 1954), p. 48.

5 Theodore Spencer, *Shakespeare and the Nature of Man* (New York, 1965), ix.

6 Jane Routh and Janet Wolff (eds.), *The Sociology of Literature: Theoretical Approaches* (University of Keele, 1977), p. 3.

7 Marc Bloch, *The Historian's Craft* (Manchester, 1963), trans. Peter Putnam, p. 65.

8 C. Wright Mills, *The Sociological Imagination* (New York, 1959), p. 5.

9 Monroe Berger, *Real and Imagined Worlds: The Novel and Social Science* (Cambridge, Mass., 1977).

10 Boris Eichenbaum, 'Literary Environment', Ladislav Matejka and Krystyna Pomorska, (eds.), *Readings in Russian Poetics* (Cambridge, Mass., 1971), p. 61.

11 John Speirs, *Poetry Towards Novel* (London, 1971), p. 283.

12 Ibid., p. 11.

13 Ibid., p. 11.

14 Ibid., p. 284.

15 Watson, *Story of the Novel*, xii.

16 Victor Neuburg, *Popular Literature* (Penguin, 1977), intro.

17 Reinhard Kuhn, *The Demon of Noontide Ennui in Western Literature* (Princeton, 1976), p. 5.

18 John Bryson (ed.), *Matthew Arnold: Poetry and Prose* (London, 1954), p. 768.

19 Perhaps the best example is Dorothy Van Ghent's essay 'On *Great Expectations*' from her *The English Novel: Form and Function* (New York, 1961).

20 Several topics of interest to this study have been treated influentially by Leo Spitzer, *Linguistics and Literary History: Essays in Stylistics* (New York, 1962).

21 In his *Language of Fiction* (London, 1966) where the idea is developed in both theoretical and practical criticism.

22 See *Validity in Interpretation* (Yale, 1975).

23 I have argued this case in a chapter, 'The Man and his Times', of my *Dickens, Money and Society* (Berkeley, 1968).

24 August 5, 1844.

25 (London, 1978).

26 Ibid., pp. 7-8.

27 It is well known that the entire Tennyson family, including the poet himself, were subject to periods of mental stress.

28 Karl Marx and Friedrich Engels, *The Communist Manifesto* in Harold Laski (ed.), *Communist Manifesto: Socialist Landmark* (London, 1948) pp. 122-3. The fact that we are dealing with translation here (by Samuel Moore, with assistance from Engels, for the English edition of 1888) should be noted. If anything, however, this reinforces the point of the wide availability of language related to the melodramatic mode.

29 These plays, and the atmosphere generated in their performance, are described in detail by James L. Smith, *Melodrama* (London, 1973).

30 Jack Stillinger (ed.), (Oxford, 1971) p. 85.

31 F. Rahill, *The World of Melodrama* (London, 1967), p. 107.

32 Several of which are detailed in the notes to this chapter.

33 Peter Brooks, *The Melodramatic Imagination: Balzac, Henry James, Melodrama and the Mode of Excess* (Yale, 1977), p. 15.

34 Alexis de Tocqueville, *The Old Regime and the Revolution* (London, 1969), trans. Stuart Gilbert.

35 *Melodrama*, p. 16.

36 'Preface' in R. L. Brett and A. R. Jones (eds.), *Lyrical Ballads* (London, 1965), p. 249.

37 *Biographia Literaria* (London, 1906), Satyrane's Letters 11, p. 290.

38 Rahill, p. 155.

39 Quoted by David Grimsted, *Melodrama Unveiled: American Theatre and Culture 1800-1850* (London, 1968), viii.

40 Rahill, p. 8.

41 Quoted by Edgar Johnson, *Charles Dickens: His Tragedy and Triumph* (Penguin, 1979), pp. 357-8.

42 Pp. 34-5.

43 Rahill, p. 85.

44 (London, 1966), pp. 215-6.

45 Mrs Gaskell, *Mary Barton*, Chapter 6.

46 Berger, p. 10.

47 *An Inquiry* (London, 1977), p. 165.

48 (London, 1979).

49 Ibid., pp. 141-2.

50 See Lucien Goldmann, *Towards a Sociology of the Novel* (London, 1977), trans. Alan Sheriden.

51 Gramsci's own ideas, complex and fragmentary as they are, can be examined first hand in A. Gramsci, *Selections from the Prison Notebooks* (London, 1971), trans. and ed. Quintin Hoare and Geoffrey Nowell-Smith.

52 (Oxford, 1977), pp. 108-9.

53 Ibid., p. 83.

54 *Politics and Letters*, p. 137.

55 (London, 1958), p. 70.

56 *Politics and Letters*, p. 255.

57 Ibid., p. 255.

58 *Sociology of Knowledge*, pp. 27-8.

59 'Sociology and Literature', *The Common Pursuit*, pp. 202-3.

60 *The Historian's Craft*, p. 146.

61 Section 7.

62 'Literary Environment', *Russian Poetics*, p. 56 (see note 10).

63 *Practical Criticism and Literary Sociology*, xii.

64 *Tintern Abbey*, lines 105-7.

65 *18 Lectures on Industrial Society* (London, 1968), pp. 27-8.

66 Erich Auerbach, *Mimesis: The Representation of Reality in Western Literature* (New York, 1957), trans. Willard Trask, p. 391.

67 (Penguin, 1965), pp. 86-7.

68 *The Novel and Society* (London, 1966), p. 113.

69 *Rise of the Novel*, p. 9.

70 (Oxford, 1961), p. 139.

71 See Marilyn Butler, *Jane Austen and the War of Ideas* (Oxford, 1975) and Gary Kelly, *The English Jacobin Novel 1780-1805* (Oxford, 1976).

72 *The Rise of the Novel*, pp. 160-1.

73 *The Historian's Craft*, p. 151.

74 *The Waning of the Middle Ages* (Penguin, 1955), p. 55.

75 H. T. Dickinson (ed.), *Politics and Literature in the Eighteenth Century* (London, 1974), ix.

76 *The Sociological Tradition* (New York, 1966), p. 22.

77 *Mimesis*, p. 227.

78 *Marxists on Literature: An Anthology* (Penguin, 1975), p. 19.

79 *On Realism* (London, 1973) p. 108.

80 (London, 1979).

81 Ibid., p. 15.

82 Ibid., p. 14.

83 Vol. 28, p. 66.

Chapter 2

1 (London, 1977), p. 54.

2 Ibid., p. 82.

3 (London, 1978), pp. 256-7.

4 Ibid., p. 260 and p. 265.

5 For a non-Marxist reading of Defoe's socio-economic context see M. E. Novak, *Economics and the Fiction of Defoe* (Berkeley, 1962).

6 *Robinson Crusoe* presents a problem with regard to references as it is not divided into chapters; page references are given to an edition widely available to students, the Penguin.

7 Saturday, February 3, 1713.

8 Chapter Nine, Conclusions.

9 Page references are given to the Everyman edition of *Moll Flanders* (London, 1930).

10 February 20, 1817 in *Jane Austen: Selected Letters 1796-1816* (Oxford, 1954), selected and ed. by R. W. Chapman, p. 190.

11 John Robert Moore, *Daniel Defoe: Citizen of the Modern World* (Chicago, 1958), p. 306.

12 Moore, p. 311.

13 *The Rise of the Novel*, p. 105.

14 Pat Rogers (ed.), *Defoe: The Critical Heritage* (London, 1972), p. 75.

15 Watt, p. 30.

16 *Rise of the Novel*, Chapter 6.

17 Ibid., p. 111.

18 Ibid., p. 111.

19 *The Novel and Society* (London, 1966), p. 114.

20 *Fictions* (London, 1976), trans. C. and T. Burns, pp. 14-15.

21 Chapter references are used for this and subsequent novels unless otherwise indicated.

22 Watt, p. 106.

23 Quoted by G. H. Ford, *Dickens and His Readers* (Princeton, 1955), p. 136.

24 A. R. Humphreys, 'Fielding and Smollett', *The Pelican Guide to English Literature* Vol. 4 *From Dryden to Johnson* (Penguin, 1968), p. 326.

25 *The Augustan Vision*, p. 31.

26 *English Literature and Society in the Eighteenth Century* (London, 1904), p. 43.

27 *The Eighteenth-Century Background: Studies On the Idea of Nature in the Thought of the Period* (Penguin, 1962), p. 17.

28 Ian Watt, p. 32; Leslie Stephen, pp. 28 and 27.

29 *The Augustan World*, pp. 186-7.

30 'Afterword' to the Signet edn. (1964), p. 471.

31 Signet, p. 478.

32 *Rise of the Novel*, p. 146.

33 Peter Laslett, *The World We Have Lost* (Methuen, 1965), p. 5.

34 Marquis of Lansdowne (ed.), *The Petty Papers: Some Unpublished Writings of Sir William Petty* (London, 1927), p. 212.

35 Charles Henry Hull (ed.), *The Economic Writings of Sir William Petty* (Cambridge, 1899), p. 244.

36 Quoted by Dorothy George, *England in Transition* (Penguin, 1953), p. 10.

37 *Sociology of Knowledge*, p. 198.
38 *Augustan Vision*, p. 105.
39 *Rise of the Novel*, p. 99.
40 *Stability and Strife*, p. 90.
41 *Sincerity and Authenticity* (Oxford, 1974), p. 19.
42 *The Social History of Art* Vol. III (London, 1962), p. 45.
43 *The Long Revolution* (Penguin, 1965), p. 120.
44 *Tellers and Listeners* (London, 1975), p. 4.
45 *Fact in Fiction* (London, 1974), viii.
46 *Essays on Literature and Society* (London, 1965), p. 10.

Chapter 3

1 *Literary Essays* (London, 1956), p. 27.
2 'Clarissa Restored', *Review of English Studies* X (1959), p. 216.
3 *Samuel Richardson: Dramatic Novelist* (London, 1973), p. 161.
4 Letter to Johannes Stinstra, June 2, 1753 in John Carroll (ed.), *Selected Letters of Samuel Richardson* (Oxford, 1964), p. 233.
5 (Lexington, Kentucky, 1968), p. 4.
6 Ibid., p. 4.
7 By John Carroll in A. E. Dyson (ed.), *The English Novel: Select Bibliographical Guides* (London, 1974), p. 62.
8 See pp. 28 ff.
9 *Selected Letters*, p. 53.
10 *Rise of the Novel*, p. 130.
11 References to *Clarissa* are by volume and page number of the four volume Everyman edn. (1962) as the book is divided into cumbrously numbered letters rather than chapters.
12 Pp. 29-31.
13 *Selected Letters*, p. 197.
14 Ibid., pp. 41, 233, 234.
15 To Mrs William Murray, November 2, 1921, in Richard Ellmann (ed.), *The Selected Letters of James Joyce* (London, 1975), p. 286.
16 *Selected Letters*, p. 63.
17 Ibid., p. 85.
18 Quoted by John Preston, *The Created Self: The Reader's Role in Eighteenth-Century Fiction* (London, 1970), p. 69.
19 Quoted by A. D. McKillop, *Early Masters of English Fiction* (Kansas, 1956), p. 48.
20 *The Life of the Drama* (London, 1966), p. 201.
21 'Samuel Richardson', *Pelican Guide* Vol. 4, pp. 293-4.
22 *'Natural Passion': A Study of the Novels of Samuel Richardson* (London, 1974).
23 *Literary Essays*, p. 48.
24 Quoted in Duncan T. C. Eaves and Ben D. Kimpel, *Samuel Richardson: A Biography* (Oxford, 1971), p. 553.

25 *The English Novel* (Penguin, 1954), p. 50.

26 *The Created Self*, p. 81.

27 p. 94.

28 See for example Christopher Hill, 'Clarissa Harlowe and her Times', *Essays in Criticism* Vol. V, No. 4 (1955).

29 Denis Diderot, *Rameau's Nephew* trans. L. W. Tancock (Penguin, 1966), pp. 38-9.

30 Ibid., p. 79.

31 (London, 1972), p. 28.

32 Quotations from *Sincerity and Authenticity*, pp. 27, 34, 29, 30, 120, 34.

33 *Rameau's Nephew*, pp. 102, 103, 104.

34 *Sincerity and Authenticity*, p. 72.

35 'Manners, Morals, and the Novel', *The Liberal Imagination: Essays on Literature and Society* (New York, 1957), p. 200.

Chapter 4

1 References to *Tom Jones* are by book and chapter.

2 p. 138.

3 '*Tom Jones:* The Argument of Design', Henry Knight Miller (ed.), *The Augustan Milieu: Essays Presented to Louis A. Landa* (Oxford, 1970), p. 289.

4 Ibid., p. 292.

5 'The Voices of Henry Fielding: Style in *Tom Jones*', *The Augustan Milieu*, p. 270.

6 *The Augustan World*, p. 49.

7 *The Implied Reader* (London, 1974), p. 38.

8 Ronald Paulson and Thomas Lockwood (eds.), *Henry Fielding: The Critical Heritage* (London, 1969), xxi.

9 *The Augustan Milieu.*

10 *The Critical Heritage*, p. 394.

11 p. 111.

12 Neil Compton (ed.), *Henry Fielding: Tom Jones: A Casebook* (London, 1970), p. 55.

13 Ibid., p. 55.

14 *Rise of the Novel*, p. 280.

15 *The Sociology of Literature* (London, 1972), pp. 203-4.

16 Ibid., p. 195.

17 *Tom Jones: A Casebook*, p. 15.

18 'Fielding and Smollett', *Pelican Guide* Vol. 4, p. 316.

19 *The Augustan Vision*, p. 28.

20 *The English Novel*, p. 67.

21 *Rise of the Novel*, p. 30.

22 *Tom Jones: A Casebook*, p. 11.

23 Quoted by Dorothy George, *England in Transition*, p. 74.

24 *Rise of the Novel*, pp. 316-17.

25 Quoted in *Fielding: The Critical Heritage*, p. 438.
26 'Fielding and Smollett', p. 319.
27 R. P. C. Mutter (ed.), *Tom Jones* (Penguin, 1966), pp. 11 and 12.
28 *The English Novel*, p. 65.
29 Ibid., p. 67.
30 G. Bryson, *Man and Society: The Scottish Inquiry of the Eighteenth Century* (New York, 1968), p. 152.
31 *The Augustan Vision*, p. 54.
32 'Fielding's Social Outlook', *Philological Quarterly* Vol. XXXV, No. 1 (1956).
33 *The Historical Novel* (Penguin, 1976), trans. Hannah and Stanley Mitchell, p. 16.
34 '*Tom Jones:* The Argument of Design'.
35 Malvin R. Zirker, *Fielding's Social Pamphlets* (Berkeley, 1966), p. 64.
36 Ibid., pp. 138-9.
37 *The Idea of the Novel in Europe 1600-1800* (London, 1979), p. 195.
38 'The Argument of Design', p. 309.
39 *The English Novel*, p. 70.
40 'The Plot of *Tom Jones*', *Critics and Criticism: Ancient and Modern* (Chicago, 1952).
41 'Style in *Tom Jones*', p. 284.

Chapter 5

1 *The Common Reader* First Series (London, 1962), p. 180.
2 See Malcolm Bradbury, '*Persuasion* Again', *Essays in Criticism* Vol. 18 (1968); Norman Page, 'Orders of Merit' and Joseph Wiesenfarth, 'Austen and Apollo' in Joel Weinscheimer (ed.), *Jane Austen Today* (Athens, Georgia, 1975).
3 *Jane Austen and the War of Ideas* (Oxford, 1975), p. 278.
4 *The Importance of the Estate* (London, 1971), p. 31.
5 References to Jane Austen's novels are to chapters and, where unavoidable, book or volume and chapter. For *Persuasion* I have adopted the practice of the Penguin edition in which chapters are numbered continuously and not broken after Volume 1.
6 Introduction to *Sense and Sensibility* (1931) pp. xiii-xiv.
7 Letter to Fanny Knight, March 23, 1817, *Selected Letters*, p. 198.
8 Ibid., November 30, 1814, p. 178.
9 *The English Novel*, p. 79.
10 *On Realism*, p. 97.
11 *The English Novel: Form and Function* (New York, 1961), p. 79.
12 *The English Novel from Dickens to Lawrence* (London, 1970), p. 63.
13 R. W. Chapman (ed.), *Jane Austen's Letters to her sister Cassandra and others* (Oxford, 1964), p. 39.
14 To Cassandra, May 12, 1801, *Selected Letters*, p. 54.

15 To Cassandra, January 7, 1807, *Selected Letters*, p. 74.

16 To Cassandra, November 8, 1800, *Selected Letters*, p. 34.

17 Chapter 55.

18 'Jane Austen, Karl Marx, and the Aristocratic Dance', *The American Scholar* XVII (Summer, 1948), p. 289.

19 *The Novel and Society*, p. 41.

20 *Jane Austen and the War of Ideas*, n. 4, p. 164.

21 *Fictions* (London, 1976) trans. C. and T. Burns, p. 76.

22 *The Country and the City* (London, 1975), p. 144.

23 *The War of Ideas*, p. 164.

24 *Sincerity and Authenticity*, pp. 15-16.

25 Speck, *Stability and Strife*, p. 52.

26 *Mimesis*, pp. 323-4.

27 *Sincerity and Authenticity*, pp. 110-11.

28 Quoted in B. C. Southam, *Jane Austen: The Critical Heritage* (London, 1968), p. 250.

29 Ibid., p. 264.

30 Admiral Sir Herbert Richmond, 'The Naval Officer in Fiction', *Essays and Studies* Vol. XXX (1944), p. 16.

31 In her diary for 1780, quoted by Richmond, p. 17.

32 *English Social History* (London, 1942), p. 499.

33 Quoted in G. M. Young, *Victorian England: Portrait of an Age* (Oxford), p. 4.

34 Michael Lewis, *England's Sea Officers* (London, 1948), n. 1, p. 69.

35 Michael Lewis, *A Social History of the Navy 1793-1815* (London, 1960), p. 42.

36 Ibid., p. 33.

37 Ibid., p. 30.

38 *Critical Heritage*, p. 9.

39 *The War of Ideas*, p. 170.

40 *Sincerity and Authenticity*, p. 76.

41 Quoted by R. W. Chapman, *Jane Austen: Facts and Problems* (Oxford, 1950), p. 76.

42 *The English Jacobin Novel 1780-1805* (Oxford, 1976), Preface.

43 Henry James, *The Portrait of a Lady* (London, 1968), Vol. 5 The Bodley Head Henry James, Preface, p. 20.

44 *The War of Ideas*, p. 280.

45 Ibid., p. 291.

46 See Alan Friedman, *The Turn of the Novel* (New York, 1966).

47 *The Improvement of the Estate*, pp. 181 and 201.

48 '*Persuasion* Again,' p. 392.

49 *The Country and the City*, p. 143.

50 Afterword to the Signet edition of *Persuasion* (New York, 1964), pp. 241-2.

51 *Mimesis*, p. 322.

52 Quoted by David Grimsted, *Melodrama Unveiled: American Theatre and Culture 1800-1850* (London, 1968), p. 11.
53 Op.cit., p. 183.
54 *The Common Reader*, p. 183.

Chapter 6

1 See p. 8.
2 *The Historical Novel* (Penguin, 1976) trans. Hannah and Stanley Mitchell, p. 92.
3 Ibid., p. 92.
4 *Politics and the Novel* (New York, 1957), p. 19.
5 *The Historical Novel*, p. 290.
6 *The Victorian Historical Novel 1840-1880* (London, 1978), p. 102.
7 Op.cit., p. 15.
8 See the Norton Critical Edition (New York) of *Vanity Fair*, n. 8, p. 65.
9 'Society in Thackeray and Trollope,' *Pelican Guide* Vol. 6, p. 144.
10 J. Y. T. Grieg, *Thackeray: A Reconsideration* (London, 1950), p. 100.
11 *The Crazy Fabric* (1965, reprinted Arno, 1973), p. 77.
12 *The Exposure of Luxury: Radical Themes in Thackeray* (London, 1972), p. 21.
13 *The Mirror in the Roadway: A Study of the Modern Novel* (New York, 1970), p. 112.
14 Henri-A. Talon, 'Thackeray's *Vanity Fair* Revisited: Fiction as Truth,' in John Butt (ed.), *Of Books and Humankind: Essays and Poems Presented to Bonamy Dobrée* (London, 1964), p. 118.
15 Op.cit., p. 20.
16 *Vanity Fair* (Penguin, 1968), Notes, p. 799.
17 Humphry House, *The Dickens World* (Oxford, 1941), p. 32.
18 See Arthur Pollard (ed.) *Thackeray's Vanity Fair: A Casebook* (London, 1978), pp. 202-3.
19 Speck, *Stability and Strife*, p. 123.
20 See Speck, *Stability and Strife* and G. E. Mingay, *English Landed Society in the Eighteenth Century* (London, 1962).
21 *Novels of the Eighteen-Forties*, p. 157.
22 G. N. Ray, *Thackeray: The Uses of Adversity* (New York, 1955), p. 411.
23 *The Exposure of Luxury*, p. 121.
24 *The Uses of Adversity*, p. 416.
25 Ibid., p. 416.
26 *Thackeray: A Casebook*, p. 265.
27 Ibid., p. 75.
28 *The Uses of Adversity*, p. 397.
29 Avrom Fleishman, *The English Historical Novel: Walter Scott to Virginia Woolf* (London, 1971), p. 148.
30 Introduction to *Vanity Fair* (Penguin, 1968), p. 8.

31 *Thackeray the Novelist* (London, 1954), p. 35.

32 *A Reconsideration.*

33 Chapter 21.

34 Quoted by Miriam Allott, *Novelists on the Novel* (London, 1965), p. 77.

35 Quoted by Iser, *The Implied Reader*, p. 113.

36 See Wayne C. Booth, *The Rhetoric of Fiction* (Chicago, 1961) and Barbara Hardy, *Tellers and Listeners* (London, 1975).

37 *Middlemarch*, 'Finale.'

38 *Writing Degree Zero* (London, 1967) trans. Annette Lavers and Colin Smith, p. 35.

Chapter 7

1 Op.cit., pp. 31-2.

2 In *The Dyer's Hand* (London, 1948), p. 408.

3 M. H. Abrams, *A Glossary of Literary Terms* (New York 1971), p. 102.

4 See Edmund Wilson, 'Dickens: the two Scrooges', *The Wound and the Bow*, (Boston, 1941).

5 See his review of *Little Dorrit* in the *Edinburgh Review* 106 (1857). Dickens replied in *Household Words*, August 1, 1857.

Chapter 8

1 Quoted in Gordon S. Haight, *George Eliot: A Biography* (Oxford, 1968), p. 29.

2 See Gordon S. Haight, *A Century of George Eliot Criticism* (London, 1966), pp. 112-13.

3 *Pelican Guide* Vol. 6, p. 141.

4 Letter to Mme Eugène Bodichon, October 2, 1876 in Gordon S. Haight (ed.), *The George Eliot Letters* (Oxford, 1954-56), Vol. 6, p. 290.

5 '*Daniel Deronda* and the Landscape of Exile', *Essays in Literary History* XXXVII (September, 1970), p. 446.

6 *The English Novel*, p. 77.

7 This preoccupation forms an important link with one of George Eliot's most admired writers, the Jane Austen of *Persuasion*.

8 Book third, chapter nine.

Chapter 9

1 (Cambridge University Press, 1981), ix-x.

2 The phrase is Keats's, from a letter to John Hamilton Reynolds, May 3, 1818; in Robert Gittings (ed.) *Letters of John Keats* (Oxford, 1970), p. 96.

3 See Chapter 1.

4 For a thorough discussion see John Sturrock, *The French New Novel* (London, 1969).

5 *Tropisms AND The Age of Suspicion* (London, 1964), trans. M. Jolas.

6 *Sincerity and Authenticity*, p. 135.

7 *Marxism and Form* (Princeton, 1971), p. 79.

8 *Snapshots and Towards a New Novel* (London, 1966), trans. Barbara Wright.

9 *The Meaning of Contemporary Realism* (London, 1963), trans. John and Necke Mander, p. 48.

10 *Russian Poetics.*

11 *The Gates of Horn* (New York, 1963), ix.

12 *The Realist Novel in England: A Study in Development* (London, 1974), x.

13 See Friedman, *The Turn of the Novel.*

14 p. 28 and 44.

15 *Middlemarch*, 'Finale'.

16 *Rise of the Novel*, pp. 324-5.

17 Booth develops what seems an unanswerable case that all narrative devices are admissible; the criterion for judgement is artistic success or failure rather than the nature of the narrative strategy itself.

18 *Joseph Conrad: A Personal Reminiscence* (London, 1924), Part III, Section ii.

19 *Rise of the Novel*, p. 328.

20 p. 11.

21 Preface to *The House of the Seven Gables* (1851).

22 *The Liberal Imagination* (London, 1950).

23 *The Individual and Society in the Middle Ages* (London, 1967), p. 102.

24 *The Waning of the Middle Ages*, p. 255.

25 *Individual and Society*, pp. 43-4.

26 'Manners, Morals, and the Novel', *The Liberal Imagination*, p. 205.

27 See p. 33.

28 See pp. 33-4.

29 In *Towards a Sociology of the Novel.*

Select Bibliography

This bibliography makes no attempt at completeness. The 'Further Reading' sections concluding each chapter, including the bibliographies mentioned there, should permit a systematic approach to the problems raised by this book. The following list is simply an attempt to suggest the reach of an interest in the relationship between literature – culture even – and society, by way of some books of general interest and others which deal with very specific topics.

BADCOCK, C. R., *Lévi-Strauss: Structuralism and Sociological Theory* (London, 1975).

BYRD, MAX, *London Transformed: Images of the City in the Eighteenth Century* (London, 1978).

CAUDWELL, CHRISTOPHER, *Reality: A Bourgeois Philosophy* (New York, 1970).

ELIADE, MIRCEA, *Myth and Reality* (New York, 1968).

GRYLLS, DAVID, *Guardian and Angels: Parents and Children in Nineteenth-Century Literature* (London, 1978).

HARDWICK, ELIZABETH, *Seduction and Betrayal: Women and Literature* (London, 1974).

HEILMEN, R. B., *Tragedy and Melodrama: Versions of Experience* (London, 1968).

HEMMINGS, F. W. J. (ed.), *The Age of Realism* (London, 1974).

HOGGART, RICHARD, *Speaking to Each Other*, 2 vols, (London, 1970).

KNIGHT, E., *A Theory of the Classical Novel* (London, 1969).

KOVACEVIC, IVANKA, *Fact in Fiction: English Literature and the Industrial Scene 1750-1850* (Leicester, 1975).

LASCELLES, MARY, *The Story-Teller Retrievers of the Past* (Oxford, 1982).

LEMON, LEE and REIS, MARION (eds.), *Russian Formalist Criticism* (Lincoln, Nebraska, 1965).

LOWENTHAL, LEO, *Literature, Popular Culture and Society* (New Jersey, 1961).

MOORE, BARRINGTON, *Social Origins of Dictatorship and Democracy* (Penguin, 1969).

MARCUSE, HERBERT, *Reason and Revolution: Hegel and the Rise of Social Theory* (New York, 1954).

POLANYI, KARL, *The Great Transformation* (New York, 1944).

SEKORA, JOHN, *The Concept of Luxury in Western Thought* (London, 1978).

SIMMEL, GEORG, *Philosophy of Money*, trans. Bottomore, Tom and Frisby, David (London, 1978).

WATT, IAN, *The Novelist as Innovator* (London, 1965).

WEBB, IGOR, *From Custom to Capital: The English Novel and the Industrial Revolution* (London, 1981).

WEBER, MAX, *Economy and Society* edited by Wittich, Guenther and Claus (Berkeley, 1978).

Index